Spirit of God, Spirit of Christ

Ecumenical Reflections on the *Filioque* Controversy

SPCK
London
WORLD COUNCIL OF CHURCHES
Geneva

Faith and Order Paper No. 103

Cover: The Holy Trinity, wall painting in the Church of the Panagia Koubelidiki, Greece.

Several of the texts included in this volume were translated into English from the original French or German. We would like to express our thanks to the Language Service of the World Council of Churches, and to Donald Allchin and Alasdair Heron for these translations.

Cover design: Paul May
ISBN: 2-8254-0662-7 (WCC)
ISBN: 0-281-03820-1 (SPCK)
© 1981 World Council of Churches, 150 rte de Ferney, 1211 Geneva 20, Switzerland

Printed in Great Britain by Ebenezer Baylis and Son Ltd., The Trinity Press, Worcester, and London.

Contents

Preface v

PART I: MEMORANDUM

The *filioque* clause in ecumenical perspective 3

PART II: ESSAYS

A. HISTORICAL ASPECTS

The procession of the Holy Spirit according to certain later Greek
Fathers 21
                                                       Markos A. Orphanos

Historical development and implications of the *filioque* controversy . 46
                                                      Dietrich Ritschl

B. DEVELOPMENTS IN THE VARIOUS TRADITIONS

Towards an ecumenical agreement on the procession of the Holy Spirit
and the addition of the *filioque* to the Creed 69
                                                      André de Halleux

The *filioque* clause: an Anglican approach 85
                                                      Donald Allchin

The *filioque* in the Old Catholic churches: the chief phases of theological reflection and church pronouncements 97
                                                     Kurt Stalder

The *filioque* in recent Reformed theology 110
Alasdair Heron

C. OPENING A NEW DEBATE ON THE PROCESSION OF THE SPIRIT

The question of the procession of the Holy Spirit and its connection
with the life of the Church 121
Herwig Aldenhoven

The *filioque* yesterday and today 133
Boris Bobrinskoy

A Roman Catholic view of the position now reached in the question
of the *filioque* 149
Jean-Miguel Garrigues

Theological proposals towards the resolution of the *filioque*
controversy 164
Jürgen Moltmann

The procession of the Holy Spirit from the Father and his relation to
the Son, as the basis of our deification and adoption 174
Dumitru Staniloae

PREFACE

In the last two years two consultations were organized by the Faith and Order Commission of the World Council of Churches to study the famous controversy over the *filioque* formula in the Niceno-Constantinopolitan Creed. Ways and means of bringing this difficult question nearer to solution were examined by a small group of theologians from the Eastern Orthodox and various western traditions. The first consultation (26–29 October 1978) produced a report which was then submitted to a wider circle of specialists for their comments. The text of this report was thoroughly revised at the second consultation (23–27 May 1979) and then presented to the Faith and Order Standing Commission in the summer of 1979. The Commission set the seal of its approval on it to the extent of recommending that it be shared with the churches. The present volume contains the report in its final form as well as the papers presented at the two consultations.

Why did the Faith and Order Commission undertake this study? The answer is simple: the addition of the words "and from the Son" to the text of the Nicene Creed is one of the issues which divided East and West for many centuries past and still divides them today. The restoration of unity is inconceivable if agreement is not reached on the formal and substantial justification for this formula. The fact that individual western churches have already broached the question in discussions with the Orthodox Church lends added urgency to the ecumenical debate. After a careful consideration of all aspects of the matter, the Old Catholic Church has come to the conclusion that the *filioque* is not to be recited in the liturgy. The Anglican Communion is seriously considering taking the same step. If separate decisions are to be avoided, it is essential that the churches should consider the question of the *filioque* together. The way to communion among the churches can be opened up only by an agreement for which they take joint responsibility.

The only meaningful context in which to raise and deal with the special question of the eternal procession of the Spirit from the Father and of the role played by the Son in this procession is that of the trinitarian understand-ing of God. The question of the *filioque* thus becomes an opportunity to develop together the meaning of the Trinity. And could any undertaking be more important than this for the development of common theological, spiri-tual and liturgical perspectives?

The report establishes that the words "and from the Son" are an addition and it concludes, therefore, that all churches should revert to the original text of the Nicene Creed as the normative formulation. This does not mean simply "dropping" the addition. Rather we must investigate further the problem which the West sought to solve by this formula. The report attaches the greatest importance to the readiness of the churches to engage in a new discussion about God. That the understanding of God is not a matter of controversy and can therefore be omitted from the dialogue is an assumption which has often been made in the ecumenical movement. In view of the enormous and novel challenges of our time, theology is faced anew with the question of how we are to speak of God on the basis of the revelation in Christ.

Cordial thanks are due to those who took part in the consultations for making their papers available for publication. But I would like especially to express our gratitude to the Johann Wolfgang van Goethe Foundation for welcoming both meetings in the beautiful premises of Schloss Klingenthal near Strasbourg; the warm hospitality of Dr Marie-Paule Stintzi contributed much to the success of the conversations.

*   *   *

Sixteen centuries have passed since the Council of Constantinople (381) in which the Niceno-Constantinopolitan Creed originated. Received by the Church as the expression of the common apostolic faith it has tragically also become a source of disagreement and disunity. The findings of this ecu-menical debate are offered for discussion in a year in which the Council is commemorated by the churches in response to the call of Ecumenical Patri-arch Dimitrios I. May the common reflection on the meaning of the Creed inaugurate a century in which the common calling and the unity of the churches will become more visible!

LUKAS VISCHER

PART I
MEMORANDUM

THE FILIOQUE CLAUSE
IN ECUMENICAL PERSPECTIVE

Preliminary note

The following memorandum has been drawn up by a group of theologians from eastern and different western traditions who met at Schloss Klingenthal near Strasbourg, France, 26–29 October 1978 and 23–27 May 1979. An initial draft was composed after the first meeting and circulated for comment to a number of other specialists. At the second meeting, the document was revised and expanded in the light of their reactions. A large number of specially prepared papers was presented at these meetings.

I. Introduction

The Niceno-Constantinopolitan Creed, often called simply "the Nicene Creed", which dates from the fourth century, has for over 1500 years been regarded as a primary formulation of the common faith of the Christian people. It has been used in many ways in the worship and teaching of different churches throughout the world, and holds a unique place as the Creed which is most widely received and recognized throughout the various Christian traditions.

There have, however, been significant differences between churches in the use that they have made of this Creed and in the authority they have ascribed to it. In the Eastern Orthodox churches it displaced all other credal formulations and came to be seen as *the* authoritative expression of the faith. In the western Church it only more gradually came into regular use alongside other, distinctively western formulae: the so-called Apostles' and Athanasian Creeds. It became and has remained the Creed regularly used in the Roman Catholic mass. At the Reformation, many of the Protestant churches (including the Anglican) continued to use it, or made reference to it in their own confessions of faith, though some have in effect ceased to make any use of it at all.

Alongside these variations in attitude and practice, there is a further contrast between the broad eastern and western traditions. In the West the wording of the third article was expanded by the addition of the "*filioque* clause". This supplemented the description of the Holy Spirit as "proceeding from the Father" with the Latin *filioque*, "and (from) the Son". In the background to this lay certain differences between the eastern and western approaches to understanding and expressing the mystery of the Trinity. The clause itself was one of several principal factors in the schism between East and West in the Middle Ages, and has continued to the present day to be a matter of controversy and a cause of offence to the Orthodox churches. So the Nicene Creed itself has come to be a focus of division rather than of unity in common faith.

Three distinct issues may be recognized in this situation. First, there is the divergence of approach to the Trinity. Second, we are presented with the particular problem of the wording of the Creed and the *filioque*. Third, the question needs to be faced of the standing and potential ecumenical significance of the Nicene Creed itself. All of these matters have taken on a new urgency and relevance in our present time. There is a widespread feeling that, especially in the West, the trinitarian nature of God needs again to be brought into the centre of Christian theological concern. The new ecumenical climate of recent years poses afresh the question of a reconciliation between East and West – a question which inevitably involves that of the *filioque*. This in turn gives a new sharpness to the question whether the Nicene Creed itself can again be received and appropriated afresh as a shared statement of the Christian faith. These questions are a challenge to all the churches; they are placed on the agenda by our present theological and ecumenical setting; and they deserve to be widely and seriously considered.

II. The Nicene Creed and the filioque clause

A. THE HISTORY AND RECEPTION OF THE NICENE CREED

In spite of its name, this Creed is not in fact that of the Council of Nicea (A.D. 325). In the form in which it has been handed down, it dates from the Council of Constantinople in A.D. 381, though it does include the main emphases of the original formulation of Nicea, if not always in exactly the same words. The full text of the Creed was reproduced by the Council of Chalcedon in A.D. 451, and since then it has been seen as the classical and definitive expression of the orthodox Christian faith as developed and articulated in the controversies of the fourth and fifth centuries.

In the Eastern Orthodox churches, this same Creed was also seen as the heir and beneficiary of the instruction made by the Council of Ephesus (A.D. 431) that no other Creed than that of Nicea should be used. The force of this regulation was primarily directed against any attempt to return behind the affirmations of the Council of Nicea concerning the full divinity of Jesus Christ; but it came in the East to have a further significance as ratifying the sanctity of the Creed framed at Constantinople, which was seen as possessing the same authority, and with it, the same exclusive status.

In the West, by contrast, the process of "reception" of this Creed was a slower one in the sense that while its canonical authority was not questioned, its actual use in the life and teaching of the Church was for many centuries distinctly limited. The western Church already possessed and continued to use the various local forms of the Old Roman Creed, from which in the eighth century the "Apostles' Creed" finally evolved; and also the "Athanasian Creed", which is not in any way connected with Athanasius, but dates from sixth century Gaul. The use of the Nicene Creed spread gradually through the western Church, and it was only as late as ca. 1014 that its singing was introduced into the liturgy of the mass in Rome itself. It was at the same time that the addition of the *filioque* was sanctioned by the Pope.

B. THE ADDITION OF THE FILIOQUE

Although the *filioque* was officially added to the Creed throughout the western Church only in the eleventh century, its history runs back very much further. As early as the fourth century, some Latin writers spoke of the Holy Spirit as "proceeding from the Father and the Son", or "from both", or in other similar ways directly linked the person of the Son with the procession of the Spirit. This understanding was developed further by Augustine in the early fifth century, and between his day and the eighth century it spread throughout the West. What may be called *"filioque* theology" thus came to be deeply anchored in the minds and hearts of western Christians. This represents the first stage of the development and the necessary background to what followed.

The next stage was the appearance of the *filioque* in official statements – e.g. the Canons of the Council of Toledo in A.D. 589 – and in the Athanasian Creed. At that time there was no apparent intention thereby to oppose the teaching of the Church in the East. (Many scholars have thought that the main concern was to counter western forms of Arianism by using the *filioque* as an affirmation of the divine status of the Son.)

By the end of the eighth century the *filioque* had come in many places in the West to be added to the Nicene Creed itself – one of these places being the court of the Emperor Charlemagne at Aachen. Charlemagne and his theologians attempted to persuade Pope Leo III (795–816) to ratify the alteration; but Leo, though seeming to agree with the theology of the *filioque*, refused to sanction an addition to the wording of the Creed which had been drawn up by an Ecumenical Council and reaffirmed by others. The expanded form of the Creed continued, however, to be widely used in the West; and two centuries later Pope Benedict VIII (1012–1024) finally authorized and approved it. Since then the western form of the Creed has included the *filioque*.

Attempts were made at the Councils of Lyons (1274) and Florence (1439) to impose the *filioque* on the East. These attempts were unsuccessful, however, and their effect in the long run was to intensify the bitterness felt in the eastern Church at the unilateral action of the West – not least because of the *anathema* which Lyons laid on those who rejected the clause. Eastern and western theologies of the Trinity and of the procession of the Holy Spirit came very much to stand over against each other, and the differences in approach which the *filioque* problem highlighted hardened into what were felt to be mutually exclusive positions.

While the Reformers were very critical of many of the developments in medieval theology, the question of the *filioque* was not seriously raised in the sixteenth century. Most Protestant churches accepted the clause and its underlying theology and continued to subscribe to both. It has only been much more recently that a new perspective has opened up. The last hundred years have brought many fresh contacts between East and West and enabled a new dialogue between them – a dialogue that is still growing today. The question of the *filioque* is now being discussed in a climate very different from that of the medieval Councils.

In this new climate, the possibility of returning to the original wording of the Creed has suggested itself to more than one western Church. The Old Catholic churches already began to make this change in the nineteenth century; the Lambeth Conference of 1978 has asked the churches of the Anglican Communion to consider doing the same; other churches too are exploring the question. It is our hope that yet more will give it serious consideration. Even those which make relatively little (or even no) use of the Nicene Creed have an interest in the matter in so far as they too are heirs of the western theological tradition and concerned both with the issues involved in the *filioque* and the progress of the ecumenical movement.

III. The Trinity and the procession of the Holy Spirit

The *filioque* question demands some consideration of the relation between the doctrines of the Trinity, of the "eternal procession" and of the "temporal mission" of the Holy Spirit. This is offered in the following four sub-sections which deal in turn with the Church's faith in and experience of the triune God (A), with biblical reflections upon the Spirit and the mystery of Christ (B), with the implications of the Spirit's temporal mission for relations between the persons of the Trinity (C), and with the way in which the Church always has to do with the Father, Son and Holy Spirit (D).

A. From its beginnings in the second and third centuries, the doctrine of the Trinity was intended to be a help for Christian believers, not an obstacle or an abstract intellectual superimposition upon the "simple faith". For it was in simple faith that the early Christians experienced the presence of the triune God; and it was in that presence that were gathered and held together the remembrance of the God of Israel, the presence within the congregation of the crucified and risen Christ and, from Pentecost, the power to hope in God's coming Kingdom which is the future of humankind.

This perception, celebrated in worship, strengthened and renewed by word and sacrament, and expressed in the individual and corporate lives and actions of believers, was not "dogmatic" or "conceptual" in the sense of enabling them to distinguish between "the advent of the risen Christ", "the presence of the Spirit" and "the presence of the Father". Their experience was – as it still is today – of the unity of the triune God. Both their prayerful acceptance and their rational understanding of this gift of God's presence, however, were articulated in terms of his triune life and being. This enabled the early Church – as it enables the Church today – to see itself as belonging within the story which God began with Abraham and Sara, which culminated in the coming, teaching, suffering, death, resurrection and ascension of Jesus Christ, and which marks out the way of the Church ever since Pentecost.

It was for this reason that the early Fathers gave witness to God's activity in Israel, his speaking through the prophets, in Jesus of Nazareth, and in the apostolic Church, as the activity of the triune God. They did not deduce their theological conclusions from a preconceived trinitarian concept. So, too, today in any reconsideration of trinitarian concepts as they have come to be developed, it is desirable that we should retrace and follow through the cognitive process of the early Church. The communion of the Church as articulated in ecclesiology seems to be the appropriate theological starting point for re-examining the function of trinitarian thought in the Church's faith, life and work. God is received, thought of and praised in the Church as God in his triune life: as Creator and God of Israel, as God the Logos and Son, as God the Spirit. It is this insight which preserves the biblical and historical roots of Christian faith in the living God.

B. The most personal Christian experience grafts us into the very heart of the mystery of Christ: sharing in the work of salvation, we are introduced into the divine life, into the heart of the deepest trinitarian intimacy. It is thus that, through the whole experience of the Church, the mystery of Christ is realized in a trinitarian perspective of salvation. New life in Christ is inseparable from the work of the Spirit. In its depths, the Church is nothing other than the manifestation of the risen Lord, whom the Holy Spirit renders present in the eucharistic community of the Church. There is a profound correspondence between the mystery of the Church and of Christian life on the one side, and the earthly life and work of Jesus himself on the other. It is thus not possible to speak of the mystery of Christ, of his person and work, without at once speaking not only of his relation to the Father, but also of the Holy Spirit.

In the earthly life of Jesus, the Spirit seems to be focused in him. The Spirit brings about his conception and birth (Matt. 1:18, Luke 1:35), manifests him at his baptism in the Jordan (Mark 1:9–11 and par.), drives him into the desert to be tested (Mark 1:12–13 and par.), empowers him in his return to Galilee (Luke 4:14) and rests in fullness upon him (Luke 4:18). It is thus in the permanent presence of the Spirit that Jesus himself lives, prays, acts, speaks and heals. It is in the Spirit and through the Spirit that Jesus is turned totally towards the Father, and also totally towards humankind, giving his life for the life of the world. Through his passion, his sacrifice on the cross "through the eternal Spirit" (Heb. 9:14), and his resurrection by the power of the Spirit (Rom. 8:11, etc.), it is in the Spirit that henceforth Jesus comes to us in his risen body, penetrated and suffused by the energies of the Spirit, and communicating to us in our turn power from on high. The humanity of Christ, full of the Holy Spirit, is real and authentic humanity; and it is by the Holy Spirit that we, too, become a new creation (John 3:5), sharing in the humanity of Christ (Eph. 2:15). We are "christified", "made christs", in the Church by the indwelling in us of the Holy Spirit who communicates the very life of Christ to us, who in Christ makes us the brothers and sisters of Christ, and strengthens us in our new condition as the adopted children of the heavenly Father.

The Spirit thus appears in the New Testament at once as he who rests upon Jesus and fills him in his humanity, and as he whom Jesus promises to send us from the Father, the Spirit of Truth who proceeds from the Father (John 15:26). The Spirit therefore does not have an action separate from that of Christ himself. He acts in us so that Christ may be our life (Col. 3:4), so that Christ may dwell in our hearts by faith (Eph. 3:12). The Spirit, who proceeds from the Father, is also therefore the Spirit of Jesus Christ himself (Rom. 8:9, Phil. 1:19) who rests in him (Luke 3:22, John 1:32–33), in whom alone we can confess Jesus as Lord (I Cor. 12:3), the Spirit of the Son (Gal. 4:6). These and many other New Testament passages reflect the Church's deep experience of the Spirit-filled and Spirit-giving being of Jesus himself. Here can be seen a full and constant reciprocity of the incarnate Word and the Holy Spirit, a reciprocity whose depths are further revealed in the fact that the sending of the Spirit had as its result the formation of the mystical body of Christ, the Church. This reciprocity must be emphasized as a fundamental principle of Christian theology. It is from this interaction, at once christological and trinitarian, that the divine plan for the salvation of the world is to be viewed in its continuity and coherence from the beginning of creation and the call of Israel to the coming of Christ. Further, all the life of the Church, indeed all Christian life, carries the imprint of this reciprocity from the time of Pentecost till the final coming of Christ. If it loses that vision, it can only suffer grievously from its lack.

C. The points of the Holy Spirit's contact with God's people are manifold. While one might be inclined to connect the coming of the Spirit exclusively with Pentecost, it must be remembered that any such limitation tends towards Marcionism in its patent neglect of the Old Testament witness to the presence and activity of the Spirit in Israel. Moreover, the Spirit is confessed to have been instrumental in the coming of Christ ("conceived by the Holy Spirit"), and to have been the life-giving power of God in his resurrection. Jesus during his ministry promised the sending of the Spirit, and the earliest Christians understood the pouring out of the Spirit at Pentecost to be the fulfilment of that promise. Thus the Spirit *precedes* the coming of Jesus, is active *throughout* his life, death and resurrection, and is *also sent* as the Paraclete by Jesus to the believers, who by this sending and receiving are constituted the Church. This chain of observations suggests that it would be insufficient and indeed illegitimate to "read back" into the Trinity only those New Testament passages which refer to the sending of the Spirit by Jesus Christ.

In the New Testament, the relation between the Spirit and Jesus Christ is not described solely in a linear or one-directional fashion. On the contrary, it is clear that there is a mutuality and reciprocity which must be taken into account in theological reflection upon the Trinity itself. The "eternal procession" of the Spirit of which trinitarian theology speaks as the ground which underlies and is opened up to us in his "temporal mission" cannot be properly characterized if only one aspect of the latter is taken into account. This raises certain questions about the *filioque*. Does it involve an unbiblical subordination of the Spirit to the Son? Does it do justice to the necessary reciprocity between the Son and the Spirit? If its intention is to safeguard the insight that the Holy Spirit is truly the Spirit of the Father *in Jesus Christ*, could other arguments and formulations defend that insight as well or even better? Is it possible that the *filioque*, or certain understandings of it, may have been understandable and indeed helpful in their essential intention in the context of particular theological debates, but yet inadequate as articulations of a full or balanced doctrine of the Trinity?

In approaching these questions it is imperative to remember that any reference to the Trinity is originally *doxological* in nature. This is all the more important in our own time, when talk of God is so severely challenged and trinitarian thinking so obviously neglected. Doxology is not merely the language of direct prayer and praise, but all forms of thought, feeling, action and hope directed and offered by believers to the living God. Doxological affirmations are therefore not primarily definitions or descriptions. They are performative and ascriptive, lines of thought, speech and action which, as they are offered, open up into the living reality of God himself. Trinitarian thought in the early Church originated within that doxological context, and only within it are we able to speak of the "inner life" of the triune God. Further, as fathers like Athanasius and Basil made clear, all such doxological references to that inner life must be checked by reference back to the biblical message concerning God's activity and presence with his people.

D. Conceptual distinctions between the "economic" and "immanent" Trinity, or between "temporal mission" and "eternal procession" should not be taken as separating off from each other two quite different realities which must then be somehow re-connected. Rather, they serve the witness to the triune God as the living God. In calling upon God, we turn and open ourselves to the God who is none other than he has revealed himself in his Word. This calling upon his name is the essential expression of doxology, that is, of trust, praise and thanks that the living God from eternity to eternity was, is and will be none other ("immanent Trinity") than he has shown himself to be in history ("economic Trinity").

In our calling upon him, the mystery of the Trinity itself is actualized. So we pray with Christ and in the power of the Spirit when we call on God his Father as *our* Father. So too we have a share in the joy of God when we allow ourselves to be told again that "for us a child is born". So too we pray in the Holy Spirit and he intercedes in us when we call on the Father in the name of the Son. In the calling upon the Father, the Spirit who proceeds from the Father, and we who worship in the Spirit, witness to Jesus Christ (John 15:26–7). The Spirit who proceeds from the Father of the Son is he whom the risen and ascended Christ sends, and by whose reception we are made the children of God.

IV. Theological aspects of the filioque

A. THE APPROACHES OF EASTERN AND WESTERN TRINITARIAN THEOLOGY

⌐In its origins the Latin tradition of the *filioque* served as an affirmation of the consubstantiality of the Father, Son and Holy Spirit, and also gave expression to the deeply-rooted concern in western piety to declare that the Spirit is the Spirit of the Son. The theology of Augustine marked a definite stage in the development of this tradition by articulating with particular clarity its fundamental concern for the oneness of the divine being, and by setting out on that basis to conceive of the Trinity in terms of a dialectic of oneness-in-threeness and threeness-in-oneness. In subsequent interpretation and application, this approach crystallized into a formal system which became the standard western teaching, and to which all the authority of the name of Augustine himself was attached. The introduction in the West of the logical procedures of medieval scholastic theology brought this form of trinitarian thinking to a new level of definition. One result of this development was to make dialogue with the East increasingly more difficult: hence arose the polemical frustrations of medieval controversy.

The eastern tradition of teaching about the Holy Trinity had from the beginnings somewhat different emphases. A central concern from the time of the Cappadocians in the late fourth century has been to affirm the irreducible distinctiveness of each of the divine hypostases (or, in the term more familiar in the West, "persons") of the Father, Son and Holy Spirit and at the same time, the uniqueness of the Father as the sole principle (ἀρχή), "source" (πηγή) and "cause" (αἰτία) of divinity. Thus, while Greek theologians could and did use such expressions as "from the Father through the Son", they could not accept the western "from the Father and the Son" as a suitable formulation for describing the procession of the Holy Spirit. This difference in emphasis, combined with the virtual absence in the East of the scholastic methods developed in the medieval West, made it difficult for the eastern Church to appreciate the western attitude. The controversies of the ninth century between Constantinople and the West – controversies, it must be said, which were as much political as theological – were the occasion of a further definition of the eastern position in the teaching of Patriarch Photius and his famous formula, "the Spirit proceeds from the Father *alone*". This tradition was continued and further developed by the work of Gregory the Cypriot and Gregory Palamas. Both these writers sought to respond to the controversy with the West by distinguishing between the *procession* of the Spirit from the Father and an "eternal *manifestation* of the Spirit through the Son".

What is striking is that, despite the evident differences between East and

West before the eleventh century, communion was maintained between them. The two traditions of trinitarian theological teaching, though divergent and at times in friction with each other, were not considered to be mutually exclusive. In the seventh century indeed, a notable attempt to explain and reconcile them was made in the work of Maximus the Confessor, a Greek Father who spent a large part of his life in the West. Only after the eleventh century did the two traditions come to be felt to be altogether irreconcilable.

B. Two central issues

In the debate between East and West about the *filioque*, two sets of questions can be seen as central. The first has to do with the traditional eastern insistence that the Spirit proceeds from the Father "alone"; the second with the western concern to discern a connexion between the Son and the procession of the Spirit.

1. Procession from the Father "alone"

According to the eastern tradition, the Holy Spirit proceeds from the Father *alone* for the following reasons:

a) The Father is the principle and cause of the Son and the Holy Spirit because it is an "hypostatic" (or "personal") property *of the Father* (and *not* of the shared divine nature) to "bring forth" the other two persons. The Son and the Holy Spirit do not derive their existence from the common essence, but from the hypostasis of the Father, from which the divine essence is conferred.

b) On the ground of the distinction between *ousia* ("being" or "essence") and hypostasis – which corresponds to the difference between what is "common" or "shared" and what is "particular" – the common properties of the divine nature do not apply to the hypostasis, and the distinctive properties of each of the three hypostases do not belong either to the common nature or to the other two hypostases. On account of his own hypostatic property, the Father derives his being from himself, and brings forth the Son and the Holy Spirit. The Son comes forth by γέννησις ("generation" or "begetting"), and his hypostatic property is to be begotten. The Holy Spirit comes forth by ἐκπόρευσις ("procession"), and that is his own distinctive hypostatic property. Because these hypostatic properties are not interchangeable or confused, the Father is the only cause of the being of the Son and of the Holy Spirit, and they are themselves caused by him.

c) In no way does the Father communicate or convey his own particular hypostatic property to either of the other two persons. Any idea that the Son together with the Father is the cause of the Holy Spirit's "mode of existence" (τρόπος τῆς ὑπάρξεως) was felt in the East to introduce two causes, two sources, two principles into the Holy Trinity. It is of course impossible to reconcile any such teaching with the divine μοναρχία ("monarchy") of the Father, that is, with his being the sole "principle" (ἀρχή).

d) In asserting in its theology, though not in the wording of the Creed, that the Spirit proceeds from the Father alone, the eastern Church does not believe that it is adding to the meaning of the original statement of the Creed. It holds, rather, that it is merely clarifying what was implicit in that original wording but had come to be denied by the West.

From a western point of view, which at the same time appreciates the concerns of the eastern tradition, it may be said that neither the early Latin Fathers, such as Ambrose and Augustine, nor the subsequent medieval tradition ever believed that they were damaging the principle of the Father's "monarchy" by affirming the *filioque*. The West declared itself to be as much attached to this principle as were the eastern Fathers. But by describing the Son as the "secondary cause" of the procession of the Holy Spirit, the doctrine of the *filioque* gave the impression of introducing "two principles" into the Holy Trinity; and by treating the Son in his consubstantiality and unity with the Father as the origin of the person of the Holy Spirit, it seemed to obscure the difference between the persons of the Father and the Son.

Nonetheless, an important fact remains. Quite apart from the – more or less happy or unhappy – formulations of the *filioque* advanced in western theology (which one must be careful not to treat as dogmas), and even if western Christians are prepared simply to confess in the original terms of the Creed that the Holy Spirit "proceeds from the Father" (without mentioning any secondary causality on the part of the Son), many would still maintain that the Holy Spirit *only proceeds from the Father as the Father is also Father of the Son*. Without necessarily wishing to insist on their own traditional understanding of a logical priority of the generation of the Son over the procession of the Spirit, they believe nonetheless that the trinitarian order (or, in Greek, τάξις) of Father-Son-Holy Spirit is a *datum* of revelation confessed by the Creed itself when it declares that the Spirit is to be "worshipped and glorified together with the Father and the Son". Thus they might indeed be ready to confess that the Holy Spirit proceeds "from the Father alone"; but by this they would not mean, "from the Father in isolation from the Son" (as if the Son were a stranger to the procession of the Holy Spirit), but rather, "from the Father alone, who is the only Father of his Only-begotten Son". The Spirit, who is not a "second Son", proceeds in his own unique and absolutely originated way from the Father who, as Father, is in relation to the Son.

2. The place of the Son in relation to the procession of the Holy Spirit

The Creed in its original form does not mention any participation of the Son in the procession of the Spirit from the Father, nor does it indicate the relationship between the Son and the Spirit. This may be because of the conflict with various current heresies which subordinated the Spirit to the Son, and reduced him to the level of a mere creature. However this may be, the absence of any clear statement on the relation between the Son and the Holy Spirit faces dogmatic theology with a problem which the West in the past attempted to solve by means of the *filioque*. In the Creed's lack of clarity on the point lies at least one of the roots of the divergence between later eastern and western theology of the Trinity. This means that even if agreement were reached on returning to the original wording of the Creed, that by itself would not be enough. In the longer term an answer must be given to the question of the relation between the Son and the Holy Spirit.

The observations which follow are advanced as a suggestion on the way in which western theology might move forward towards a closer understanding with the East, while still maintaining its concern to link the persons of the Son and the Spirit:

a) The Son's participation in the procession of the Spirit from the Father cannot be understood merely in terms of the *temporal mission* of the Spirit, as has sometimes been suggested. In other words, it cannot be restricted to the "economy" of the history of salvation as if it had no reference to, no bearing upon and no connexion with the "immanent" Trinity and the relation within the divine life itself between the three consubstantial persons. The freedom of God in his own being and as he acts in history must always be respected; but it is impossible to accept that what is valid for his revelation of his own being in history is not in some sense also valid for his eternal being and essence.

b) There is a sense in which it is correct to say that the Holy Spirit proceeds from the Father *alone* (ἐκ μόνου τοῦ Πατρός). This "alone" refers to the unique procession of the Spirit from the Father, and to his particular personal being (ὑπόστασις or *hyparxis*) which he receives from the Father. But it does not exclude a relationship with the Son as well as with the Father. On the one hand, the procession (ἐκπόρευσις) of the Spirit must be distinguished from the begetting (γέννησις) of the Son; but on the other hand this procession must be related to the begetting of the Son by the Father alone. While the Holy Spirit proceeds from the Father alone, his procession is nevertheless connected with the relationship within the Trinity between the Father and the Son, in virtue of which the Father acts *as Father*.

The begetting of the Son from the Father thus qualifies the procession of the Spirit as *a procession from the Father of the Son*.

c) From this fundamental thesis, two things follow. *First, it should not be said* that the Spirit proceeds "from the Father and the Son", for this would efface the difference in his relationship to the Father and to the Son. *Second, it should be said* that the procession of the Spirit from the Father presupposes the relationship existing within the Trinity between the Father and the Son, for the Son is eternally in and with the Father, and the Father is never without the Son. Eastern theology has traditionally emphasized the first of these two conclusions. The Latin Fathers were already exploring the implications of the second long before the *filioque* had finally been clarified and introduced into the Creed.

d) Along these lines, western trinitarian theology could come to understand the procession of the Holy Spirit in the way suggested by such patristic formulations as "the Spirit proceeds from the Father and receives from the Son". This underlines the fact that the Son is indeed not alien to the procession of the Spirit, nor the Spirit to the begetting of the Son – something which has also been indicated in eastern theology when it has spoken of the Spirit as "resting upon" or "shining out through" the Son, and insisted that the generation of the Son and procession of the Spirit must be *distinguished* but not *separated*. Differences certainly remain still in this area, for eastern theology is not easily able to agree that there is any *priority* of the generation of the Son over the procession of the Spirit, and desires rather to emphasize the "simultaneity" of the two, and to see the one as "accompanying" the other. Nonetheless, there does open up here a field for further exploration. So far as western theology is concerned, the Spirit could then be seen as receiving his complete existence (hypostasis) from the Father, but as existing in relation to both the Father and the Son. This would follow the principle that because the Father is the source of divinity, the Spirit does proceed from him "alone". At the same time, however, it would express what that principle alone and by itself cannot: the relation of the Spirit as a person within the Trinity to the Son as well as to the Father. The *filioque*, on this suggestion, would have valid meaning with reference to the relationship of the three hypostases within the divine triunity, but not with regard to the procession of the complete and perfect hypostasis of the Spirit from the Father.

e) These suggestions raise the further question of whether new or at least alternative formulations might be found which could express what the *filioque* validly sought to convey. Several old-established expressions have been mentioned in this section of the memorandum, viz:

– the Spirit proceeds from the Father of the Son;
– the Spirit proceeds from the Father through the Son;
– the Spirit proceeds from the Father and receives from the Son;
– the Spirit proceeds from the Father and rests on the Son;
– the Spirit proceeds from the Father and shines out through the Son.

These and possibly other formulations as well deserve to be given attention and consideration in future discussion.

V. The relevance of the question

These ancient controversies about what at first sight seems to be a strictly limited point of doctrine have, we believe, an unexpectedly urgent relevance. The study of the *filioque* question can be the point of entry into a wider exploration of the person and work of the Holy Spirit, of the relation of the Spirit to Jesus Christ, and indeed of the whole of trinitarian theology. The feeling that in all the western traditions something has been lacking in our experience and understanding of the Holy Spirit has grown rapidly in recent years. This tendency has carried with it a sense that the doctrine of the Trinity as such has come to appear remote and abstract to many, indeed very many Christian people. As Lesslie Newbigin writes: "It has been said that the question of the Trinity is the one theological question that has been really settled. It would, I think, be nearer the truth to say that the Nicene formula has been so devoutly hallowed that it is effectively put out of circulation." [1] In the western Christian world, while the churches continue to repeat the trinitarian formula, the trinitarian experience seems distant from many ordinary Christians. To them the word "God" is more likely to evoke thoughts of a supreme Monad than of the triune being of the Father, the Son and the Holy Spirit.

In the course of our discussions, we have realized that the question of the Trinity is one which is very far from being "settled". We have found in this fact not only a source of difficulties which have still to be tackled and overcome, but also at the same time a source of hope. In many different quarters it seems as if these basic articles of the Christian faith were coming to be the centre of new enquiry and fresh reflection. While we have not been able to agree as to how far the addition of the *filioque* clause was the cause of the differences between East and West on this whole subject, we have come to see that at least it has become a sign or indication of an underlying difference in theological approach. For the first ten centuries of the Christian era this difference was contained within a unity of faith and

---

[1] *The Open Secret*, Grand Rapids, Mich., Eerdmans, 1978, p. 30.

sacramental communion; since then it has been one of the primary causes of the continuing division between Orthodoxy on the one side and the Roman Catholic, Anglican and Protestant churches on the other. Within the last century, however, this situation has begun to change. First among the Old Catholics, then amongst Anglicans and others, the position of the *filioque* clause in the Creed has come under question. The whole matter of trinitarian theology has begun to be approached afresh. It has seemed to many that the balance and fullness of trinitarian doctrine, the reciprocity of the action of the Son and the Spirit, have been to some extent obscured in the West. It is not at all easy to trace the links of cause and effect in such areas. We do not say that the doctrine of the *filioque* was the cause of these developments. It may be that they have other origins. But certainly there is an interaction between one point of doctrine and others, between teaching and faith, between doctrinal formulations and the growth of Christian life.

In our discussion two points in particular have been suggested as opening up the wider bearing of the *filioque* debate. Both have figured especially in modern discussion of the issue. As they arise out of the concern to see the doctrine of the Trinity in connexion with the experience and practice of the Church, we must take them seriously into account.

A. On the one hand, it can be argued that the *filioque* underlines the fact that the Holy Spirit is none other than the Spirit of Jesus Christ; that this understanding of the Spirit is fundamental to the New Testament witness; and that the *filioque* is a necessary bulwark against the dangers of christologically uncontrolled "charismatic enthusiasm", dangers against which the churches today need to be on guard.

In no way would we wish to underplay the significance of this concern. At the same time, the Spirit too must not be "quenched" (I Thess. 5:19). Justice can be done to both sides of the matter only if in our speaking of the relation between the Spirit and the Son we do not give the impression of a one-sided dependence of the Spirit upon Christ, but express the reciprocity between them mentioned above in Section III B.

B. On the other hand, it can be maintained that the *filioque* subordinates the Holy Spirit to Christ; that it tends to "depersonalize" him as if he were a mere "instrument" or "power"; and that this tendency can also encourage a subordination of the Spirit to the Church in which the Church itself becomes hardened in authoritarian institutionalism.

This warning, too, must be taken seriously. It is admittedly an open question whether and how far connexions of this kind can be historically demonstrated in the development of the western Church. Nevertheless, this danger too can only be met and countered on solid theological ground by the recognition of the reciprocity and mutual interaction of the Son and Holy Spirit.

VI. Recommendations

We therefore recommend:

— A. That the new possibilities of discussion about the meaning of our faith in God, Father, Son and Holy Spirit, which are now opening up, and which we have begun to explore in this memorandum, should be pursued by all the churches; and that there should be a deeper effort to see how this faith is to be expressed in the forms of Christian worship, in the structures of the Church, and in the patterns of Christian life, so that the Holy Trinity may be seen as the foundation of Christian life and experience. This will require in particular a new sensitivity to the person and work of the Holy Spirit as the one who in his fullness both rests upon Jesus Christ and is the gift of Christ to the Church, the Lord and Giver of life to humankind and all creation.

— B. That the original form of the third article of the Creed, without the *filioque*, should everywhere be recognized as the normative one and restored, so that the whole Christian people may be able, in this formula, to confess their common faith in the Holy Spirit:

> And we believe in the Holy Spirit,
>> the Lord and Giver of life,
>> who proceeds from the Father,
>> who with the Father and the Son together is
>>> worshipped and glorified,
>> who spoke by the prophets.

— C. That the different churches should respond to these suggestions in ways appropriate to their own historical and theological situations. For some, this will involve a more living appreciation of formulae whose authority has never been questioned. For others, it will mean a wholly new appreciation of the value and significance of this ancient ecumenical confession of faith. For some in which the Creed is constantly used in public worship, it will imply liturgical changes which will need to be introduced step by step. In all these various ways a renewed reception of the Nicene Creed can play a vital role in the growing together of the separated Christian traditions into the unity of faith.

PART II
ESSAYS
A.
HISTORICAL ASPECTS

THE PROCESSION OF THE HOLY SPIRIT
ACCORDING TO CERTAIN
LATER GREEK FATHERS*

MARKOS A. ORPHANOS

Photius

Until the time of Photius, the issue of the procession of the Holy Spirit had been a matter of theological speculation. With Photius, it became a highly controversial point. Photius, in his discussion of the subject, almost singles out the idea of the Holy Spirit's procession through the Son and deals mainly with the procession of the Holy Spirit from the Father alone.

Photius treats the subject under the following presuppositions: (*a*) a distinction must be made between the properties belonging to the divine nature and those belonging to the hypostases; (*b*) what is common in the Holy Trinity is common to all three hypostases what is hypostatic is individual and belongs only to the corresponding hypostasis; (*c*) the hypostatic properties are uncommunicable and unconfused; (*d*) the Father is related to the Son and to the Holy Spirit as their unique cause of being and it is by him that they are caused.

The faculty of proceeding the Holy Spirit, argues Photius, is a hypostatic property of the Father and not of the common divine nature.[1] Therefore, it by no means belongs to another πρόσωπον of the Holy Trinity. Any participation of another Person is contrary to the uncommunicability and the unconfusedness of the hypostatic properties. Because the Father, as Father,

---

* This is the second part of a paper entitled "The Procession of the Holy Spirit According to Certain Greek Fathers". The first part, dealing with the ideas on the procession of the Holy Spirit of some ancient Greek Fathers such as Origen, Athanasius, the Cappadocians, Epiphanius, Cyril of Alexandria, Theodoret of Cyprus, Maximus the Confessor, Ps. Dionysius the Areopagite and John of Damascus, has been omitted because to some extent they are discussed in other papers in this volume.
● Markos A. ORPHANOS (Greek Orthodox) is lecturer at the Theological Faculty of the University of Athens, Greece.
[1] *De S. Spiritus Mystagogia* 15, PG 15, PG 102, 293AB.

begets the Son and proceeds the Holy Spirit, any share of the Son in the procession of the Holy Spirit would imply that the Son shares the hypostasis of the Father or stands for it, or that he is a part of the Fathers hypostasis. Such a notion, however, changes the Holy Triad to diad and introduces the misbelief of Son-Fatherhood (υἱοπατρία).[2]

Photius goes on to say that if the Father proceeds the Holy Spirit, not on the grounds of his hypostasis but on the grounds of his nature, then not only will the Son participate in the procession of the Holy Spirit but also the Holy Spirit himself will take part in his own mode of existence.[3] The double procession, continues Photius, makes the Father a simple name, deprived of meaning and sense; the property characterized by that word no longer belongs exclusively to him and the two divine hypostases are confused in one sole person. That is, however, the view of a Sabellius, or rather of some other half-Sabellian monster.[4]

The procession of the Holy Spirit from the Father and the Son, says Photius, results also in the opposite conclusion, namely, the plurality of the hypostases. If the Son is begotten from the Father, and the Holy Spirit proceeds from the Father and the Son, then the Holy Spirit must produce something else, on account of the equality of the divine Persons. This, of course, implies that instead of three we must have four hypostases and even more. Then the triune God is blemished and Christianity is diverted to the Greek polytheism.[5]

The Father, emphasizes Photius, is the unique cause (αἴτιον) of the mode of being of the Son and the Holy Spirit who are αἰτιατὰ and he by no means communicates his own particular property to the other two Persons. Any idea that the Son together with the Father is the cause of the Holy Spirit's mode of existence introduces to the Holy Trinity two causes and two principles. Of course, this is not possible and cannot be reconciled with the divine monarchia of the Father.[6]

Photius argues that the causal participation of the Son in the procession of the Holy Spirit introduces two principles and diverts the Orthodox faith to the gnosticism of Marcion and Manes,[7] because, he says, the procession of the Holy Spirit from the Son must be the same or a different one from

---

[2] *Ibid.* 16, PG 102, 293AB.
[3] *Ibid.* 17, PG 102, 325A.
[4] *Ibid.* 9, PG 102, 289A.
[5] *Ibid.* 37, PG 102, 317A.
[6] *Ibid.* 11, PG 102, 292AB.
[7] *Ibid.* 7, PG 102, 316A; *Encyclica ad Archiepiscopales Thronos . . .* 17, PG 102, 729A.

that of the Father. If it is the same, then the Son communicates the hypostatic property of the Father. If it is different, then it must be an opposition between the Father and the Son.[8] In this line of thought, Photius maintains that the *filioque* introduces two principles of which the one is unoriginated (ἄναρχος) and the other originated (ἀρχομένη). This introduces two causes. With two causes, however, the Trinity becomes formed of four hypostases, because the hypostasis of the Holy Spirit is subject to a kind of division. This is so because the Holy Spirit derives his existence from two causes, namely, the Father as a first cause and the Son which is a cause which has been caused.[9]

Photius goes on to say that if we are going to accept the notion that the Son as a cause produces the Holy Spirit, then we must acknowledge that the Father's procession of the Holy Spirit is imperfect. This, however, contradicts the perfection of the Father. On the other hand, if to the perfect cause, the Father, we add another one, the Son, this cause must be imperfect and inferior in comparison to the first. The insertion of such a ἡμίτομον cause into the internal relations of the Holy Trinity, however, introduces to the Holy Trinity the Greek mythologies of hippocentaurs and makes the Holy Trinity a monster.[10]

According to Photius, the Son cannot be considered as a common cause of the Holy Spirit's procession with the Father, because this would imply that the procession is a common property of the Father and of the Son. Since all things common to the Father and to the Son are in any case common to the Spirit, the Holy Spirit must thus proceed from himself. Even he will be principle of himself and at the same time both cause and caused. Nevertheless, Photius says, not without irony, even the myths of the Greeks never fabricated such an idea.[11]

The procession of the Holy Spirit also from the Son, states Photius, leads to another absurdity, namely, it makes the Father both a direct and an indirect cause of the Holy Spirit's procession. The Father is a direct cause because he begets the Son directly and proceeds the Holy Spirit. He is an indirect cause because he proceeds the Holy Spirit through the Son. But this does not happen even in the creation of the compound and changeable nature.[12]

---

[8] *Ibid.* 17, PG 102, 729A.
[9] *De S. Spiritus Mystagogia* 14, PG 102, 293A; *Ibid.* 43, PG 102, 321BC.
[10] *Ibid.* 7, PG 102, 288BC; 31, PG 102, 317C–318A; 44, PG 102, 321BC.
[11] *Ibid.* 44, PG 102, 321C.
[12] *Ibid.* 42, PG 102, 341A.

The participation of the Son in the procession of the Holy Spirit, continues Photius, not without some exaggeration, introduces the impious notion that the Holy Spirit is the Grandson of the Father, an erroneous conception which the Fathers from Athanasius onwards have vigorously refuted. Photius says that it leads also to the heresy of Macedonius putting the Holy Spirit in a state of inferiority. While the Father and the Son possess the faculty of the procession of the Holy Spirit, the Holy Spirit, despite his equality with the Father and the Son, is deprived of the possibility to beget the Son and to come out of himself.[13]

The procession of the Holy Spirit from the Son is not supported by biblical evidence. The words of our Lord "for He (i.e. the Holy Spirit) shall receive of mine and shall show it unto you", according to Photius, do not mean that the Holy Spirit receives from the Son, but from the Father. The meaning of "receiving" is not the same as that of "proceeding".[14] In this particular verse "receiving" does not mean the causal derivation of the Holy Spirit's being from the Son, but simply the proclamation of things to come.[15] Even Christs declaration "he shall receive of mine" implies that the Holy Spirit receives the accomplishments from the Father, as his cause, and he himself bestows them on the disciples in order to encourage them for the sufferings to come.[16] St Paul's statement "God hath sent forth the Spirit of his Son into your hearts, crying Abba, Father" does not suggest that the Son is the cause of the Holy Spirit's existence, but simply that the Holy Spirit is consubstantial and invariably of the same nature as the Son. The Holy Spirit is called the "Spirit of the Son" because of his homoousion with the Son. He is also called "Spirit of the Christ" because he anoints Christ in his human nature.[17]

Nevertheless, Photius admits that there is only one cause, according to which the Holy Spirit proceeds from the Son, not, of course, in the mode of his being but in his temporal mission to the world. It is the result of the perichoresis of the divine hypostases and their common energies.[18]

The innovation of the *filioque*, Photius goes on to argue, is not supported by the Tradition of the Church, because neither in the divine words of the scriptures nor in the human words of the Fathers was it verbally enunciated that the Spirit proceeds from the Son.[19] Photius, of course, was aware that

---

[13] *Ep. ad Archiepiscopum et Metropolitam Aquileiensem* 9, PG 102, 801D.
[14] *De S. Spiritus Mystagogia* 21–23, PG 102, 300A–301C.
[15] *Ibid*. 29, PG 102, 309C.
[16] *Ibid*. 30, PG 102, 312B.
[17] *Ibid*. 51, PG 102, 329B.
[18] *Ibid*. 23, PG 102, 388AB.
[19] *Ibid*. 5, PG 102, 285A.

according to the partisans of *filioque* certain Latin Fathers such as Ambrose, Augustine and Jerome taught that the Holy Spirit proceeds from the Son. But he maintains that they were falsified or that they did not speak in dogmatic terms, or that as human beings they were fallible. In the last case it would be better to gloss over their error and not to glory in it.[20]

Even if Ambrose or Augustine in the West taught the procession of the Holy Spirit from the Son, Photius continues, a great number of Roman Pontiffs such as Celestine, Leo the Great, Vigilius, Agatho, Gregory the Great, Hadrian I, Leo III, Benedict III, John VIII and Hadrian III held the opposite view, namely, that the Holy Spirit proceeds from the Father.[21] The same teaching was also pronounced by six of the seven Ecumenical Councils, clearly implying that the *filioque* clause has no foundation either in scriptures or in the Tradition of the Church.[22]

Photius' doctrine on the procession of the Holy Spirit being only from the Father is rigorous, comprehensive and convincing. It is a pity, however, that because of his strong polemical manner in discussing this issue, he was prevented from treating the subject thoroughly. Thus he does not fully discuss the procession of the Holy Spirit through the Son, even though it was a traditional teaching of the previous Greek Fathers. On the other hand, Photius' interpretation of the relevant biblical passages seems sometimes to be far-fetched. The same can be argued with regard to Photius' criticism and refutation of the arguments of his opponents and partisans of the doctrine of *filioque.* Nevertheless, Photius' doctrine on the procession of the Holy Spirit has had a tremendous influence upon the Byzantine theology of the *filioque*. The authors who oppose the doctrine of *filioque* turn again and again to Photius' treatises and derive arguments and ideas from them.

Gregory the Cypriot

Among the numerous Byzantine theologians who have been involved in the question of the procession of the Holy Spirit, Gregory (or George) the Cypriot, Patriarch of Constantinople, deserves a noteworthy place. Gregory, in his dispute with John Veccos, first an opponent and then a defender of *filioque*, was able to clear up some points in regard to the procession of the Holy Spirit which had been vague.

Gregory follows the Greek patristic tradition, arguing that the Father, on account of the divine monarchia and the unconfusedness of the hypostatic

---

[20] *Ibid.* 71–72, PG 102, 352BC – 353A.
[21] *Ibid.* 87–89, PG 102, 376A–380A.
[22] *Ibid.* 5, PG 102, 285AB.

properties, is the sole source and principle of the Son and the Holy Spirit.[23]
The Father causally sends forth the Holy Spirit on the grounds of the
common essence, because the Father alone is the begetting deity and the
divine source and the only source of the whole deity (θεογόνος θεότης καὶ
πηγαία θεότης καὶ μόνη πηγὴ τῆς ὅλης θεότητος).[24] The Father, Gregory
goes on to say, is the principle and cause of the Son and the Holy Spirit, not
because they derive their existence from the essence of the Father, but
because they owe their mode of being to the hypostasis of the Father,
through which the divine essence is conferred.[25]

Indeed, because of the identity of essence, the Holy Spirit is also from
the essence of the Son and not from his hypostasis.[26] Any derivation of the
Holy Spirit's mode of existence from the hypostasis of the Son is contrary
to the teaching of the Fathers, who plainly teach that the Father is the
begetting deity (θεογόνος θεότης) from whom come forth the Son by way
of generation and the Holy Spirit by way of procession.[27]

Gregory also repeats the well-known patristic argument that the Father
is the unique cause of being of the Son and the Holy Spirit who are caused
(αἰτιατά). Thus, none of that produced by a cause (αἰτιατὰ) can be a cause
in itself or with the Father produce himself or another αἰτιατόν. Gregory
the Cypriot argues with Photius in saying that the procession of the Holy
Spirit from both introduces two principles and two causes in the Holy Trinity.
This even makes the procession of the Holy Spirit from the Father imperfect,
an idea which is contrary to the perfection of the Father.[28]

Gregory was aware that John Veccos rejected that there are two principles
or two causes in the Holy Trinity and that he argued that, although the Son
participates in the causal derivation of the Holy Spirit, there is only one
principle and cause, namely, the Father. Veccos continues that it is due to
the fact that the Sonly cause (υἱϊκὴ αἰτία) leads up to the Fatherly cause
(πατρικὴ αἰτία).[29] This notion was also common to the Latins who maintained that, despite the Sons participation in the causal procession of the
Holy Spirit, the Holy Spirit comes out only from one cause, because the
Father is the primordial source and the Son a joint cause.

---

[23] *De processione Spiritus Sancti* PG 142, 283A; 299A; *Scripta Apologetica* PG 142,
235C, 271C.
[24] *De Processione Spiritus Sancti* PG 142, 271AB.
[25] *Ibid*. PG 142, 270D – 271A.
[26] *Ibid*. 271ABC.
[27] *Ibid*. 272D.
[28] *Ibid*. 281B, 271CD; *Scripta Apologetica* PG 142, 255C.
[29] *Scripta Apologetica*, PG 142, 235C.

However, Gregory does not accept this argument and insists that the notion that the Holy Spirit derives his being from the two causes or from one, because the second is referred to the first, is blasphemous. It is not founded biblically and is not consistent with the teaching of the Fathers. Therefore, says Gregory, as far as the Holy Spirit's causal procession is concerned, it is neither from nor through the Son, but from the Father alone.[30]

Speaking against the assertion of Veccos that the expression "through the Son" implies the *filioque* (because the preposition "through" bears the same meaning as the preposition "from"), Gregory maintains that this is a misconception. Indeed, the Holy Spirit proceeds "through" the Son, but this procession refers to his eternal manifestation (ἀΐδιον ἔκφανσιν) and not to his essential derivation. When Veccos identifies the expression δι' Υἱοῦ with the expression ἐκ τοῦ Υἱοῦ he commits himself to a great blasphemy against the Spirit.[31]

Thus, while from Photius onwards the formula δι' Υἱοῦ was confined to the mission of the Holy Spirit in time, it is to Gregory's merit that he applies it also to the eternal manifestation of the Spirit through the Son. Gregory explains that many Fathers have taught that the Holy Spirit proceeds through the Son, but they apply this procession not to the Holy Spirit's causal mode of being but to his manifestation. The cause of the hypostatic existence of the Holy Spirit remains the Father alone.[32]

This manifestation, which Gregory describes in terms such as ἔκφανσις, φανέρωσις, πρόεισις, refers not to the Holy Spirit's causal mode of being but to the manner according to which his being exists. The ἔκφανσις is different from the ἐκπόρευσις. The first applies to the manifestation of the Holy Spirit, the second to his very mode of being.[33]

In order to distinguish the procession as mode of existence of the Holy Spirit from his manifestation, Gregory the Cypriot makes an important distinction between the verbs ὕπαρξιν ἔχειν and ὑπάρχειν. Thus, the Holy Spirit owes his cause of existence to the Father alone, but he exists in the Son and rests in him, shining forth and revealing himself through or from the Son.[34] According to Gregory, this distinction between ὕπαρξιν ἔχειν and ὑπάρχειν makes plain that the Holy Spirit proceeds in his hypostatic being

---

[30] *Ibid.* PG 142, 256AB.
[31] *Ibid.* PG 142, 250B.
[32] *Ibid.* PG 142, 250A.
[33] *Ibid.* PG 263AB; 265D–266A.
[34] *De Processione Spiritus Sancti*, PG 142, 275C–276A.

from the Father alone. Yet, in his manifestation in this "economy" the Holy Spirit proceeds from the Father and also from the Son. The Holy Spirit, having from the Father his very being, rests and abides in the Son, from whom he is shining forth and bestowed.[35]

The Holy Spirit, explains Gregory, exists eternally in the Son and is manifested through him, but this existence and manifestation must not be confused with the Holy Spirit's eternal causal mode of existence which is due to the Father alone. In order to illustrate this distinction, Gregory uses the well-known analogies of the sun, its radiance, and its light, as well as of the spring, its river and its water.[36] Gregory argues that it is recognized that the very Paraclete shines and manifests itself eternally by the intermediary of the Son, as light shines from the sun by the intermediary of rays. But that does not mean that it comes into being through the Son or from the Son.[37]

This manifestation of the Holy Spirit through the Son, explains Gregory, refers to the eternal life of the Holy Trinity, but also to the temporal mission of the Holy Spirit. Yet, a clear distinction must be made between the Holy Spirit's emission and his mode of existence. The temporal mission is a common act of the three divine Persons resulting from their common will and energy. The mode of the Holy Spirit's existence, however, depends on the Father's hypostasis. Therefore, Veccos and his followers are wrong in transferring the idea of the Son's participation in the divine energies to the internal relations of the Holy Trinity and particularly to the mode of being of the divine Persons.[38]

Gregory distinguishes between the principle and cause of the Holy Trinity which is the Father alone, and the principle cause of the creation which is the whole Holy Trinity. These two principles must not be confused, because it would result in a confusion between the Holy Trinity and the creation. Therefore, continues Gregory, as far as the creation of the world is concerned, the Father, the Son and the Holy Spirit, on the ground of their common nature, will, power, and energy, create in common as one principle and one cause the created order. This common energy is a property of the divine nature and does not confound the hypostatic properties. However, with regard to the mode of being of the Holy Spirit, the unique principle and cause is the Father in his hypostatic property. Any participation of the Son in the mode of being of the Holy Spirit implies that either this procession

---

[35] *Scripta Apologetica* PG 142, 266CD.
[36] *Ibid.* PG 142, 251AB; *De Processione Spiritus Sancti* PG 142, 285C; 287BC.
[37] *Ibid.* 240BC; 285AB.
[38] *Ibid.* 282D – 283A.

is imperfect or that the two Persons are confounded into one because the property of proceeding the Holy Spirit is a hypostatic property of the Father.[39]

It is obvious that Gregory considers the question of the Holy Spirit's procession from the Father and his manifestation from the Father through the Son from the point of view of distinction between the divine essence and the eternal uncreated energies of God. Of course, Photius, following suit to other Fathers, had accepted this distinction between the essence and the energies of God, but he had restricted these energies to the gifts of the Holy Spirit. By opposing the eternal procession of the Holy Spirit from the Father to the Spirit's temporal mission from the Son, he had accepted the procession of the Holy Spirit through the Son as a consequence of the Incarnation. Gregory the Cypriot, however, accepts this manifestation (ἔκ-φανσις) of the Holy Spirit through the Son as an eternal act. Gregory continues that it is his eternal manifestation as an energy, coming out from the Father and through the Son, that the previous Fathers had in mind when they said that the Holy Spirit proceeds from the Father διὰ τοῦ Υἱοῦ διὰ τοῦ προσεχῶς ἐκ τοῦ πρώτου or that the Holy Spirit is ἐξ ἀμφοῖν or he is ἴδιον τοῦ Υἱοῦ.[40]

Gregory's contribution to the doctrine of the Holy Spirit's procession is remarkable. In underlining this, John Meyendorff is correct when he writes: "Instead of simply repeating Photius' formulas about the 'eternal procession' of the Holy Spirit from the Father alone and the 'emission in time' by the Son, Gregory recognized the need to express the permanent relationship existing between the Son and the Holy Spirit as divine hypostases and he spoke of an 'eternal manifestation of the Spirit by the Son'." [41] Gregory's doctrine was taken and developed by his namesake, Gregory of Palamas, to whom we now turn our attention.

Gregory Palamas

Gregory Palamas discusses the issue of the procession of the Holy Spirit mainly from two points of view: (*a*) his causal procession from the Father alone, and (*b*) his energetic procession (κατ᾽ ἐνέργειαν) from the Father through or from the Son.

As far as the Spirit's causal procession is concerned, Gregory follows the

---

[39] *Ibid.* 281BD–282AD; 294D–295A; *Scripta apologetica* PG 142, 242BC.
[40] Gregory obviously had in mind Fathers such as Gregory of Nyssa, Epiphanius, Cyril of Alexandria, John of Damascus, Maximus the Confessor, etc.
[41] *A Study of Gregory Palamas*, London, Faith Press, 1964, p. 13.

Greek patristic tradition, arguing that the hypostasis of the Father is the unique cause, origin and source of the Son's and the Holy Spirit's divinity and existence. The Father is the cause of the divine unity not only because his nature is one, but also because the Son and the Holy Spirit coming out from the Father go back to this one and unique Person.[42]

According to Gregory Palamas, the procession of the Holy Spirit from the Father alone is based on John 15:25 and the Tradition of the Church. Of course, the Niceno-Constantinopolitan Creed, Palamas admits, does not say plainly that the Holy Spirit proceeds from the Father alone, as it does not state that the Son is begotten from the Father alone. Nevertheless, it is self-evident because the Father is the only cause of being of the two other Persons of the Trinity who are caused (αἰτιατά).[43] The procession (ἐκπό-ρευσις), explains Palamas, is a property of the hypostasis of the Father and not of the divine essence. If it is accepted as a common property of the nature, the Holy Spirit should then also proceed from himself. In this case, however, the Holy Trinity becomes four Persons. On the other hand, if this procession (ἐκπόρευσις) is a common property of the Father and the Son, and the Holy Spirit is deprived of it, then the Holy Spirit is alienated from the divine nature.[44]

Gregory goes on to say that because the procession of the Holy Spirit is a hypostatic act of the Father, the double procession introduces two causes and origins in the Holy Trinity, since the Father and the Son are two distinctive hypostases.[45] The threat of introducing to the Holy Trinity two origins is in no way ruled out by the assertion that the Father and the Son constitute a sole origin of the Holy Spirit. This is absolutely contrary to the θεογόνον which is an incommunicable hypostatic property of the Father.[46] On the other hand, if the θεογόνον were to be attributed to the Son, it would lead to another misconception, namely that the Son is of the same hypostasis as the Father.[47] Therefore, Gregory points out, the procession of the Holy Spirit from the Father alone safeguards the monarchia and rules out the danger of introducing into the Holy Trinity two principles and two causes.[48] He says that it is necessary to distinguish between the origin of the

[42] Λόγος ἀποδεικτικός 1.8, Bobrinskoy, Συγγράμματα Γρηγορίου Παλαμᾶ 1, p. 133; *Ibid.* 1–23, p. 52, 49; 1.2, p. 31, 4–17.
[43] *Ibid.* 1.6, p. 33, 28–34, 5; 1.15, p. 43, 23–26.
[44] Ἐπιστολὴ πρὸς ᾽Ακίνδυνον 4.7, Meyendorff, 1, p. 209, 15, 19.
[45] *Ibid.* 1.7, p. 34, 15–19.
[46] Λόγος ἀποδεικτικός 1.15, Bobrinskoy, 1, pp. 43, 16–44, 24.
[47] *Ibid.* 1.22, p. 81, 28–30.
[48] *Ibid.* 1.49, p. 70, 16–19.

Holy Trinity, which is the Father alone, and the origin of the creation, which is the Triune God.[49] According to this distinction, the Father alone is the origin and the root of the Holy Trinity. The Father sends out the Son by way of generation and the Holy Spirit by way of procession. The Father as the unique principle (ἀρχὴ) is the cause of the unity of the Holy Trinity and its hypostatic differentiation.[50] The three divine Prosopa as a trihypostatic principle, argues Palamas, create together because they possess one sole energy and will.[51] Their activity from the Father through the Son is realized in the Holy Spirit.[52] On the basis of the distinction between the Fatherly principle (πατρικὴ ἀρχὴ) and the triadic principle (τριαδικὴ ἀρχὴ), the statement of Gregory of Nazianzus that the Son is ἡ ἐκ τῆς ἀρχῆς ἀρχὴ does not mean that the Son is the origin of the Holy Spirit but the origin of the creation, which comes into being by the common act of the three divine hypostases.[53] Any confusion of these two principles results in the confusion between the divinity and the creation, for either the creatures have the same mode of being as the Prosopa of the Holy Trinity, or the divine hypostases – and particularly the Holy Spirit – come into being like the created order, namely, by the will and energy of God.[54]

The idea of the double procession of the Holy Spirit, Gregory maintains, leads to the same misconception, because the statement *tanquam ab uno principio* refers not to "theology" but the the divine "economy", namely, the participation of the Son in the creation of the world.[55] On the contrary, the clear distinction between the Fatherly principle (πατρικὴ ἀρχὴ) and the triadic principle (τριαδικὴ ἀρχὴ) presupposes the participation of the Son in the act of the creation and excludes any notion of the Son's participation in the causal mode of being of the Holy Spirit.[56]

Over and over again Gregory refers to the hypostatic procession of the Holy Spirit and his manifestation. The mode of being and the manifestation of the Holy Spirit, Gregory argues, are two aspects of the mystery of the Holy Spirit. The Holy Spirit derives his existence from the Father, yet he exists eternally in the Son and rests in him.[57] The Son participates in the

---

[49] Ἐπιστολὴ πρὸς ᾽Ακίνδυνον 1.5, Meyendorff, p. 207, 24–25.
[50] Λόγος ἀποδεικτικὸς 1.15, Bobrinskoy, pp. 43, 16–44, 24.
[51] Περὶ ἑνώσεως καὶ διακρίσεως 21, *Mantzarides*, 2, p. 84, 13–15.
[52] Ἐπιστολὴ πρὸς ᾽Ακίνδυνον 1.5, p. 207, 24–25.
[53] *Ibid.*
[54] *Ibid.* 1.14, pp. 24–25.
[55] Λόγος ἀποδεικτικὸς 1.15, p. 44, 1–2.
[56] Ἐπιστολὴ πρὸς Βαρλαὰμ 1.21, Meyendorff, 1, p. 236, 15–237, 3.
[57] Λόγος ἀποδεικτικὸς 2.73, p. 144, 14–21.

manifestation (ἔκφανσις) of the Holy Spirit. Therefore, Gregory continues, the Spirit pours itself out from the Father through the Son and, if you like, from the Son.[58] Comparing the causal procession of the Holy Spirit with his energetic (κατ' ἐνέργειαν) procession, he maintains that the Holy Spirit belongs to Christ by essence and by energy, because Christ is God; nevertheless, according to essence and hypostasis it belongs but not proceeds,[59] whereas, according to energy, it belongs and proceeds. Because of the perichoresis and the consubstantiality of the hypostases, the Son and the Holy Spirit are of the other (τοῦ ἄλλου) but not from the other (ἐξ ἄλλου).

On account of the difference between the causal and the manifesting (ἐκφαντορικὴ) procession of the Holy Spirit, Palamas explains, when certain Fathers assert that the Holy Spirit comes forth "from both" or "through the Son" or "from the Son", they are referring to the common energy of these divine hypostases and not to the mode of existence of the Holy Spirit. Therefore, Palamas suggests, when you understand that the Holy Spirit proceeds from the two, because it comes essentially from the Father through the Son, you should understand this teaching in the following sense: it is the powers and essential energies of God which pour out and not the divine hypostasis of the Spirit.[60]

The hypostasis of the Holy Spirit, Gregory continues, does not come out from the Son, nor is it shared (μεθεκτὴ), i.e. it is not communicated to any creature. Only the divine grace and energy are participated in (μεθεκταί).[61] On the other hand, when the Fathers speak about the procession of the Holy Spirit through or from the Son, they connect this procession with the divine essence and not with the hypostasis of the Son. Everything, however, which comes out commonly from the divine essence is energy and not hypostasis.[62]

Gregory Palamas goes on to say that because the divine essence as well as the hypostases are not shared (ἀμέθεκτοι) and only the divine energies can be communicated (μεθεκταί), on Pentecost and in other cases where the Holy Spirit was bestowed by Christ, it was not the hypostasis of the Holy Spirit but his charismata that were transmitted. The granting of the divine energies is a common act of the Holy Trinity which starts from the Father, comes through the Son and is realized in the Holy Spirit.[63]

[58] *Ibid.* 1.29, p. 54, 23–24.
[59] *Ibid.* 2.29, p. 105, 17–21.
[60] *Ibid.* 2.20, p. 96, 23–28.
[61] *Ibid.* 2.48, p. 122, 14–17.
[62] *Ibid.* 2.69, pp. 140, 19–141, 3.
[63] Περὶ ἑνώσεως καὶ διακρίσεως 21, *Mantzarides*, p. 84, 10–15.

On account of this distinction between the divine essence and the divine uncreated energies, the Holy Scriptures referring to the Holy Spirit speak on the one hand of "the Spirit" with the definite article and on the other hand of "Spirit" without the article. In the first case the essential derivation is implied while in the second the gifts of the Holy Spirit, i.e. his energies. Therefore, when our Lord infused the disciples with the Holy Spirit he did not say "receive ye the Holy Spirit" (as is commonly translated in English) but simply "receive Holy Spirit", that is to say βραχύ τι τοῦ πνεύματος, his energy, and not his essence or hypostasis.[64]

Thus the participation of the Son can be accepted only in the sense of the energetic (κατ' ἐνέργειαν) procession of the Holy Spirit and by no means can it be transferred by induction to his mode of existence. The energies of the Holy Spirit are a result of the common free will and activity of the Holy Trinity. However, the hyparxis of the Holy Spirit is an act of the hypostasis of the Father. Therefore, the Son participates in the mission and the energies of the Holy Spirit, but the Holy Spirit owes his existence to the Father alone.[65]

According to Palamas, the energetic (κατ' ἐνέργειαν) procession of the Holy Spirit from the Father through the Son is eternal and it becomes temporal when the Father and the Son will it. The energy as uncreated pre-exists its realization and manifestation, therefore, his being a Spirit is precontemplated on the Son emanating from him only according to time (ἐπὶ τοῦ Υἱοῦ προθεωρεῖται τὸ εἶναι αὐτοῦ Πνεῦμα τοῦ ἐξ αὐτοῦ εἶναι, εἰ καὶ μὴ κατὰ χρόνον).[66]

In order to illustrate the eternal existence of the common energies in the Holy Trinity and their temporal manifestation, Palamas uses for the first time in the Greek patristic tradition the analogy of "love" (ἔρως) which was introduced in the West by Augustine[67] and used by others. Thus, according to Palamas, the Spirit of the Word from on high is like a mysterious love of the Father towards the Word mysteriously begotten; it is the same love as that possessed by the Word and the well beloved Son of the Father towards him who begat him; this he does in so far as he comes from the Father conjointly with this love and this love rests, naturally, on him.[68] Gregory, referring to the Incarnate Logos, argues that the Holy Spirit is indeed the

---

[64] Λόγος ἀποδεικτικὸς 2.6, p. 83, 3–6.
[65] *Ibid.* 2.26, p. 102, 10–15.
[66] *Ibid.* 2.14, p. 92, 1–3.
[67] *De Trinitate* IX.X.15, PL 42, 968–969.
[68] *Capita Physica Theologica* 36, PG 150, 1145A.

Spirit of the Son as well, but He receives this from the Father, because of his attribute as the Spirit of Truth, Wisdom and the Word; since Truth and Wisdom are words appropriate to the Genitor.[69]

Gregory Palamas is obviously referring, on the one hand, to the eternal relations within the Holy Trinity and particularly to the mutual use (χρῆσις) of the Holy Spirit from the Father and the Son, and on the other hand, to the Holy Spirit's temporal mission. However, this "love" which "comes from the Father conjointly with this love" is by no means the hypostasis of the Holy Spirit coming into existence from the Father and the Son, because in his use (χρῆσιν) the Son already possesses the Holy Spirit and this "love" abides in him. But the Son possesses the Holy Spirit because he comes out from the Father in his existence.[70]

If we take into account that, according to Palamas, every name applied to God refers to his energy and not to his essence or hypostasis, this characterization of the Holy Spirit as "love", used by the Father and the Son, applies not to the hypostasis of the Holy Spirit but to the common energy which is the love of the Triune God. It exists eternally in God and is manifested in time coming out from the Father through the Son and the Holy Spirit.[71]

That Gregory Palamas by this image of love, strange to the eastern tradition, is referring to the energetic procession (κατ' ἐνέργειαν) of the Holy Spirit and not to his causal existence is clear from his explanation that the Holy Spirit is pre-eternal joy of both the Father and the Son. As common to both as concerns its use (χρῆσις), hence it is sent by both only to those who are worthy, but being only of the Father, as far as its existence is concerned. Therefore, the Holy Spirit proceeds alone from the Father as concerns its existence.[72] By this clear distinction between the καθ' ὕπαρξιν procession of the Holy Spirit from the Father alone and his κατ' ἐνέργειαν from the Father through the Son or from the Father and the Son, Palamas excludes the idea of *filioque*. The double procession of the Holy Spirit, to Palamas' judgment, introduces confusion or relativism of the hypostases and their hypostatic properties. In the case in which the Father and the Son, as one principle, proceed the Holy Spirit, then they are confused into a φυσικὴ

---

[69] *Ibid.*
[70] Λόγος ἀποδεικτικὸς 2.26, p. 102, 12–15.
[71] Περὶ ἑνώσεως καὶ διακρίσεως 21, p. 84, 10–15.
[72] *Capita Physica Theologica* 36, PG 150, 1145A.

ἀδιακρισία and the Holy Spirit himself as the unity of the two hypostases is not clearly distinguished as a hypostasis.[73]

On the other hand, the distinction between the καθ' ὕπαρξιν and the κατ' ἐνέργειαν procession of the Holy Spirit safeguards man's participation in the uncreated grace, i.e. the common energies of the Triune God, and at the same time excludes the danger of polytheism.[74]

Mark of Ephesus

Mark Eugenicus, Metropolitan of Ephesus, arguing against the Latins and the pro-unionists at the Council of Florence and later against those who had subscribed to its Decree or accepted its pronouncement that the Holy Spirit has his essence and his subsistent being from the Father and the Son simultaneously and proceeds from both eternally as from one principle and one spiration,[75] insists that the Holy Spirit derives his hypostatic hyparxis from the Father alone.[76]

I am not going to discuss Mark's arguments in defence of the Holy Spirit's procession from the Father alone or the implications of the twofold procession of the Holy Spirit, but I should like to underline briefly his criticism of the presupposition and theological foundations of *filioque* as they were presented by his contemporaries.

The first point which draws Mark's criticism is the Latin theory that the Holy Spirit proceeds from the Father and the Son, but as from one principle and cause and by one spiration.[77] Mark argues that this is unacceptable, because the twofold procession of the Holy Spirit as from one principle makes the Father and the Son two principles or confuses their Persons.[78]

Since the Father is the unique "cause" and the Son "caused", the Son can never be cause (αἴτιον) not only because this contradicts the uniqueness of the Father's causality[79] but also because it makes the Son cause and at the same time caused (αἴτιο-αἰτιατόν) which is absurd.[80] On the other hand, the "cause" and the "caused" cannot be put together and make one principle

---

[73] A Radovic: *The Mystery of the Holy Trinity According to St. Gregory Palamas* (in Greek), Thessaloniki, 1973, p. 150.

[74] *Theophanes* 20–21, Mantzarides, 2, pp. 245–248.

[75] *Conciliorum Oecumenicorum Decreta (Jedin)*, Freiburg im Bresgau, 1962, p. 502, 39–45.

[76] *Capita Syllogistica* 31 (Petit) PO 15, p. 401; *Confessio Fidei* (Petit), PO 15, p. 435.

[77] *Conciliorum Oecumenicorum Decreta*, p. 502, 39–45.

[78] *Capita Syllogistica* 24, p. 393.

[79] *Ibid.* 18, p. 388.

[80] *Ibid.* 34, pp. 402–3.

and cause, just as the Father cannot be Father and Son or the Son Son and Father.[81] The notions of "cause" and "caused" imply logical opposition, but according to the Latin tradition the opposition of relations produces distinction and differentiation of the Persons and not unity of them.[82]

Mark also objects to the Latins' argument that just as Father, Son and Holy Spirit in creating the world are not three principles but one, without losing their hypostatic individualities, in the same way Father and Son proceeding in common the Holy Spirit are not two principles but one without confusion or mixture.[83] Following Gregory the Cypriot[84] and Gregory Palamas,[85] Mark explains that there is a difference between the triadic principle (τριαδικὴ ἀρχὴ) which is the principle and cause of the creation and the Fatherly one (πατρικὴ ἀρχή) which is the principle of the divinity.[86] As far as the creation of the world is concerned, the three divine Persons, on the ground of their common energy, power and will, create jointly as one principle.[87] But it is not so with the existential procession of the Holy Spirit, which is a hypostatic faculty of the Father alone.[88] The induction of the mode of being of the Holy Spirit from the mode of being of the created order would cast the Holy Spirit down to the rank of the creation.[89]

On the ground of the distinction between these two principles the statement of Gregory of Nazianzus that the Son is ἡ ἐκ τῆς ἀρχῆς ἀρχὴ[90] does not mean that the Son is principle of the Holy Spirit but principle of the creation, because, conjointly with the Father and the Holy Spirit, he created it.[91] It is noteworthy, Mark says, that Gregory, referring to the existential relation of the divine Prosopa, calls them "'Άναρχον καὶ ἀρχὴ καὶ τὸ μετὰ τῆς ἀρχῆς".[92] Thus he makes clear that the Holy Spirit comes forth not from the ἀρχὴ, i.e. the Son, but with the ἀρχή from the Unoriginated ἀρχή i.e. the Father.[93] The procession of the Holy Spirit from the Father and the Son

[81] *Ibid.* 18, p. 388.
[82] *Ibid.*
[83] *Ibid.* 41, p. 408; 46, p. 411.
[84] *De Processione Spiritus Sancti*, PG 142, 281BD–282AD; *Scripta Apologetica* PG 142, 242BC.
[85] Ἐπιστολὴ πρὸς Ἀκίνδυνον 1.5, Meyendorff, p. 207, 14–30.
[86] *Capita Syllogistica*, 32, p. 401.
[87] *Ibid.* 41, p. 408.
[88] *Ibid.*
[89] *Ibid.* 1, p. 370.
[90] *Oratio* 45, 9, PG 36, 633C.
[91] *Capita Syllogistica* 1, p. 371.
[92] *Oratio* 42, 15, PG 36, 476A.
[93] *Capita Syllogistica* 1, p. 372.

as from one joint principle and cause, Mark maintains, is impossible, because the faculty of being principle and cause is a hypostatic or personal property.[94] As such, however, it distinguishes the Persons and does not unite them.[95] As long as the Son is considered as a principle of the Holy Spirit's procession, therefore, diarchy can in no way be excluded from the Holy Trinity, since everything which naturally owes its being to the two cannot be considered as coming from one.[96] On the other hand, the diarchy and the danger of introducing two causes cannot be avoided by considering the Son as the ἄμεσον or πόρρω cause and the Father as the ἔμμεσον or πορρωτέρω or διὰ τοῦ προσεχοῦς.[97] These notions indicate opposed relations which result in the distinction of those principles and not in their identity. Therefore, Mark concludes, οὐκ ἄρα ἕν αἴτιον ὁ Πατὴρ ἔσται καὶ ὁ Υἱὸς ἀντικείμενα αἴτια ὄντα.[98]

Also the twofold procession of the Holy Spirit as from one principle is not possible even if he proceeds "from" the Father "through" the Son. Everything which derives its existence from someone through some other owes its existence to two causes. Every human being coming into existence "from a man" "through a woman" has two causes and two principles[99] just as Jacob born from Abraham through Isaac has two causes of his being in spite of the fact that the one is ἔγγυον and the other ἐγγύτερον.[100] Thus, concludes Mark, as long as the Son is a principle of the Holy Spirit's procession in no way can diarchy in the Holy Trinity be avoided.[101]

The second point of Mark's criticism concerns the meaning of the prepositions "from" (ἐκ) and "through" (διὰ) in respect to the procession of the Holy Spirit. At the Council of Florence they were accepted as synonymous[102] and on this ground the notion that the Holy Spirit proceeds "from the Father through the Son" was considered to be identical to the notion that he proceeds "from the Father and from the Son". Thus the Latins have argued that the Latinizers have accepted that the procession of the Holy Spirit "through" the Son implies that the Son as well as the Father is the cause or

---

[94] *Ibid.* 11, p. 388.
[95] *Confessio Fidei*, 2, p. 439.
[96] *Capita Syllogistica* 1, p. 370.
[97] *Ibid.* p. 370; *Ibid.* 10, p. 382; *Ibid.* 42, p. 408.
[98] *Ibid.* 19, p. 389.
[99] *Ibid.* 42, p. 408.
[100] *Ibid.* 39, p. 407.
[101] *Ibid.* 40, pp. 407–8.
[102] *Relatio de rebus a se gestis* 5, (Petit) PO 15, p. 447.

principle of the Holy Spirit.[103] Therefore, the *filioque* clause was not an innovation but the common faith of East and West, expressed only in two slightly different formulas, lawfully added to the Creed for good and sufficient reasons.[104]

In refuting this idea, Mark argues with the previous Greek Fathers that the prepositions "from" and "through" bear the same meaning and imply causality only when they refer to the creation or to the energetic manifestation of the Holy Spirit and never to his mode of being.[105] Indeed, Mark admits, certain Greek Fathers, in referring to the procession of the Holy Spirit, have said that he "proceeds from the Father through the Son". However, they meant not the mode of being of the Holy Spirit but his consubstantiality with the Father and the Son. Maximus the Confessor underlines this by stating that the Holy Spirit proceeds substantially from the Father through the ineffably generated Son.[106]

On the other hand, by the formula "through the Son" certain Fathers have suggested not the Holy Spirit's origin but his procession which is simultaneous with the begetting of the Son from the Father. Therefore, "through" here means not "from" but "with" or "together" as Gregory of Nyssa makes clear.[107]

That these prepositions bear a quite different meaning, Mark goes on, is proved by the fact that the Greek Fathers, referring to the procession of the Holy Spirit, never say that he proceeds "from" the Son or "through" the Father but "from" the Father "through" the Son. This "through the Son" procession of the Holy Spirit is applied by the Fathers to the Holy Spirit's energetic manifestation.[108] Therefore, they do not use it alone but always in connection with the Father's participation in it and in the formula "from the Father through the Son".[109] Thus, Mark concludes, the phrase "from the Son" – with reference to the procession of the Holy Spirit – implies not principle or cause but channel through or with which something is manifested, conveyed, known or given.[110]

The third point to which Mark comes over and over again is the Latins' view that the existing "order" in the enumeration of the divine Prosopa of

---

[103] *Conciliorum Oecumenicorum Decreta*, pp. 501, 35–502, 5.
[104] *Ibid.*
[105] *Confessio Fidei* 7, pp. 436–437.
[106] *Capita Syllogistica* 10, p. 381; *Confessio Fidei* 1, p. 436.
[107] *Capita Syllogistica*, 38, pp. 406–7.
[108] *Ibid.* 20–21, pp. 389–391.
[109] *Confessio Fidei* 1, p. 438.
[110] *Ibid.* 437.

the Holy Trinity corresponds to their order of origin and nature. Thus the Holy Spirit being third in order after the Father and the Son derives his being from both.[111] In Mark's opinion such an ontological order does not exist in the Holy Trinity. Not because the Holy Trinity is ἄτακτος but because it is above any kind of order.[112] Therefore the divine Prosopa, as Gregory of Nazianzus has already said, are pronumerated and connumerated and subnumerated.[113] When the Latins recall Basil's statement: "Even if the Holy Spirit is third in dignity and order, why need he be third also in nature?" [114] to prove their case, they misinterpret it. Basil does not say that there is an order of nature in the Holy Trinity, but arguing in supposition he allows for the sake of argument that if the Holy Spirit is third in order and dignity, even so he is not third in nature.[115]

If in the formula of baptism,[116] Mark goes on, the Father comes first, the Son second and the Holy Spirit third, it is because things which are to be enumerated have to be mentioned one after another. The Father, possessing as cause a logical priority towards the Son, comes first; the Son as caused second and the Holy Spirit perforce comes third. He comes third not only because he is συμπληρωτικὸν of the Holy Trinity, but because if he were to come second it would imply that he was also a Son of the Father.[117]

In Mark's judgment, even if we accept that there is a certain "order" in the Trinity on account of the triune deity, it by no means leads to *filioque*. This is made clear by Basil[118] who states that the Spirit proceeds from the Father alone and depends on the Son, that is to say he is placed in order after him, not because he proceeds from him but because he is apprehended with him.[119] "Dependent on" and "be caused of" are two quite different things. The first implies not more than "ordered with" while the second points to the cause and principle of being.[120] Thus, Mark concludes, while the "order" of confessing or pronouncing the names of the divine Prosopa and their enumeration does not point to the double procession of the Holy Spirit, the Latin notion of ontological and natural order introduces to the

---

[111] *Capita Syllogistica* 6, pp. 376–8.
[112] *Ibid.* p. 377.
[113] *Oratio* 34, 15, PG 36, 253D–256A.
[114] *Adversus Eunomium* 3.1, *Garnier* 1, 272BC.
[115] *Mansi* 31A, 869CD.
[116] Math. 28, 19.
[117] *Capita Syllogistica* 6, pp. 376–7.
[118] *Ps Basil*, Ep. 38,4, *Courtonne*, 1, pp. 84–5.
[119] *Capita Syllogistica* 6, p. 377.
[120] *Ibid.*

Trinity subnumerations (ὑπαριθμήσεις) and degradations (ὑποβαθμίσεις) which could easily lead to the subordination of the hypostases.[121]

The fourth point of Mark's criticism refers to the theory of Thomas Aquinas according to which only opposed relations of origin distinguished the divine Prosopa. These opposite relations exist between Father and Son as well as between Father and Holy Spirit because paternity and procession produce opposite relations and consequently distinctions. But as the Holy Spirit cannot be really distinct of the Father unless he proceeds from the Father, in the same way he cannot be really distinct from the Son unless he proceeds from the Son. On this ground the idea of the Son as an origin for the procession of the Holy Spirit – indeed connected to the first origin, the Father – is necessary and the *filioque* clause well founded.[122]

Opposing this theory, Mark remarks, with the Fathers previous to him, that the distinction of the hypostases is grounded not in their opposite relations and not in their different origins, but only in their different modes of being from the one principle and origin, i.e. the Father.[123] The mode of being of the Son by way of generation and that of the Holy Spirit by way of procession, as perfect acts of the Father's hypostatic faculty, clearly distinguish them from their own origin and cause, i.e. the Father, as well as from among themselves. For this reason, Mark continues, although the Holy Spirit does not proceed from the Son, the two are really distinct both by their constitution and by their mode of being.[124]

In opposition to the Thomistic theory of different origin and opposite relations, Mark underlines the distinction of hypostases κατὰ τὴν ἀντίφασιν, which is the result of their different mode of being and their individual properties. Thus between "unbegotten", "begotten" and "proceeding" or the "cause" and those "caused" there is a distinction according to the ἀντίφασις but not according to their opposite relations and their different origins. This distinction κατὰ τὴν ἀντίφασιν on the one hand safeguards the hypostatic differentiation of the divine Prosopa, and on the other is in accordance with the teaching of the eastern Fathers, who consider the Father as the unique principle of the Holy Spirit and reject any participation of the Son in the Spirit's mode of being.[125]

Mark does not leave unnoticed the existing difference between the hy-

---

[121] *Ibid.* 43, p. 409.
[122] *Ibid.* 13, p. 384. For Thomas Aquinas' arguments cf. *Summa Theologica* 1a, 28, 1–4.
[123] *Capita Syllogistica* 13, p. 384.
[124] *Ibid.* 25–26, pp. 396–7.
[125] *Ibid.* 13, pp. 384–5.

postatic procession of the Holy Spirit and his mission or energetic manifestation and criticizes the partisans of *filioque* that their failure to pay the required attention to it leads them to confusion of the existential (καθ' ὕπαρξιν) and the energetic (κατ' ἐνέργειαν) procession of the Holy Spirit.[126]

Following the other Greek Fathers, Mark says that the mission of the Holy Spirit is a common act of the three divine Prosopa and takes place in time and for a particular purpose.[127] This mission does not belong to the eternal hypostatic properties, but to the *ad extra* activities of the Holy Trinity. Thus John 16:7 is applied not to the hypostatic procession of the Holy Spirit but to his grace, power and manifestation, i.e. his energetic procession.[128]

Christ, Mark goes on to say, by his infusion of the Holy Spirit on his disciples after the resurrection, gave to them neither the essence nor the hypostasis of the Holy Spirit, but his energy.[129] Also on the day of Pentecost neither the essence nor the hypostasis of the Holy Spirit was manifested and bestowed but his energy, which coming from the Father through the Son in the Holy Spirit is common or rather identical to the three divine Prosopa.[130] Therefore, the distinction between *ousia* and *energies* in God is of cardinal importance for the proper answer to the question of the procession of the Holy Spirit.

Mark Eugenicus summarizes successfully the Greek patristic tradition on the issue of the procession of the Holy Spirit, not simply by repeating the arguments of previous Fathers but by advancing their reasoning and putting the problem in the perspective of his own time. Indeed, his explanation bears a polemical nuance. This is because he has advanced his arguments in a difficult situation, fighting against the Latins and the Greek pro-unionists, acting as the main defender and representative of the Greek patristic traditional line. For this reason he sometimes goes to extremes and discredits his opponents' arguments. He reacts to the Decree of Florence by his insistence upon the procession of the Holy Spirit from the Father alone, basing his arguments upon the teaching of ancient Fathers. Tracing the implications of *filioque* he follows to a large extent the line of Photius and in refuting the foundations of *filioque* and the arguments of his opponents

---

[126] *Ibid.* 4, p. 373.
[127] *Ibid.*
[128] *Ibid.* p. 375.
[129] *Ibid.* 8, pp. 375–6.
[130] *Ibid.* 4, pp. 375–6.

in favour of it, he mainly follows the line of reasoning used by Gregory Palamas.[131]

Mark's discussion on the distinction between *ousia* and *energies* and its implications for the question of the procession of the Holy Spirit is rather limited, because he was prevented by the Emperor from discussing this topic at the Council of Florence. Nevertheless, it is quite clear that he does treat the subject of the procession of the Holy Spirit from this angle and the existing difference between the divine essence and the divine uncreated energies determines his whole discussion on the subject of the Holy Spirit's procession.

Mark himself was considered by theologians belonging to the traditional patristic school as the "criterion" of the sound doctrine[132] and the "bright and great and godly wise herald of truth".[133] It is not surprising, therefore, that his teaching on the procession of the Holy Spirit has had a tremendous influence among his contemporaries as well as upon later Orthodox theologians until the present day.

Conclusion

If we are to draw some conclusions, we may summarize the account given by saying that the idea according to which the Holy Spirit derives his being equally and coordinally from the Father and the Son is foreign to Greek patristic theology. This is neither accidental nor a mere obstinate attitude of the Greek Fathers towards the Latin tradition, but the natural outcome of their theological insight and their approach to the mystery of the triune God-head.

The earlier Greek Fathers – particularly after the Cappadocians clearly distinguished between *ousia* and *hypostasis*, common or natural, and individual or hypostatic properties, which are not interchangeable or confounded – steadfastly argued that the Father is the principle, cause and fountain-head of deity. Thus, the Father, deriving his being from himself, brings forth from his essence, but on the capacity of his hypostatic property, the Son by way of generation, and the Holy Spirit by way of procession. He confers to them his whole essence but he does not communicate to them his hypostatic

---

[131] See on this topic A. Schmemann: Ὁ ἅγιος Μάρκος ὁ Εὐγενικὸς, 34 (1951), pp. 34–43; 230–241.

[132] *Marci Ephesii, Morientis Oratio ad Amicos,* Petit, PO 15, p. 489.

[133] Cf. C. Tsirpanlis, *Mark Eugenicus and the Council of Florence*, Thessaloniki 1974, p. 107.

property of begetting and proceeding. Therefore, the Father remains the unique "cause" of being of the Son and of the Holy Spirit who are "caused".

On this basis the later Greek Fathers discussed and developed further the issue of the procession of the Holy Spirit and on this ground they came up against the different approach on the subject by their Latin counterparts. The Latin doctrine of a twofold procession of the Holy Spirit from the Father and the Son was rejected by the Greeks who felt that such a notion introduces two principles and two causes to the Holy Trinity. This, of course, could not be reconciled with the idea of the divine monarchia of the Father, which was a keystone of faith.

The Latins' explanation that the Holy Spirit proceeds in a primordial sense from the Father who endowed the Son with the capacity to produce the Holy Spirit is such a way that the Son is not the "cause" but a "joint-cause", did not satisfy the Greek Fathers. In disagreement with the pro-unionists, they thought that this idea leads to diarchy or to confusion of the hypostases. If the Father and the Son, they objected, proceed the Holy Spirit in their distinct hypostatic faculties then two causes and two principles are introduced into the Holy Trinity. If this occurs as from one Person then the confusion of the hypostases is inevitable. If from their common essence then the Holy Spirit on account of his common essence must participate in his own mode of being.

The double procession of the Holy Spirit as from one cause, the Greek Fathers maintained, is impossible not only because the Father proceeds the Holy Spirit as a perfect "cause" and producer, but also because the capacity of being "cause" is a hypostatic and individual property, and as such un-communicable. The hypostatic properties distinguish and by no means unite the Prosopa. On the other hand, the "cause" and that which is "caused" cannot be a joint cause, because their difference implies distinction and not unity.

The Greek Fathers were in agreement with the Latins who maintained that the Father, the Son and the Holy Spirit made jointly the created order acting as one cause and principle – and not three – without confusion of their own hypostases. They were in disagreement, however, with the Latins' inference that this can also be applied to the mode of being of the Holy Spirit. The conviction of the Greek Fathers was that the τριαδικὴ ἀρχὴ as the common cause of the creation must not be confused with the πατρικὴ ἀρχὴ which remains the unique cause of being of the Son and of the Holy Spirit.

Any induction of the mode of being of the Holy Spirit from the mode of being of the creation was felt by the Greek Fathers to confuse creation and divinity.

The later Greek Fathers were not prepared to accept the idea of the double procession of the Holy Spirit as a necessary consequence of his opposed relations of origin towards the Father and the Son. To their understanding it is not the opposite relations of origin that are the foundation and cause of the hypostatic existence and differentiation of the divine hypostases, but the different mode of being of the Son by way of generation and of the Holy Spirit by way of procession from their unoriginated unique principle and cause, i.e. the Father.

The Greek Fathers were also cautious and rejected the Latins' conclusion that the "order" of manifestation and names of the divine Prosopa implies their existential and natural order as well. For the Greeks there is no ontological order whatsoever in the Holy Trinity. If in the formula of baptism in the doxology and the confession of the Holy Trinity the Father comes first, the Son second and the Holy Spirit third it is so because the Father, as "cause", possesses a logical priority over the Son and the Holy Spirit who are "caused". The Son naturally comes second and the Holy Spirit perforce third, because if he came after the Father then he must be Son.

The *filioque* controversy gave to the later Greek Fathers the opportunity to thoroughly study and develop the idea of difference between *ousia* and *energies* in the Triune God – a topic which rests in the insight of the earlier Greek Fathers – and, in the light of this distinction, to consider the question of the procession of the Holy Spirit. This outlook enabled them to make a clear distinction between the Holy Spirit's essential derivation and his energetic manifestation. On this ground they argued that the καθ' ὕπαρξιν procession of the Holy Spirit is quite different from his κατ' ἐνέργειαν procession. In his καθ' ὕπαρξιν procession the Holy Spirit proceeds from the Father alone, yet in his κατ' ἐνέργειαν or κατ' ἔκφανσιν he comes out from the Father through the Son and even from the Father and from the Son, because all divine energies are realized from the Father through the Son in the Holy Spirit. Thus the prepositions "from" and "through", according to the Greek Fathers, bear the same meaning and they can be interchanged only when referring to the Holy Spirit's energetic manifestation. In respect to his essential derivation the Holy Spirit proceeds "from" the Father and by no means "from" or "through" the Son.

By this distinction between essence and energies the Greek Fathers were able not only to avoid any confusion between the mode of being of the Holy Spirit and his energetic manifestation or his activities, but also to point out that this κατ' ἐνέργειαν procession of the Holy Spirit "through" the Son is eternal and as such must not be restricted or confused with his temporal mission.

It is true that, in dealing with the procession of the Holy Spirit, the Greek Fathers, particularly the ancient ones, are not always explicit or clear-cut in their account. We have to remember, though, that the issue became a theological problem for the Greek Fathers only in the ninth century. Therefore, early authorities such as Gregory of Nyssa, Epiphanius, Didymus of Alexandria, Cyril of Alexandria, etc., in a time when the issue of the procession of the Holy Spirit was undefined, unclarified and unsettled, made statements which, if they are to be evaluated in themselves and with later standards, can be interpreted in the sense of *filioque*. This conclusion, though, cannot be maintained when these statements are considered within the whole trinitarian thought of those Fathers.

In spite of certain ambiguities, one point, I think, is beyond question, namely, that the "consensus" of the Greek Fathers never tolerated a hypostatic procession of the Holy Spirit *a patre filioque* even in the sense of *ex utroque tamquam ab uno principio et unica spiritione*.

HISTORICAL DEVELOPMENT AND IMPLICATIONS OF THE FILIOQUE CONTROVERSY

DIETRICH RITSCHL

The Church in the West, in a long theological development, has added the word *filioque* to the phrase "the Holy Spirit . . . who proceeds from the Father" in the Niceno-Constantinopolitan Creed, the only truly ecumenical creed in Christianity. The thesis is that the Spirit proceeds from the Father *and* from the Son. This reference to the procession of the Holy Spirit would be completely misunderstood if it were taken to be something other than a reference to an inner-trinitarian process. "Within" the triune God, within the "immanent Trinity", the Holy Spirit is to be understood as experiencing an eternal *processio* from both the Father and the Son. To understand the controversy over this issue,[1] one must let one's thoughts sink into the classical trinitarian modes of argumentation. The theologian will then discover – perhaps much to his surprise – that the issue is of considerable relevance to our contemporary understanding of the Church, of ethics, of authoritative teaching and – last but not least – of the various forms of the charismatic movement in our time. It could be argued, of course, that it is daring to move such subtle issues of inner-trinitarian speculations to the centre of attention, especially at a time when many of us find it difficult to speak about God at all. However, it could well be the case that the very study of this subtle issue will show that western theology has suffered for a long time from a tendency to speak of God "in general", i.e. not of God as the triune God. Such modalistic tendency (the reduction of Father, Son and Spirit to three aspects of the Godhead, as it were) would indeed create difficulties for "God-talk".

• Dietrich RITSCHL (Swiss Reformed) is professor of systematic theology at the University of Mainz, Federal Republic of Germany.
[1] Cf. my briefer account of this controversy, "Geschichte der Kontroverse um das Filioque", in *Concilium*, Vol. 10, October 1979, pp. 499–504.

Behind the controversy lies a conception of the Trinity which is different in the eastern and the western parts of the early Church. The controversy itself, however, had at its centre at all times the unilateral decision of the West to add an important trinitarian clause to the ecumenical creed. It is difficult throughout the history of the controversy to draw dividing lines between theological and political thoughts and sentiments. The early western theologians' incomplete understanding of the intricacies of eastern theology, and the eastern theologians' difficulties in appreciating western church historical developments, as well as their criticism of Roman papal authority, added much to the complexity of the controversy. The situation is further burdened by the fact that western theology did not display any convincing consistency in defending the *filioque* theologically. Medieval theologians, notably Anselm and Thomas Aquinas, advanced justifications which were quite different from the traditional "double procession" as taught by Augustine or in the "Athanasianum".

The western Church's addition of the *filioque* to the Nicene Creed[2] has been refuted by theologians of the Orthodox churches at different stages of the history of the controversy[3] for at least three reasons. The addition is said to be: (*a*) non-canonical, i.e. not based upon ecumenical council decisions, (*b*) not grounded in the New Testament and in early tradition, and (*c*) dogmatically untrue and of dangerous consequences. Orthodoxy today can look back on an impressive array of defenders of the original text of the Nicene Creed, reaching from John of Damascus to Patriarch Anthimos' reply to Pope Leo XIII in 1894.

The problem of dealing with this controversy today presents itself on two levels:

1. Is the *filioque* merely an addition to the text of the Nicene Creed – an addition which contemporary Orthodox theologians could perhaps tolerate or explain historically as a typical expression of Ambrosian-Augustinian trinitarian thoughts? Or is the *filioque* the symptom of a deep difference in the eastern and western understandings of the Trinity and, in consequence,

---

[2] Western theology had the *filioque* long before the whole western Church had it. The council decisions of Toledo in 446–7 and in 589 (the *filioque*-phrase in the council of 400 is most likely a later addition) are only part of the story. Not until the early eleventh century was the *filioque* officially sung in the western mass.

[3] Cf. the classic history by H. B. Swete, *On the History of the Doctrine of the Procession of the Holy Spirit from the Apostolic Age to the Death of Charlemagne*, 1876; also M. Jugie, "Origine de la controverse sur l'addition du Filioque au symbole," *Revue des Sciences philosophiques et théologiques*, 28, 1939, pp. 369ff.; also François Dvornik, *Le schisme de Photius, histoire et légende*, Paris, Editions du Cerf, 1950.

of piety and worship, of the dogmatic understanding of the meaning of the presence of Christ as well as of the Holy Spirit's contact with the Church and with humankind?

2. The *filioque* is considered in the East and in the West in quite different ways and an entirely different degree of importance is assigned to it in the two parts of the Church. This is so not because of different historical analyses, but primarily because of the fact that the West assigns at least as much dignity to the Apostles' Creed as it does to the Nicene Creed. Moreover, the importance of fixed credal formulations is seen differently in East and West. (There are, of course, among the various western traditions, further differences of evaluation which need to be taken into account, i.e. between the Roman Catholic Church, the Anglican community and the different Protestant denominations. Example: the writer of this paper is free to favour the Orthodox critique of the *filioque* without getting into difficulties with the church which ordained him.)

These two levels of the problem will have to be kept in mind by those who search for a possible consensus on the *filioque* question. A promising analysis of the issue depends upon a proper distinction between the historical and the systematic aspects of the question. In the following account of the history of the controversy and of its implications, we will proceed from a brief summary of the external historical developments to a discussion of the theological issues from the point of view of history of doctrine and conclude by briefly describing the more recent stages of the dispute. Parts II and III will pay special attention to the systematic-theological aspects.

I. A brief account of the external evidence of the controversy

The bare facts and years of the history of the controversy provide an exceptionally incomplete picture of the issue in question. This is surprising only if one considers the controversy a matter of conciliar decisions. It is, however, much more than that. The councils of Toledo[4] and the synods of Gentilly, Frankfurt, Friuli and Aachen promulgated decisions which by no means represented the official teaching of the pope in Rome, although the concept of the *filioque* unquestionably did represent a theological tendency in Latin theology if not a necessary corollary of the generally accepted trinitarian concepts of Tertullian,[5] Novatian,[6] Ambrose[7] and Augustine.[8]

---

[4] The many councils of Toledo (from 400 until the sixteenth century, cf. *Migne PL* 84, 327–562) reflect the special problems of the Church in Spain: Arianism (Priscillianism), the Muslim occupation, the reconquest, the replacing of the Mozarabic rite, etc.

Moreover, the official decisions of the Church in the East, especially at Constantinople, must be seen in the context of problems connected with the Latin Church's missionary strategy and activity among the Slavs (Bulgaria in particular) and other tensions with Rome,[9] not to speak of the fact that the Latin West had at best understood half of what the Cappadocian Fathers had been teaching about the Trinity. The classical Eastern Orthodox concepts concerning the Trinity and the Holy Spirit were known to the West (and to Augustine in particular) only in the form of summarized end-results. The background of these results was not understood.[10] Nor did the eastern theologians, at the crucial time of the controversy, understand the difficult situation of the Church in Spain in relation to new forms of Arianism, or the peculiar interests of the Frankish Church at the time of Charlemagne. In other words: the problem of the addition of the *filioque* has its context in peculiar developments of history and in gradually evolving theological positions; the possibilities for a consensus faded away with the increasing lack of understanding of the other Church's tradition and current problems.

The following list of events and dates, representing a selection of relevant stages in the history of the controversy, is, therefore, no more than a schematic presentation of a problem which is, in fact, much broader.

EVENTS AND TEXTS

WEST	EAST
Early fifth century: *filioque* in liturgical use in Spain (against Priscillianism?) Toledo (446/ 47)	
Athanasianum[11] ("Spiritus s. a Patre et Filio . . . procedens", 22)	
589 3rd Council of Toledo[12]	
633 4th Council of Toledo[13]	

---

[5] *Adv. Praxean* (after 213).

[6] *De trinitate* (before 250).

[7] The three books *De Spiritu sancto*.

[8] *De trinitate* (399–419) and *ep.* 11 and 120.

[9] Cf. François Dvornik, *Byzance et la primauté romaine*, Paris, Editions du Cerf, 1964.

[10] Cf. B. Altaner's summary of his investigation into the question of the western reception of eastern theology in *Revue bénédictine*, 62, 1952, pp. 201ff.–215.

[11] Cf. J. N. D. Kelly, *The Athanasian Creed*, New York, 1964, esp. pp. 86–90.

[12] Texts in A. Hahn, *Bibliothek d. Symbole u. Glaubensregeln*, Breslau, 1897, 3rd edition, pp. 232ff.

[13] *Ibid.*, pp. 235f.

After 742: John of Damascus, *Expos. fid. orth.* I, 8, 12, advances the first eastern refutation of the *filioque*

767 Synod of Gentilly

794 Synod of Frankfurt

796 Synod of Friuli: Paulinus of Aquileia (d. 802) defended the *filioque* (*Migne PL* 99, 9–683)

Struggle between Frankish and eastern monks at St Sabas monastery in Jerusalem over the formers' use of the *filioque*

808 Leo III writes Charlemagne that he believes the *filioque* to be correct but does not want it included in the Creed

809 Charlemagne asks Theodulf of Orléans (d. 821) to write his *De Spiritu Sancto*[14] Synod of Aachen, *filioque* included in the Creed

810 Synod in Rome: Leo III declares the *filioque* orthodox but does not want it included in the Creed; two silver plaques with the text of the unaltered Nicene Creed exposed at St Peter's in Rome

810 Alcuin's *De processione Spiritus S.*

858 Photius replaces Ignatius as Patriarch

863 Pope Nicholas I confirms Ignatius as Patriarch

Emperor Michael III persuades the pope to reopen the matter

The Latin Church claims Bulgaria

867 Photius (patriarch) condemns missionary activity of Rome in Bulgaria and rejects the *filioque* Council of Constantinople excommunicates Pope Nicholas Also 867: Ignatius reinstated

869 Rome anathematizes Photius

870 Rome condemns Ignatius' claim on Bulgaria Papal legates to Constantinople sign the Creed without *filioque*

869 Council of Constantinople confirms Rome's condemnation of Photius

877 Ignatius dies; Photius again patriarch

---

[14] *Migne PL* 105, 187ff.

and confirm Photius' reinstallation (so F. Dvornik against older research)

892 Rome excommunicates Photius? (Dvornik thinks this a later forgery)

1009 Pope Sergius IV includes the *filioque* in his statement of faith addressed to Constantinople

1014 Pope Benedict VIII[16] officially adds the *filioque* to the Nicene Creed (pressured by Emperor Heinrich II) as part of the Roman mass

1274 Council of Lyons,[17] reunion attempted Eastern delegates accept the *filioque* (and papal supremacy)

1438/39 Council of Florence, the patriarch and all Orthodox delegates (except Mark of Ephesus) signed the *filioque* as well as other points of Roman doctrine

879–80 Council of Constantinople recalls decision of 869

886 Emperor Leo VI deposes Photius

Cf. Photius' *Liber de Spiritus S. mystagogia*[15]

Pope Sergius' namesake, Patriarch Sergius, omits the pope's name from the official diptychs (such has happened before by mistake)

Emperor Michael VIII (1259–82) reapproaches Rome in need of help against the Turks

Eastern churches recall the agreement of the delegates to Lyons

No official proclamation of the decision in Byzantium until 1452

29 May 1453: destruction of Constantinople (after combined Orthodox and Roman service at Hagia Sophia early on same day)

The actual "*filioque* controversy", as it is treated in history books, is connected with the name of Patriarch Photius, a learned theologian and a problematic personality. His doctrine – procession "from the Father alone" – was theologically grounded and politically defended. But since Photius had no western counterpart to match his theological and philosophical learning, the West resorted to almost exclusively political manoeuvring in combatting his position. This attitude remained typical of the western Church until and including Pope Benedict's official addition of the *filioque* to the text of the creed. Benedict VIII himself was certainly more interested in the wars against Saracens and Greeks than in theology. A potentially serious theological controversy was reduced to political power struggles. The lucidity

---

[15] *Migne PC* 102; cf. in addition to Dvornik the older article "Photius" by F. Kattenbusch, in *RE* (3rd ed., 1904), pp. 374–393.

[16] *Migne PL* 142, 1060f.

[17] Denz. 460–63.

of Augustine's trinitarian thoughts and the helpful attempts of explaining the differences between East and West by Maximus the Confessor in the seventh century seemed to have disappeared from the memory of the participants of the struggle. The Councils of Lyons and of Florence, with their attempts to impose the *filioque* upon the eastern Church, brought no solution and created much bitterness on the part of eastern Christians. The final mass, sung by Greeks and Latins together on the morning of 29 May 1453, the day of the destruction of Constantinople – fourteen years after the Council of Florence – is like a funeral song to a constructive theological exchange between East and West.

The thin contacts between the churches of the Reformation and eastern Orthodoxy did not lead to a re-examination of the *filioque* question. The confession books of the Reformation maintained the *filioque*, partly because of the relatively high esteem for the Athanasianum. One of the few experts on western theology in the East, Cyril Lukaris (murdered in 1638), did not reopen the discussion either. But Peter Mogila, also very familiar with western thought, attacked the *filioque* in his *Orthodox Confession* together with papal primacy.

The development since the seventeenth century can again be listed according to significant events, whereby the theological positions of the Anglican and the Old Catholic churches become increasingly relevant to the *filioque* question.

EVENTS AND TEXTS

WEST	EAST
Seventeenth century: various theological writers in England reconsider the *filioque* in the interest of contact with Eastern Orthodoxy	In Peter Mogila's *Orthodox Confession* (1642–3) the *filioque* (and papal primacy) are called separating issues
1742 Pope Benedict XIV considers the *filioque* not as *conditio sine qua non* for union with the Orthodox Church[18]	
Nineteenth century: several English theologians advocate the deletion of the *filioque* from the Nicene Creed	

---

[18] Cf. however, the *professio fidei Orientalibus (Maronitis) praescripta*, Denz. 1459–1473.

1874/5 Consultations between Old
Catholic and Orthodox Churches
in Bonn, with Anglican
representation. Old Catholics
begin with process of deletion of
the *filioque*

1894 Pope Leo XIII appeals to
Orthodox churches to unite with
Rome

Patriarch Anthimos of Constantinople
replies that union is acceptable if
Rome can demonstrate full
consensus in doctrine until ninth
century, including the proof that
the *filioque* has been taught by the
early eastern Fathers

1912 Anglican-Orthodox consultations
in St Petersburg, continued by
1931 Joint Doctrinal Commission[19]
which was reconstituted later and
1973 met in Oxford and
1976 in Moscow
1978 Lambeth Conference recommends
the deletion of the *filioque* clause[20]

This very brief summary requires some preliminary comments. It is obvious from the outset that the actual development of the controversy was interwoven with political interests and conflicts. But to observe this does not permit the conclusion that the issue as such was a political one. It was not. The issue is a trinitarian question, *viz.* an entirely different development of concepts and expectations concerning trinitarian theology in East and West. More helpful than the reference to political and church-political interests would be the observation that East and West operated with "irreducibly diverse forms of thought", as Avery Dulles puts it in quoting W. Kasper.[21] But even after having insisted on this way of approaching the famous controversy one must proceed to an investigation at a deeper level. Nor will it suffice to list the passages in the few Greek Fathers who openly teach a

---

[19] See *Anglo-Russian Theological Conference*, ed. H. M. Waddams, London, Faith Press, 1958; also H. A. Hodges, *Anglicanism and Orthodoxy*, London, SCM Press, 1955, and the essays by N. Zernov and G. Florovsky in *A History of the Ecumenical Movement*, ed. R. Rouse and S. C. Neill, London, 1954.
[20] See *Report of the Lambeth Conference 1978*, pp. 51f.; also *Anglican-Orthodox Dialogue, The Moscow Statement . . . Joint Doctrinal Commission 1976*, London, SPCK, 1977, ed. K. Ware and C. Davey, pp. 97ff., with a history of the dialogue, pp. 4–37.
[21] Avery Dulles, SJ, *The Survival of Dogma*, Garden City, NY, Doubleday, 1973, p. 167.

filioque-concept,[22] or the statements of some more recent Orthodox theologians who seem to tolerate the *filioque*.[23]

The tension which erupted in the *filioque* controversy has its roots in the
different trinitarian concepts in the Latin and Greek churches. These differences, in turn, are part of different forms of piety and of expectations
regarding the accessibility of God or of the Holy Spirit. Without being able
to go into a full investigation of these important areas, it will be necessary
to list at least some of the basic trinitarian concepts which lie behind these
other differences between the two parts of the Church.

II. The theological issues behind the controversy

The decision is arbitrary where to begin in describing the development of
patristic trinitarian thought. If one is interested in the philosophical and
systematic conditions available to the early Fathers for articulating trinitarian
concepts, one might best look at the details of Aristotelian influence upon
Greek theology in the fourth century, especially the second half and – with
regard to Latin theology – one would have to look at Ambrose's and
Augustine's peculiar ways of appropriating Plotinus' philosophy (merged
with Aristotelian and Stoic cosmology). If, however, one focuses on the
history of theology in the narrower sense, the proper starting point in the
East would be Athanasius[24] and the fuller development of his thoughts in
the Cappadocians[25] and in Didymus the Blind and Evagrius; in the West it
would undoubtedly be Tertullian.[26] With regard to the roots of the
filioque-problem one would have to look also at early conciliar decisions,
i.e. the synod of Alexandria in 362 which was expressly confirmed in Constantinople in 381. Moreover, one would have to bear in mind that the
whole conceptuality – in the East and in the West – would not have been
possible without Plotinus' philosophical categories. These analyses cannot,
of course, be carried out here. The purpose of the following observations is

---

[22] One passage in Cyril of Alexandria (*Thesaurus de . . . trinitate* 34), one in Epiphanius, also Ephraem Syrus, and others.
[23] Moderate: the Russian theologian V. Bolotov; radical: Pavel Svetlov.
[24] Cf. D. Ritschl, *Athanasius*, Zürich, EVZ, Theologische Studien 76, 1964; T. F.
Torrance, "Athanasius: A Study in the Foundations of Classical Theology", *Theology
in Reconciliation*, London, 1975, pp. 215–266, and Theodore C. Campbell, "The
Doctrine of the Holy Spirit in the Theology of Athanasius", *Scottish Journal of
Theology*, November 1974, pp. 408–440.
[25] Still important Karl Holl, *Amphilochius v. Ikonium in seinem Verhältnis zu den
grossen Kappadoziern*, Tübingen, 1904.
[26] Cf. John Burleigh, "The Doctrine of the Holy Spirit in the Latin Fathers", *Scottish
Journal of Theology*, June 1954, pp. 113–132.

merely to provide some material for the understanding of the fact that the theology of the Church in the East could not possibly have produced the *filioque* concept whereas the Church in the West could perhaps not have done without it.

A. ATHANASIUS AND THE CAPPADOCIANS

Theology in the East only gradually learnt to distinguish between οὐσία and ἐνέργεια and between οὐσία and ὑπόστασις, or ὑπόστασις and πρόσωπον. It is clear, however, that, after the work of the Cappadocians the distinction between οὐσία and the ἐνέργειαι had become absolutely essential for Greek theology. Although the "energies" in God cannot be separated from his οὐσία it is impossible for the believers to reach God in his very own οὐσία which transcends all beings, names and concepts. Any being has its being only in the ἐνέργειαι of (or within) God and it is in participating in God's energies that the believers can enter into communion with God. This view, the heart of Orthodox theology, fully developed by Gregory Palamas, is basically present in Athanasius. The terms were not clear in Athanasius and it is not surprising that the western Church was able to claim Athanasius as well. But the substance of later theology in the East was already present in Athanasius and the claim by the Cappadocians that they legitimately continued Athanasius' approach is mostly justified. (However, modern research has shown that there were other theologians who influenced the Cappadocians, but their importance was suppressed because of lack of orthodoxy in certain points; one such example is Apollinaris of Laodicea[27] whom Harnack calls the "great teacher of the Cappadocians" [28].)

Athanasius teaches in *Contra Arianos*, and later in *Ad Serapionem*, that Father, Son and Holy Spirit dwell in one another, that the Spirit is not to be thought of on a lower level than the Son, and that the believers' participation in God is a participation of the Spirit.[29] The word is the bridge in this participation. Since the word is in the Father, and since the word and the Spirit participate fully in the Father, and since the word is with the believers (and in them), so the believers are *in God in the Spirit*. In this construction

---

[27] Cf. E. Mühlenberg, *Apollinaris von Laodicea,* Göttingen, 1969 and T. F. Torrance, "The Mind of Christ in Worship: The Problem of Apollinarianism in Worship", in *Theology in Reconciliation*, pp. 139–214.
[28] A. v. Harnack, *DG* (4th ed.), II, p. 295.
[29] D. Ritschl, "Die Einheit mit Christus im Denken der griechischen Väter", *Konzepte*, Ges. Aufsätze Bd. I, Bern 1976, pp. 78–101, and ch. II in *Memory and Hope, An Inquiry Concerning the Presence of Christ*, New York, London, Collier Macmillan, 1967.

of both the Trinity and the believers' participation in God, the phrase "through the Son" is quite appropriate. In fact, the διὰ τοῦ Υἱοῦ was (and is) a proper theological formula in Eastern Orthodoxy, although its similarity with the western "from the Son" resulted over the centuries in a distrust of eastern theologians for the originally proper concept. Athanasius still teaches clearly that God is "over all" and also "through all and in all", that the Son is "through all" and the Spirit "in all". This is the basis for speaking of the vicarious work of the Spirit on behalf of those who are "in the Spirit". There is a communion of the Spirit with the believers which is grounded in the communion of the Son who is in the Spirit and the Spirit who is in the Son. The incarnation of the word is, in turn, the ground for the believers' reception of the Spirit. However, the Spirit so fully participates in both, the Father and the λόγος and this for reasons of a total unity of God's being and activity (ἐνέργεια), that there are some reasons for questioning the later Eastern Orthodox theologians' claim that Athanasius too is a crown witness of the distinction between the οὐσία and 'ἐνέργειαι in the triune God. It could be argued that Athanasius' concept of God making himself present *through* the Word and *in* the Spirit tends to identify God's "being in himself" with the way the believers recognize him. The ultimate abolition of the distinction between the immanent and the economic Trinity is, of course, dear to western theology. (It is, e.g., *the* basic theological-epistemological thesis in Karl Barth's dogmatics.) It could be argued further that in this point the West has understood Athanasius better than has later Byzantine theology. Since our interest here is not in Athanasius' theology as such but in the eastern trinitarian concepts which necessitated a denial of the *filioque*, we can leave undecided the problem just mentioned.

The Cappadocians' interest is characterized by their emphasis on the oneness of the three persons in the Trinity (against Neo-Arians) as well as on the differentiation of the three ὑποστάσεις within the unity of the three (against the charge that they taught "two sons"). Whereas Basil is the first to rethink the term ὑπόστασις although without clearly defining the Spirit's eternal procession, Gregory Nazianzen introduced the notion of ἐκπόρευσις, while Gregory of Nyssa reflected upon the continuation of this thought by speaking of the "through the son"-concept. All three of them, of course, accepted the ὁμοούσιον of the Spirit. The reasons they give for this are connected always with the insight that the believers' knowledge of God would be incomplete or impossible if the Spirit were a κτίσμα. Thus from the outset the soteriological argument and the direct reference to the liturgy in worship are part of the whole theological reflection.

Basil faces honestly the problem of the Spirit's neither being ἀγέννητον nor γεννητόν nor being a κτίσις[30], and in *De spiritu sancti* he appears to teach the procession of the Spirit from the Son, although Holl,[31] denying that he means to do that, says rather that Basil, referring here to the inner τάξις within the Trinity, actually distinguishes between an inner order and the outer appearances of the πρόσωπα. With regard to the recognizable πρόσωπα the order is – as it was in Athanasius – *from* the Father *through* the Son *in* the Spirit. With regard to the inner-trinitarian relations, however, Basil does not have available a concept for the Holy Spirit equivalent to the γεννησία of the Son.

The situation is somewhat different in Gregory Nazianzen in that he – despite fundamental agreement with his teacher Basil – places much emphasis on the origination of the Spirit. A basic text for him is John 15:26. The notion of ἐκπόρευσις permits him to define the ἰδιότης of the Spirit, a notion parallel to the γεννησία of the Son. Gregory's trinitarian interest is, as it was for Basil, intimately connected with the spiritual condition of the believers whose ψυχή he distinguishes from the νοῦς. It is the νοῦς that is to reach similarity with God (τελείωσις). This construction operates with the notion of ἀγεννησία, γέννησις and ἐκπόρευσις. This Gregory considers sufficient proof against the charge that he teaches δύο υἱοί in God. It is important to note that Gregory Nazianzen does not use the phrase ἐκπόρευσις διὰ τοῦ Υἱοῦ or something like it. Thus Gregory goes beyond Basil in providing a clear and helpful terminology, but it cannot really be said that his five theological *Orations* provide complete clarity on the question of the origination of the Spirit.

Gregory of Nyssa, of course, also bases his thinking on the trinitarian thinking of Basil but he adds a complex of thoughts concerning absolute goodness, evil and the original state of man. The influence of Origen and in general of Neo-Platonism is more noticeable than in Basil and Gregory Nazianzen. An interest in a kind of history of salvation, i.e. of the soul's gradual approach towards God, is closely connected with his concept of the Trinity. Gregory's teaching presupposes an immanent concept; God is ἡ ζωοποιὸς δύναμις. This δύναμις operates *immanently* in a threefold way: πηγὴ μὲν δυνάμεως ἐστὶν ὁ Πατὴρ, δύναμις δὲ τοῦ Πατρὸς ὁ Υἱὸς, δυνάμεως δὲ πνεῦμα τὸ Πνεῦμα "Αγιον.[32] This immanent Trinity works towards the outside, but in such a fashion that it is always clear that the Father is the πηγὴ, the source, that the ἐνέργεια is with the Son and the τελείωσις with

---

[30] *Contra Eunom.* III, *Migne PG* 29, 668B.
[31] *Op. cit.*, p. 141.
[32] *Migne PG* 45, 1317 (*adv. Maced.*).

the Spirit. The Father is ἀγέννητος, the Son is μονογενής. Again: there is only *one* Son in the Trinity. It could be argued that Gregory of Nyssa places all emphasis on the economic concept of the Trinity. It is more plausible, however, to say that this is not so. The Father is αἴτιον, the Son and the Spirit are ἐκ τοῦ αἰτίου. It follows clearly: no *filioque* concept is being taught. The αἰτία of the Spirit is in the Father, but the Son mediates in the works of the Trinity *ad extra*. The Holy Spirit is διὰ τοῦ Υἱοῦ and not *from* the Son. This distinction between eternal origination and economic mediation is of great importance. The Cappadocians, like all Orthodox theologians of the East, leave no doubt that the inner or immanent Trinity is a mystery into which human thought cannot penetrate.[33] All the more important is the work of the Spirit, the theological understanding of which Gregory of Nyssa translated into mystical-ascetic thoughts which, in turn, influenced Ps. Dionysios Areopagita and, through him, most of eastern tradition. This combination of practical piety and worship with the complicated trinitarian thoughts is the most characteristic feature of Eastern Orthodoxy. From the point of view of our interest in the *filioque*, the most important dogmatic assertion of classical eastern theology is the insight that God the Father is the πηγὴ, the source, and ῥίζα, the root, of the Godhead with its dynamic energies which reach and transform (or transfigurate) the believers in the Spirit who, in turn, is in the Son as the Son is in him. It is correct to say, therefore, that the Spirit reaches the believers διὰ τοῦ Υἱοῦ, but it is meaningless to say that the Holy Spirit eternally originates from the Father *and from* the Son, as though there were two sources or two roots.

The difference between East and West on the addition of the *filioque* to the Nicene Creed is an expression of the differences concerning the epistemological relation between the economic and an immanent concept of the Trinity.

B. EARLY WESTERN CONCEPTS OF THE TRINITY

Although a synod in Rome in 382 accepted the trinitarian dogma of Constantinople of 381, it cannot be said that the West had fully understood the eastern trinitarian theology. Nor has Augustine – whose conception of the Trinity became the western concept – fully apprehended the decision of the second ecumenical council in 381 and of the Cappadocians' teaching on

---

[33] Cf. Vladimir Lossky, *The Vision of God*, London, Faith Press, 1963, also his *The Mystical Theology of the Eastern Church*, London, Clarke, 1957, with his emphasis on the difference of eastern and western spirituality in relation to the single procession of the Holy Spirit, a concept which alone permits the transfiguration or deification of the believer in Christ.

the Trinity. There were language barriers – and more than that. Augustine stood deeply in the tradition of Tertullian and of Ambrose and, as Harnack judges[34] – perhaps overdoing the point – Augustine would never have thought of the Trinity had he not felt himself bound to the tradition in which he stood.

Ambrose, with his interest in the Cappadocians and his admiration for Athanasius, emphasized the unity and oneness of God along with the un-searchable mystery of the Trinity, and was tending towards a practical identification of the Holy Spirit with the Father. This is historically quite understandable, but it certainly is not a valid representation of Athanasius and his followers in the East. Athanasius may have been truly presented, however, in Ambrose and Augustine's unwillingness to make much of a differentiation between the immanent and the economic Trinity. Ambrose's doctrine of the Trinity shows the same aporetic difficulties which we find in Augustine, the difficulty of harmonizing the two concepts: one in three and three in one. If this *conceptual* paradox is the mystery of the Trinity, surely the western Church celebrates another mystery than does the Church in the East.

The work of Marcellus of Ancyra[35] should be mentioned here, partly because it influenced Rufinus whose concepts of the Trinity (indebted to Cyril of Jerusalem) and of the procession of the Spirit influenced later western theology. Marcellus had taught an economic modalism, i.e. the Son and the Spirit appeared only in order to perform certain functions. It is noteworthy that Marcellus' orthodoxy was accepted at Rome in 340 and at Sardica in 343.

Pelikan[36] maintains (against Schindler) that Augustine in his trinitarian thinking was deeply influenced by Hilary of Poitiers' caution not to allow a differentiation between the economic and the immanent concept of the Trinity. Hilary implicitly taught the *filioque*. If this is the case, and also the influence of Marcellus and Rufinus on later western concepts, one would have reasons to suspect that the *filioque* of later western theology grew out of the western theological unwillingness to distinguish between the economic and the immanent Trinity. If this conclusion is correct, it would also follow that Tertullian is not really a witness for later filioquism. This can briefly be demonstrated.

---

[34] A. v. Harnack, *Grundriss der Dogmengeschichte*, 7th ed., Tübingen, 1931, p. 237.
[35] Cf. T. Evan Pollard, "Marcellus of Ancyra, A Neglected Father", in *Epektasis* (for Jean Daniélou), Paris, 1972, pp. 187–196.
[36] J. Pelikan, "Hilary on Filioque", in his *Development of Christian Doctrine*, New Haven, Yale University Press, 1969, pp. 120–141.

Tertullian's *Adversus Praxean* was occasioned by the ideas of the Mon-
archian Praxeas whose concern was not the Spirit but the relation between
the monarchy of God and the life of Jesus. Nor was Tertullian's concept of
the Trinity shaped by a special interest in the Spirit, an interest one might
suspect because of Tertullian's relation to Montanism. His concern was
rather the understanding of the economic *distributio* and *distinctio* of the
three *personae* with the one *substantia, potestas, virtus* of God, a *differentia
per distinctionem* which on the one hand guarantees the unity of the divine
substance, on the other the fact that God is not *unicus et singularis*. This he
could have only at the price of declaring the Son and the Spirit *portiones* of
the divine substance, but fully part of that substance nevertheless. In choos-
ing between a three-partition of God and inferiority of the Son and the
Spirit in relation to the Father, Tertullian chose the latter. This subordinationism, however, is not our concern here. What is interesting is the
concept of procession from the Father alone. Tertullian teaches in *Adversus
Praxean* (4) that Son and Spirit proceed merely for the purpose of creation
and revelation and that both proceed *ex unitate patri* (19). In this basic
assertion Tertullian does not differ from later Greek concepts, although, of
course, his understanding of the reasons for the procession are entirely
different from, for example, the concept of the Cappadocians. The Spirit,
who proceeds *a patre per filium*, occupies a "third grade" within the majesty
of God: the Son "*interim acceptum a Patre munus effudit Spiritum Sanctum,
tertium nomen divinitatis et tertium gradum majestatis . . .*" (30,5). However,
this still amounts to the assertion that the Spirit proceeds from the *Father*.
Tertullian teaches the mediatorship of the Son in the procession of the Spirit
from the Father, which is to say that he distinguishes between origination
and procession. "*Tertius enim est Spiritus a Deo et Filio sicut tertius a radice
fructus ex fructice et tertius a fonte rivus ex flumine et tertius a sole apex ex
radio*" (8,7). The Spirit, like the Son, is (only) a *portio* of the divine
substance, although he receives it directly, whereas the Spirit receives it
indirectly from the Father. Such reception occurred before creation, for it
was in creation that the Spirit cooperated as the third person of the Trinity
(cf. 12,3). For these reasons it does not amount to much to claim Tertullian
as a crown witness for the classical western understanding of the *filioque*, as
has often been done. A crown witness he is, to be sure, for western tendencies towards modalism.

The important innovation in Augustine is the (philosophical) decision to
think the Trinity not by beginning, as it were, with the Father, but with the
Trinity itself. The *relationes* of the three persons condition each of them in
dependence to the others, so much so, that Augustine teaches the Son's

active participation in his own sending (i.e. his incarnation). The combination of the neoplatonic idea of simplicity with the biblical concept of the personhood of God is the main thesis. All three persons of the Trinity share in these qualities which together amount to one *principium*. Augustine *must*, therefore, teach the *filioque*. The reasons he gives for this in *De Trinitate* and in the *Homilies* on *John* are elaborate and convincing – provided one shares his quasi modalistic understanding of the inner-trinitarian *relationes*. Still unsolved, however, is the problem why the Son should not be thought of as having proceeded from the Spirit, unless one interprets "conceived by the Holy Spirit" in just this way. In other words: as soon as historical references are made to Israel, to the coming of Jesus, to the Church (i.e. to "economic" dimensions), Augustine's inner-trinitarian concept does not seem to be relevant.[37] The Trinity almost becomes a perfect triangle which "in its work" *ad extra*, as it were, seems reducible to a single point. In Augustine's teaching it is merely the impact of the content of the Bible which prevents the logically possible conclusion that the Father and Son proceed from the Spirit. It is this impact, too, which persuades Augustine to teach that, although the Spirit is the symmetrical bond of love (*vinculum caritatis*) between Father and Son and proceeds from both, the Spirit proceeds *principaliter* from the Father (*De trin.* 15, 17, 29). Thus Augustine's doctrine of the "double procession", which became typical of later theology including the *Athanasianum*, was somewhat balanced by this assertion. This led at a later stage of theology (e.g. the Council of Lyons) to the idea of a single spiration, *spiratio*, by which the Spirit is said to proceed from the two sources as from one single source.

III. Implications of more recent stages of the controversy

After this survey of the development of those aspects of patristic trinitarian thought which have a bearing on the later *filioque* controversy, it is safe to conclude that the important trinitarian decisions on the *filioque* issue were made long before the controversy began. This is why the controversy itself is more of church-historical than of theological significance.

With reference to eastern theology, it must be said of course that Photius' insistence on the procession from the "Father alone" ("Photism"), further developed by Gregory the Cypriot[38] and Gregory Palamas, did present some

---

[37] Cf. my discussion of this critical interpretation of Augustine's implicit modalism in *Konzepte I* (see footnote 29), pp. 102ff. and 123–140.

[38] Cf. O. Clément, "Gregoire de Chypre, De l'ekporèse du Saint Esprit", *Istina*, 1972, No. 3–4, pp. 443–456.

new theological concepts.[39] Several eastern authors drew attention to the shortcomings of the traditional western identification between the economic and the immanent Trinity, e.g. the Bulgarian Archbishop Theophylact of Ochrid in the eleventh century. Here lie indeed the roots of the whole controversy. But decisively new theological thoughts on the Trinity and on the procession of the Spirit have not been produced by later Eastern Orthodoxy. Besides, such innovating ideas would not be in harmony with Eastern Orthodoxy's self-understanding. The emphasis on the philosophical *concepts* introduced by the Cappadocian Fathers in order to point to the mystery of the Trinity has remained typical of all later eastern theology. The question of the relation between the Son and the Spirit has remained basically unsolved.

With reference to western theology, on the other hand, it must be admitted that Anselm and Thomas Aquinas' justifications of the *filioque* do seem to have introduced new elements to the discussion. Alasdair Heron[40] makes much of the difference between Augustine and Anselm's position on the matter. He draws attention to the fact that Augustine's allowance for a procession of the Spirit *principaliter* from the Father is in Anselm[41] and Thomas Aquinas[42] given up in favour of a completely triangular concept of the Trinity. Anselm is vulnerable to Lossky's criticisms, Heron maintains, whereas Augustine – who seems to Heron to be closer to a "through-the-son-concept" – is not. Here is not the place to argue this interpretative problem. It seems that good reasons could be advanced to show that Augustine too is vulnerable to Lossky's harsh critique of implicit western modalism. Be this as it may, the Councils of Lyons and Florence show the clear influence of both Augustinian and of Anselm and Thomas' trinitarian thought. Later stages in the history of theology, for example at the time of the Reformation, do not give evidence of any new thoughts on the matter. It amounts to little to ask the question whether Luther in his opposition to A. Karlstadt and Thomas Müntzer consciously made use of filioquism in combatting the enthusiasts' claim that the Holy Spirit may also blow "outside" the realm of the written word (or if word stands for the second person

---

[39] Cf. V. Lossky, "The Procession of the Holy Spirit in Orthodox Triadology", *Eastern Church Quarterly*, 7, 1948, pp. 31ff. See also U. Küry, "Die Bedeutung des Filioque-Streites für den Gottesdienst der abendländischen und der morgenländischen Kirche", *IKZ*, 33, 1943, pp. 1ff.
[40] A. I. C. Heron, "Who Proceedeth from the Father and the Son", *Scottish Journal of Theology*, 4, 1971, pp. 149ff.
[41] *De processione Spiritus S.*, e.g. 9.
[42] *Summa theologiae*, I, q. 36, Art. 2–4.

of the Trinity, it could also be said "outside" the mission of the Son). *De facto* this is what he *did* teach and the position taken was well in line with classical western anti-Montanist thought. The emphasis in the Roman Church on papal primacy and on the institution of the Church has its perfect parallel in the Reformation churches' insistence on the primacy of the written word in its function of a criterion with which to judge the movements of the Spirit – a parallel at least with regard to the ecclesiological utilization of trinitarian thought. Moreover, the protestant authors in England who concerned themselves with the *filioque*, e.g. William Sherlock (1690), John Pearson and E. Stillingfleet (1664), either did not understand the gravity of the issue (as in the case of Sherlock), or ultimately reached a position close to filioquism. The learned nineteenth century author and hymn-writer J. M. Neale came closest to refuting the *filioque*. But new thoughts were not added. At best there was a recollection of the importance of distinguishing between the "eternal procession" and the "temporal mission" of the Holy Spirit, a distinction without which much unnecessary misunderstanding occurs.

If eastern theology has failed to provide a satisfactory explanation of the relation between the Son and the Spirit, and if western theology is right in suspecting in Eastern Orthodoxy an undue emphasis on the Father's μον-αρχία as well as an over-emphasis on (Aristotelian) philosophical concepts with which to approach the mystery of the Trinity, western theology surely has shown its shortcomings in its undue tendency to blend together Father, Son and Spirit into a monotheistically conceived "godhead" and by prematurely identifying economic with immanent trinitarian structures. Nikos Nissiotis[43] would then be right in saying that neither East nor West has produced an adequate theology of the Holy Spirit and that western "christomonism" and filioquism cannot be an economic substitute for an inner-trintarian structure.

Karl Barth[44] has provided one of the most extensive defences of the *filioque* in twentieth century theology. It is Heron's judgment that Barth follows entirely the lines of Anselm's trinitarian thought. This may indeed be the case. More important almost is the obvious tendency in Barth to see

---

[43] *Die Theologie der Ostkirche im ökumenischen Dialog*, Stuttgart, Evangelisches Verlagswerk, 1968, p. 26. Cf. also J. N. Karmiris, "Abriss der dogmatischen Lehre der orth. kath. Kirche", in P. Bratsiotis, ed., *Die Orthodoxe Kirche in griechischer Sicht*, I, Stuttgart, Evangelisches Verlagswerk, 1959, pp. 15–120, esp. 30–34.
[44] K. Barth, *Church Dogmatics*, I/1, paragraph 12 (German, pp. 496–514), Edinburgh, T. & T. Clark.

the safeguard against a free-floating spiritualism, which he rightly desires to see anchored in the immanent Trinity. While with regard to the *relationes* in the Trinity Barth argues deductively, he proceeds inductively with respect to the ultimate defence of the *filioque*: the economic desirability of making clear at all times that the Spirit of God is Christ's Spirit is seen to be rooted in the immanent Trinity. The expression of this desirability is quite understandable; the question remains, however, whether perhaps the price paid is too high, *viz.* the tendency to modalism, and hence, the lack of a dynamic doctrine of the Spirit. George Hendry[45] criticizes Barth's and ultimately Augustine's defence of the *filioque*. He does not provide, however, an alternative which could be acceptable to western and also to eastern theology. The decisions of the Old Catholics to delete the *filioque* from the Nicene Creed and the more recent Anglican recommendations have been accompanied and supported by many learned historical studies, but new theological thoughts have not really grown out of these endeavours, unless one would call the partially improved contacts with Eastern Orthodoxy a new theological result. The deeper issue, however, the solution of which alone would be ecumenically promising, is a new way of approaching the much belaboured relation between the economic and the immanent Trinity, i.e. a new way of trinitarian articulation. The old ways can altogether be intellectually analysed, all intricacies can be understood,[46] provided one invests sufficient time and patience, but these analyses as such do not produce what is needed today.

In approaching the question of the Trinity, it is important to remember that any reference to the Trinity is originally doxological in nature. This is important in our time when God-talk is so severely challenged and trinitarian thinking so obviously neglected. Doxological affirmations are not primarily definitions or descriptions, rather ascriptive lines of thought, speech and action which are offered to God himself. Trinitarian thought in the early Church originated within doxological contexts and it is only within such contexts that we can speak of the "inner life" of the triune God. But, as the early Eastern Fathers made clear, all such doxological references to that inner life must be checked by reference back to the biblical message concerning God's activity and presence with his people. Such reference will

---

[45] *The Holy Spirit in Christian Theology*, Philadelphia, 1956 (London, 1965), pp. 30–52. See also Donald L. Berry, "Filioque and the Church", *Journal of Ecumenical Studies*, summer 1968, pp. 535–554.
[46] See e.g. the issue of *Istina*, No. 3–4, 1972, devoted to this task (pp. 257–467). Cf. also Paul Henry, S.J., "Contre le 'Filioque' ", *Irénikon*, Vol. XLVIII, pp. 170–177.

show that the Spirit is confessed to have been instrumental in the coming of Christ ("conceived by the Holy Spirit"), and to have been the life-giving power of God in his resurrection. Jesus during his ministry promised the sending of the Spirit, and the earliest Christians understood Pentecost as the fulfilment of that promise. Thus the Spirit precedes the coming of Christ, is active throughout his life, and is also sent by him to the believers. This chain of observations suggests that it would be insufficient and perhaps illegitimate to "read back" into the Trinity only those New Testament passages which refer to the sending of the Spirit by Jesus.

A restructuring of trinitarian articulation will have to pay equal attention to the actual experience of the early Christians and of Christian existence today, to the "synthetic" thoughts – mostly in doxological dress – concerning God's presence in Israel, in the coming of Jesus and in the Church, as they were expressed by the earliest witnesses of trinitarian thought, and surely also to the logical and linguistic conditions of our time. One must not forget that, from its beginnings in the second and third centuries, the doctrine of the Trinity was intended to be a help for Christian believers, not an obstacle nor an abstract intellectual superimposition upon the "simple faith". For it was in simple faith that the early Christians experienced the presence of the triune God. They did not deduce their theological conclusions from a pre-conceived trinitarian concept. So, too, in our reconsideration of trinitarian concepts, it is desirable that we, in following the cognitive process of the early Church, take ecclesiology as the appropriate theological starting point for re-examining the function of trinitarian thought in the Church's faith, life and work.

B.
DEVELOPMENTS
IN THE VARIOUS TRADITIONS

TOWARDS AN ECUMENICAL AGREEMENT
ON THE PROCESSION OF THE HOLY SPIRIT
AND THE ADDITION
OF THE FILIOQUE TO THE CREED

ANDRÉ DE HALLEUX

The insertion of the word *filioque* into the liturgical creed and the doctrinal controversy on the procession of the Holy Spirit to which it gave rise continue to form part of the centuries-old controversy between Orthodoxy and Catholicism today, even though many historians and theologians are now inclined to see it as no more than a pretext, or at most the occasion, for a schism which was really engendered by the antagonism between ecclesiastical power structures and a progressive alienation of minds and hearts. The biblical, patristic, canonical and rational arguments have been rehearsed unwearyingly and with the same variations by both sides right down to and including the interconfessional symposia and colloquies of recent decades. The only real light and shade in this interminable quarrel has been the alternation between long periods of mutual incomprehension and the exchange of anathemas and short-lived attempts at reconciliation. Negative as this summary may appear, it could equally well throw into sharp relief the necessary conditions and the possibilities of a hopeful approach to this question in the present ecumenical climate. It is in this spirit that these brief reflections of a Roman Catholic theologian are offered. I speak only for myself and my purpose is not so much to present a concrete solution as rather to clear away some of the obstacles blocking the road along which the quest for a reconciliation desired by all should be pursued.

Official discussions

The Orthodox Church, which is shortly to begin an official theological dialogue with the Roman Catholic Church on the theme of pneumatology, has recently resumed similar conversations with two other western partners

• André de HALLEUX (Roman Catholic) is professor of patrology at the University of Louvain, Belgium.

– the Old Catholics and the Anglican Communion – which pick up a dialogue inaugurated in Bonn more than a century ago. This suggests that our starting point should be an appraisal of the ecumenical significance of the results already arrived at in these two recent dialogues.

At the conclusion of its meeting in Chambésy in 1975, the Joint Orthodox-Old Catholic Commission announced its rejection of the *filioque* not simply as an uncanonical addition to the Creed but also and above all as an erroneous doctrine. The procession of the Spirit from the Father *and* the Son, or even of the Father *through* the Son, is no longer recognized here as a legitimate theologoumenon as it had been by the same two partners during the Bonn conversations of a century ago. The δι' Υἱοῦ is henceforth restricted to the temporal mission of the Spirit, whose eternal procession from the Father alone is declared to be warranted by Holy Scripture, the Creed and the entire ancient Church.

Meeting in Moscow in 1976, the Joint Orthodox-Anglican Commission, while it also wished to see the *filioque* expunged from the Anglican liturgical Creed, spoke more circumspectly about the doctrinal aspect of the question. In fact the joint statement here confines itself to pointing out that the Creed should confess in biblical terms the eternal procession of the Spirit from the Father. Nonetheless, while not levelling any formal charge of error against the *filioque*, it is stated that the biblical passages which associate the Son with the Father in a relationship with the Spirit apply only to the temporal mission of the Spirit. This is tantamount, however, to denying any scriptural warrant for the Latin tradition, although in the Bonn conversations of 1875 the Anglican partner had insisted on safeguarding this tradition.

We seem therefore to be witnessing in a sense the reversal of the position which prevailed at the Council of Florence in 1439. Then, the equivalence of the δι' Υἱοῦ to the *filioque* was canonized by the Decree of Union without any reciprocal concession; in other words, while the Greeks recognized the Latin pneumatology, their own was not acknowledged. In the official dialogue today, it is the turn of the western partners of the Orthodox Church to subscribe to Photian monopatrism without any reciprocal concession. In that case, can we speak of a genuine ecumenical dialogue here? Is this not rather one more makeshift agreement, reflecting this time a reversal of the old distribution of forces which now places Orthodoxy in a theologically superior position over against a West suffering from a sense of guilt at its former complacency? In any case, the resurgence of an inflexible anti-filioquism is hardly likely to facilitate the forthcoming official conversations with the Roman Catholic Church. The latter could not abandon its own tradition without repudiating itself.

The neo-Photian theses

The most probable explanation of this doctrinal ἀκρίβεια in contemporary Orthodoxy is the evident influence of a Photian and Palamitic revival in various theological and spiritual circles during the past thirty years, exemplified especially in the neo-patristic synthesis of a Vladimir Lossky. The pneumatological theses of this school may be summarized in the following two points. The procession of the Spirit from the Father alone is a dogmatic truth based on John 15:26 and on the Niceno-Constantinopolitan Creed and confirmed by the patristic principle that, within the Trinity, the Father represents the unique source, principle and cause of the hypostatic processions. Consequently, the participation of the Son does not apply to the constitutive ἐκπόρευσις of the Spirit though certainly to the economy and temporal mission of the Spirit and possibly also to the eternal radiation and outpouring of divine energies distinct from the divine essence and its hypostases.

These theses are not novel. Their current success, however, is due mainly to the way in which the Losskian school has been able to incorporate them within the framework of a radical opposition – both structural and existential in character – between the Greek and the Latin theologies, in much the same way as the "Slavophile" thinkers of the nineteenth century had spoken of the spiritual pre-eminence of the Orthodox East in creating a profound inner unity in love analogous to the trinitarian *sobornost*, in contrast to the Latin and Germanic West with its inability to reconcile the imposed unity of Roman Catholicism with the individualist freedom of Protestantism.

The argument is that divergent attitudes and intellectual assumptions in the two sectors of Christendom have led to the development of the ancient common trinitarian tradition into two incompatible syntheses and that western theology has emerged from this development with characteristic disfigurement. Latin triadology is first of all essentialist: it has stressed the essence in God to the detriment of the persons, which are reduced to the fluid category of "relations", so much so, in fact, that the Spirit, said to proceed from the Father and the Son as from a single principle and regarded as the mutual bond between them, has been reduced (the argument runs) to a pure function of the divine unity. Next, Latin theology is rationalist. It is supposed to claim to unravel the mystery of the immanent Trinity, partly by simple inference from its economic manifestations and therefore with scant respect for the radical apophatic mystery enveloping the essence of God, and partly even on the basis of analogies with human psychology and therefore with all the risk of anthropomorphic illusions. This, it is argued, has fatal consequences for Latin ecclesiology. The subordination of charisma to the institution, of freedom to power, of the prophetic to the legalistic, of mysticism to scholasticism, of the laity to the clergy – are not all these the expression in the Roman Catholic Church of precisely this inner-trinitarian subjection of the Spirit to the Son which is implicit in Latin filioquism? And – as the ultimate expression of this ecclesiological "christomonism" – the subjection of synodal communion to the primacy of the papal jurisdiction?!

A question of motive

To make the *filioque* the master key for deciphering all the differences between Catholicism and Orthodoxy in the manner just described is to adopt an epistemology the very seductiveness of whose logic makes it suspect right from the start, given the complexity of history. Certainly there is some substance in a number of the criticisms directed at the Latin tradition by the neo-Photians and the neo-Palamites; but they sometimes prove to be so tailored to the dictates of a system as to distort and even ignore altogether the real intentions of Augustinian and scholastic theology. The Anselmian axiom concerning the procession of the Spirit – *tamquam ab uno principio* – far from expressing a congenital essentialism is simply an attempt to meet the objection that acceptance of the *filioque* would contradict the divine monarchy: if the two persons of the Father and the Son breathe the Spirit in one and the same act of mutual love, the unique originating principle undoubtedly consists in what is a supremely "interpersonal" exchange!

Nor has it been in virtue of an incorrigible rationalism that the Latin tradition has always spontaneously sought to understand the immanent Trinity in the light of the divine economy and by reflecting on the psychology of human understanding and of love; for no *hubris* need necessarily be involved when the human spirit, made as it is in the image of God, seeks to picture to itself its Creator in the light of the "vestiges" imprinted in his works and in terms of his activity in the redemptive history. On the contrary, this is the pathway proposed to us by Scripture itself and in fact followed also by the Greek Fathers themselves. However naive the confidence of scholastic theologians in the "necessary conclusions" of their syllogisms may sometimes seem, all of them worthy of the name remained aware, as a rule, of the absolute freedom of the transcendent God and of the hopeless inadequacy of every theological analogy.

It should also be emphasized that, in the Latin tradition, the trinitarian *filioque* implies no ecclesiological subordination of the Spirit to Christ, still less any "christomonism". In view of the fact that the economy of Pentecost could in no conceivable circumstances contradict the economy of the Incarnation of which it is the fulfilment – the Spirit whom Jesus sends secures the confession of him as Lord! – to play off a totally juridicized church against a purely charismatic church can never be other than a crude caricature. Moreover, it is in its trinitarian root itself that the falsity of the charge of christomonism is demonstrated: the τάξις of the spiration of the Spirit by the Son no more implies the subjection of the Spirit to the Son than the generation of the Son by the Father implies any inferiority of the Son in relation to his Father. Perhaps to a greater degree than the triadology of the Greek Fathers, that of the Latins with its preoccupation with subordination-ism never lost sight of the radical consubstantiality of the three persons. One certainly does not commit oneself to an ideology of power and domination by conceiving of the Spirit as the expression of the mutual love of Father and Son!

An empty defence

The danger of the negative approach of contemporary Orthodox neo-Photianism to Latin pneumatology is that it may provoke an equally negative defensive response on the part of Catholic theologians which would land us once more in the endless round of fruitless polemics. For example, we might respond *ad hominem* by accusing the Cappadocian Fathers themselves of trinitarian essentialism. Even for them, ὁ θεὸς can mean the common divin-ity, in contrast to the usage in the New Testament. They, too, could be accused of having reduced the subsistent hypostases to their original rela-tionships, in an unsatisfactory effort to counter Arian subordinationism, whereas it was the Latin tradition which inaugurated an authentic trinitarian personalism with the existential psychology of Augustine rounded off by the ontology of Thomas Aquinas in which the hypostasis is understood as a subsistent relationship. Then again, the charge of rationalism, too, would probably be turned against the same Cappadocians who, over-reacting to the Eunomian dialectics, laid themselves open to the charge of taking refuge in an essentially agnostic apophatism forbidding in principle any inferences from the ὅτι to the τι of God. Having thus divorced the immanent Trinity from the economy, the Palamites could then be said to have left themselves with no alternative but to re-establish the connection by thinking in terms of an eternal radiation of divine energies, somewhat on the lines of the neo-Platonic emanations, divine energies which are really distinct from the closed and impenetrable nucleus of the divine essence, whereas the Latin scholastics, for all their respect for the mystery of the divine essence would consider it nonetheless to some extent accessible to the human spirit elevated by the grace of God or by the "light of glory".

It need hardly be said that a defence of this kind takes just as little account of the positive intentions of the Greek trinitarian tradition as the criticisms it refutes fail to do justice to the real motive of the Latin triadology. Engaged in polemics, each speaker naturally tends to absolutize his own standpoint and to discredit the standpoint of his opponent. But ecumenical dialogue would require that each should recognize the truth affirmed by the other while remaining aware of his own imperfections. A balanced judgment is difficult enough even in human affairs. When it is a matter of the mystery of the one Triune God it becomes radically impossible, since here discursive thought, tackling the paradox from one side or the other, as it must, inevitably appears to come down on one side rather than on the other. Instead of reproaching the other spokesman for his different theological approach, the more appropriate procedure would be to ensure that he does not neglect the corrective supplied by the contrary affirmation. The Latins are no more to be accused of Sabellianism because of their concern for the unity of the divine nature than the Greeks are to be branded as tritheists because of their primary concern for the trinity of the hypostases.

A positive context
   This means that there is no more urgent theological task facing the ecumenical dialogue on the procession of the Spirit than the deliberate detachment of the debate from its negative and polemical context. By locating the heart of the controversy in a supposedly insuperable incompatibility between two triadologies which is the source of all the differences between ecclesiologies, anthropologies and spiritualities, the neo-Photians rule out any possibility of reconciliation right from the start. But there have always been other Orthodox theologians convinced that the difference between filioquism and monopatrism had no appreciable influence on the doctrine and life of the two churches. Moreover, to liberate the question of the procession of the Holy Spirit does not mean treating it as if it were an exercise in abstract logic, isolated from other questions in a way that would lead to dangerous distortions of perspective; it means, rather, finding a positive context for it. Instead of locating it at the very heart of our differences, we must replace it within the pneumatological tradition we still share. Within this consensus the difference will assume its true proportions.
   Most of the publications stimulated on the Roman Catholic side in recent years by the theological *aggiornamento* of the Second Vatican Council and the pentecostal or charismatic revival are primarily concerned with the ecclesiological dimension of pneumatology, including its sacramental and liturgical aspects. Since the Spirit manifests his presence from the very first page of Genesis (1:2) down to the very last page of Revelation (22:17), a

complete outline of ecumenical pneumatology based on biblical theology would have to embrace the entire redemptive history from the creation to the second coming. His prophetic function among the people of the Old Covenant would be specially emphasized by reference to the inspiration of the scriptures as well as to the anointing of kings and priests. The presentation of his role in the life of Christ – principally in his conception, baptism and resurrection – would take into account the diverse standpoints of the synoptic gospels, of Acts, of Paul and of John. His activity as the soul of the Church from the pentecostal mission down to the spiritualization of the resurrection bodies would be illustrated in sacraments and ministries, in martyrdom and monasticism, as well as in the life of Christians generally, from the profession of faith up to and including mystical experiences. In the ordinary way, nothing should prevent unanimity on all these things between Catholics and Orthodox. On the economy of the Spirit there is no significant difference between them.

It is important, moreover, to point out that the doctrinal agreement also covers the essentials of trinitarian pneumatology. The fact is that on both sides we confess the Spirit as the third person-hypostasis of the unique divine nature-essence, consubstantial-ὁμοούσιον with the Father and the Son. It may seem obvious for the contemporary theologian to acknowledge the divinity of the Holy Spirit and his personal distinction within the Trinity but we have only to read the Fathers of the fourth century to realize afresh how tremendously difficult it was for Orthodox pneumatology to shake itself free not only from subordinationism but also from a certain confusion between the Spirit, on the one hand, and his gifts, or the divine nature, or the incarnate Logos, or the risen Christ, on the other, a confusion encouraged by the imprecisions of Scripture.

Restored to this context of the common economic and trinitarian faith, the question of the Son's participation in the breathing of the Spirit by the Father could no longer be regarded as the nodal point of contradiction between two irreconcilable pneumatologies but, on the contrary, would be cut down to its true dimensions as a peripheral difference within the context of a fundamentally identical tradition.

The decrees of union

The fact remains that, historically, the doctrine of the procession of the Holy Spirit was developed in the form of strictly dogmatic definitions. At the Councils of Lyons (1274) and Florence (1439), labelled "ecumenical" by classic Roman Catholic theology, the Latins made recognition of the *filioque* the condition of a union which was soon to be rejected by the conscience of the Orthodox Church, since the latter continued to consider the monopatrist formula the only adequate way of expressing the pneumatological faith. Does not this dogmatic crystallization of the controversy constitute an insuperable barrier to any suggestion that the question should be reopened and reconsidered within the context of a legitimate theological pluralism? By strictly adhering here to the decrees of the seven ecumenical councils of the first millenium, the Orthodox Church retains the advantage of not being bound by the dogmatic formulas of the medieval and modern West. Although it has a very rich concept of tradition, conceiving this as always integrally present to it, in practice it retains the maximum spiritual freedom to define its faith. But on the Roman Catholic side, too, the ecclesiological renewal of the Second Vatican Council as well as the claims of ecumenism invite theologians to review the irrevocable judgments of previous generations.

It was, moreover, Pope Paul VI himself who, when commemorating the seventh centenary of the Council of Lyons, took the remarkable step of breaking with the custom of referring to this assembly as "the fourteenth ecumenical council" and henceforth designating it "the sixth of the general synods held in the West". Drawing attention to the all-important role of political and cultural factors, the Pope went so far as to question the voluntary character of a union which he recognized as having been imposed on the basis of formulas produced by theologians who were ill-informed about eastern realities (*AAS* 66, 620–625). The same criteria are certainly less applicable to the Council of Florence, though here again what was in practice imposed upon the Greeks was also a definition in the Latin and scholastic style. Moreover, while it would certainly be unrealistic to seek to challenge the dogmatic status of the decree of a council which both parties were agreed in acknowledging as genuinely ecumenical, it would nevertheless be anachronistic to interpret this decree in terms of a "fundamental theology" developed by Roman Catholic theologians in the nineteenth century. The pneumatological definition of the Council of Florence, unaccompanied moreover by any anathema, rests only on a rational argument and makes no explicit reference to any biblical or patristic authority.

But we have only to analyse the text of the decrees of these two medieval councils to see that they in no way reject the real intention of Orthodox monopatrism, though the latter is never expressly mentioned. The condemnation pronounced by the Council of Lyons is directed equally against those who affirmed a double procession of the Spirit as against those who rejected the *filioque*. It therefore does not touch those for whom the formula ἐκ μόνου τοῦ Πατρὸς would still be compatible with the Son's participation in a spiration wholly subjected to the primary causality of the Father. As for the decree of the Council of Florence – lacking any trace of a formal condemnation – this, too, is content to insist that all Christians should recognize filioquism as an authentic expression of the faith without thereby denying that the Photian formula can equally be so. But the outstanding feature of the decree is its concern to respect the Greek point of view far more than was the case at Lyons. In fact, by reaffirming the principle *tamquam ab uno principio*, it is now made quite clear that the *filioque*, far from excluding, actually presupposes that the Father is seen as the unique source and principle of all divinity, since it is wholly from him that the Son · derives his spirative power, the causal character of which is therefore not understood in the sense of first cause, as in the αἰτία of the Greek Fathers.

Thus, although at the two "union councils" the Latins may have persuaded the Orthodox to acknowledge filioquism without formally conceding their counter position, nevertheless the radical intention of the monarchy of the Father, which constitutes the profound truth of Photian monopatrism, is clearly respected, objectively speaking, in the decrees of these councils.

Back to the Fathers

Neither of the two parties is prevented, therefore, from reopening the dialogue on the procession of the Holy Spirit in a strictly ecumenical perspective, i.e. by reference to an axis which is central enough to sustain the clash of partial viewpoints without resort to relativism or syncretism. This common axis of reference would lead Orthodox and Catholics back to the period prior to the schism when the trinitarian theologies of the Greek East and the Latin West still coexisted peacefully in their pluriformity. Neither of the two churches would any longer require the other to accept subsequent definitions of its own theology as a canon of faith and both of them would also recognize the legitimacy of the other's distinctive theological developments. In practice, the dialogue would mean an effort on the part of each partner to explain his own patristic tradition as understood from within, i.e. with no attempt to subject his partner's tradition to his own personal criteria, but seeking rather to dig down to the deepest intentions of his Fathers in the faith instead of sticking to *florilegia* of quotations, which are always open to challenge as artificially isolated from their contexts. This is what is required of us if the two apparently conflicting pneumatologies are ever to be seen as, in reality, complementary approaches to the one divine mystery with all the considerable enrichment this discovery will bring with it.

Another advantage which this projected return to the Fathers would bring with it would be to recall theology to a greater discretion. The fact is that those who helped to develop the pneumatological dogma in the latter half of the fourth century – Athanasius and Didymus, Basil and the two Gregories, Ambrose and Damasus – were content to define the procession of the Spirit negatively, rejecting the dilemma on the horns of which the Pneumatomachi sought to impale those who refused either to regard the Spirit as a creature or to speak of him as engendered as a brother of the Son. To this the Fathers sometimes added that they regarded the positive meaning of the procession as an unfathomable mystery, with an apophatic wisdom which conspicuously relativizes the frail scaffolding of contradictory arguments accumulated since then on both sides in order to explain this mystery.

Nor should we lose sight of the fact that the patristic tradition itself was already employing current philosophical terms and arguments which were equally lacking in any absolute theological value. When they adopted such concepts as "principle" or "cause" as rational tools for their arguments, the Fathers did so doubtless with the intention of preserving the central thrust of the monotheist trinitarian faith against Arianism and Sabellianism and certainly with no notion of developing a sacrosanct metaphysic or, to use their own expression, of "physiologizing the divine". However indispensable philosophical categories may be for formulating the Christian revelation, we must never lose sight of their fundamental inadequacy to express the mystery and of the need to correct them with the dimension of transcendence. There is no guarantee, for example, that the Aristotelian concept of efficient causality explains the inner divine relationships more satisfactorily than another kind, which deny rational conceptualization, of reciprocally and simultaneously triple relations, which would nonetheless not be restricted to one simple mode of manifestation. It would be much wiser, therefore, to try to keep the ecumenical dialogue on the procession of the Holy Spirit at the level of the strictly theological affirmations of the Fathers.

Two complementary traditions

Having said that, it turns out that the history of the *filioque* and its equivalents – sometimes older, like *ab utroque* – is far more difficult to reconstruct than is sometimes claimed. This is the case even if we ignore the semantic difference between the Latin verb *procedere* and the Greek word ἐκπορεύεσθαι, as well as possible nuances in the use of such prepositions as *ex, ab,* and *de*, which are equally demonstrable as against the Greek ἐκ. Confining ourselves strictly to the Son's participation in the procession of the Spirit, the starting point will be the formula *a Patre per Filium*, attested from Tertullian (*Prax* 4) onwards. Tertullian used this phrase to show that the "economy" does not encroach on the "monarchy"; he conceived of the trinitarian processions as, so to speak, a biological diffusion of the divine substance. We find the same formula used by Hilary on the eve of the "Macedonian" controversy, only this time in a context where the purpose is to prove that the Spirit of God is not a creature (*Trin.* 12:55–57). But the *per Filium* naturally aroused suspicions of subordinationism once the Pneumatomachi, basing their arguments on John 1:3, among other texts, had presented the Spirit as the first of the beings created by the Word. This may be why Ambrose in his refutation of the Arians of Illyria preferred to express the unity of nature by saying: *procedit a Patre et a Filio* (*Spir.* 1:11, 120). But that filioquism should have become really traditional in the West can only be attributed to Augustine, the pupil of Ambrose and doctor of the West.

It should be stressed, however, that the most ancient witnesses to this tradition represent no more than one way among others of affirming the consubstantial divinity of the third person of the Trinity, which Latin theology and the Latin liturgy loved to express, moreover, in another way by calling the Holy Spirit the bond or unity of the Trinity. In the fourth and fifth centuries the Johannine writings are still expounded without a term like *procedere* (John 15:26) being given the technical meaning which was subsequently assigned to it. In a Victricius of Rouen, the origin is felt to be akin to the περιχώρησις, both terms being intended simply to show the common possession of the same substance (*PL* 20:446): in other words, at the end of the fourth century, the precise character of the procession is still not envisaged. So too in the *Tome* of Damasus, which in a sense constitutes the western counterpart to the Creed of Constantinople (381), the *de Patre* appears to be a pure synonym for *de divina substantia*, intended simply to prove that the Spirit is *Deum verum* (anath. 16).

Nor was the consubstantial dimension of the trinitarian processions unfamiliar to the tradition of the Cappadocian Fathers which is reflected in the Creed of 381. But this tradition inclined to see here the origination of the three hypostases with their incommunicable properties; deeply attached to the principle of the monarchy and causality of the Father, it had used John 15:26 to define the eternal ἐκπόρευσις of the Spirit. There is no justification for claiming these Fathers as filioquists, therefore, and the texts cited by Latin controversialists in this sense on the basis of ancient manuscripts of the writings of Basil or Gregory of Nyssa certainly seem, in the last analysis, to have been interpolations. But it is worth observing that Augustine himself fully respected the "monarchy" in regarding the Spirit as proceeding *principaliter* from the Father, where the adverb doubtless does not mean "chie-

fly" but as from the unique principle (*Trin.* 15:17, 29; *In Jn.* 99:8). It was
doubtless in order not to yield any ground to pneumatomachian subordinationism that the Cappadocian Fathers avoided giving too much promi-
nence to the Son's participation in the eternal procession of the Spirit.

But Epiphanius and, above all, the school of Alexandria, who insisted as
did the Latins on the unity of the divine nature and in speaking of the
procession did not limit their terminology to that of John 15:26, gave greater
emphasis to the fact that the Spirit of the Father and the Son is παρ'
ἀμφοτέρων (Epiph. *Pan.* 74:7–8), i.e. οὐσιωδῶς ἐξ ἀμφοῖν (Cyril *Ador.* 1).
To limit these and other affirmations of the same tenor to the mission and
to leave out the eternal source and essential roots of the economy in the
immanent Trinity would be tantamount to foisting on the standpoint of the
fourth and fifth century Fathers a dichotomy still alien to them. Moreover,
the ancient formula "from the Father through the Son" is not only typical
of the Latin tradition but is also found in abundance in the Greek Fathers,
including John of Damascus and it was this formula which was regularly
proposed as a basis of agreement in the course of attempts at union or
dialogue. It should still be capable of reconciling Orthodox and Catholics
for while it expresses the Son's participation in the procession of the Spirit,
which is what the *filioque* intends but is obscured in the Photian formula ἐκ
μόνου τοῦ Πατρὸς, at the same time it strictly safeguards the monarchy of
the Father which the *filioque* may appear to jeopardize but which is the real
concern of monopatrism. In other words, the most faithful interpretation of
the common patristic tradition could be to apply the Greek ἐκ to the relation
of the Spirit to the Father and to interpret the Latin *ex* in the *filioque* in the
sense of *per*/διά.

The Creed of Constantinople

But surely the silence of the Creed of Constantinople about any role of
the Son in the procession of the Spirit is tantamount to a deliberate denial
of any such role on the part of the authors of this basic document of
Orthodoxy? The truth is that, since the Acts of the Second Ecumenical
Council have not been preserved, the precise circumstances in which the
Creed came to be drawn up remain a matter of speculation. Nevertheless,
although some scholars go so far as to detach the *Constantinopolitanum*
completely from the Council of 381, it is generally accepted today that the
ancient tradition is correct which attributes the completion of the pneuma-
tological article of the Creed of Nicea to the Fathers of Constantinople –
Gregory Nazianzus was the second president of the Council and Gregory of
Nyssa, whose brother Basil of Caesarea had been dead for more than two

years, was present at it. It is also assumed that its extant wording represents the revision of an already Nicenized local baptismal creed. The Fathers of 381, while confessing a doctrine radically opposed to the "Macedonian" theses, would seem nevertheless to have avoided any explicit enunciation of the divinity and consubstantiality of the Spirit in order to make it easier for the Pneumatomachi of the Hellespont at some time to rally to Orthodoxy, as the Emperor Theodosius hoped they would. This then is the probable context in which we should read the clause about the procession of the Spirit from the Father.

In the implicit quotation of John 15:26 in this clause, the preposition παρά in the gospel has been changed into ἐκ. This suggests that the point of the statement relates henceforth not so much to the Pentecostal mission of the Spirit as to its procession of origin, although the participle ἐκπορευόμενον has not been put into the aorist tense like the γεννηθέντα which indicates the eternal generation of the Son. The ἐκπορευόμενον is probably not completely lacking in an "economic" connotation, therefore, any more than are the immediately preceding adjectives "Lord" and "Life giver", in which the reference to creation and redemption is semantically implicit even though they point directly to the divinity of the Spirit.

That having been said, the statement of the procession certainly appears to express an intention absolutely parallel to that of the Nicene Fathers in the second article of their Creed: to state that the Son is begotten of the Father was tantamount to excluding his creation from nothing; to state that the Spirit proceeds from the Father was likewise to signify that he is not a creature. It would therefore be wrong to see here the adoption of a position concerning the precise mode of the ἐκπόρευσις rather than a simple confession of the divinity of the Spirit, synonymous in this respect to all the other clauses of the pneumatological article. In other words, the Creed transcends the quarrel between monopatrism and filioquism. The controversy between the Greeks and the Latins on that point broke out only when each of the two parties began to claim support from the Creed for its own position.

The silence of the Fathers of Constantinople is not to be explained, therefore, by their supposed opposition to the idea that the Son participated in some way or other in the spiration of the Spirit. This silence is all the more striking, however, when we consider that it would have been much more in accord with the customary formulas of the Cappadocian Fathers had they combined with John 15:26 another traditional biblical text such as John 16:14 or Romans 8:9, affirming that the Spirit receives from the Son or referring to the Spirit as the "Spirit of Christ". The reserve evident in the Creed should probably be explained, therefore, as a deliberate precautionary

measure motivated by a given circumstance, namely, the claim of the Pneumatomachi that the Spirit was created by the Son. By omitting any reference
at all to a relationship between the Spirit and the Son, the Fathers of 381
forestalled the illegitimate inference that the Spirit is a creature and subordinate to the Son, an inference which seemed unambiguously excluded by
the ἐκπόρευσις according to John 15:26, interpreteted analogously to the
generation of the Son in the second article. The dogma of the *Constantinopolitanum* is therefore no obstacle to unity.

The addition to the Creed

Yet even supposing agreement were reached on the procession of the
Holy Spirit along the lines of the Greek and Latin Fathers before the schism,
this would still leave untouched the original offence which was always central
to the Orthodox repudiation of the *filioque*. What canonical or moral right
had the Roman Catholic Church to introduce an additional clause into the
liturgical Creed of the common faith which a decree of the Ecumenical
Council of Ephesus had forbidden anyone to alter, and to do so unilaterally,
i.e. without a new ecumenical council? The Catholic party, persuaded that
the supreme *magisterium* can and should explain the faith confessed in the
Creed, if necessary by introducing into this Creed the dogma which it has
defined, could not have sufficiently realized the seriousness of what the
Orthodox regarded as a breach of the visible sign of the doctrinal unity of
all Christians with one another and of the unity of the Church today with
the Church of the Fathers.

On the basis of advances in the historical study of the creeds during the
past century, we are in a better position to appreciate the question discussed
at length at the Council of Ferrara in 1438, namely, whether the prohibition
of the Third Ecumenical Council included *any other exposition* of the faith,
as the Greeks understood it to mean, or only any exposition of *another faith*,
as the Latins understood it to mean. We now know that the Fathers of the
fourth and fifth centuries used to cite as the faith of Nicea formulas which
verbally were sometimes very remote from the actual text of the *Nicaenum*
– which itself, unlike the *Constantinopolitanum*, was never baptismal or
eucharistic – provided that they reflected the anti-Arian dogma defined at
Nicea. This patristic freedom of formulation – as well as that of the manu-
script tradition of the two great Creeds (the clause "God (born) of God" in
the Latin liturgical text is absent in the Greek) – undoubtedly reflects the
diverse customs of the local churches. The fact remains that all the Ecumenical Councils from Ephesus onwards demonstrated their respect for the

Creed of the first two Ecumenical Councils by refraining from inserting into it the dogmatic formulas of their definitions.

There are still vast areas of obscurity in the history of the insertion of the *filioque* into the *Constantinopolitanum*. The view that the addition, first attested in Spain, was intended to combat the Arianism of the Visigoths is still repeated though it remains no more than a hypothesis lacking any convincing proof. The more likely explanation is that the *filioque* was simply transferred from ancient local symbols into that of Constantinople when this latter symbol was adopted instead. The fact that a filioquist formula first appears in the Toledan symbols is generally explained today as having been due to the influence of an anti-Priscillian letter of Pope Leo the Great (*ep.* 15:1) in which already in 447 the words *ab utroque* occur as the most normal thing in the world, though there is still no need to trace the *filioque* back to a source in the pre-Ephesian *fides romana*. Thus the insertion of the *filioque* in the Creed of Constantinople need initially have meant no more than a natural adaptation to the local tradition, reflecting doubtless a regrettable ignorance of the conciliar tradition but certainly no subjective mistrust of the Eastern Orthodox Church. On the contrary, special respect was shown to this church by the liturgical reception of its Creed since for Rome this meant sacrificing its own old "apostolic" creed.

Unfortunately, however, the addition of the *filioque* became the stone of stumbling and one of the badges of the schism. Orthodoxy has indeed sometimes been disposed to concede to the Latins by the economy of love what canonical ἀκρίβεια forbad them to concede, while Rome for its part never – except at the darkest moments – went so far as to make union conditional on the explication of the Greek creed. But is it desirable that a mutual recognition of the two traditions on the procession of the Holy Spirit should leave written into the very text of the profession of faith the bone of contention which provoked the scandal of division, even if this difference *is* a thousand years old? Many theologians on both sides admit that the pneumatological article of the Creed of Constantinople is imperfect and some have proposed that a common reformulation should be undertaken. But could any future Ecumenical Council assume the responsibility of revising the venerable text by a new dogmatic "addition"? So long as the *Constantinopolitanum* remains what it is for each of the two churches, it would be better, therefore, after theological agreement has been achieved, to restore it in its original form so that Catholics and Orthodox may in future be able to proclaim it together. It would therefore be up to the Roman Catholic Church to suppress the *filioque* of the Creed, as a token of reconciliation with the Orthodox Church but without signifying by this renunciation any repudiation of its own tradition.

Conclusion

By way of conclusion to these few thoughts in an ecumenical context, it may be permissible to place the desired agreement on the procession of the Spirit and on the addition of the *filioque* to the Creed under the twofold patronage of a convergent mutual recognition which dates back to the era when the misunderstanding which would spark off the schism first began to appear. About the year 650, Maximus the Confessor, when reminded by his compatriots that they rejected the *filioque*, explained to them in the terminology of their common eastern tradition that the "Romans" did not thereby intend any denial that the Father was the unique first cause (αἰτία) in the Trinity but meant it in the Greek sense of the procession (προϊέναι) through the Son, in order to show the divine consubstantiality (τὸ συναφὲς τῆς οὐσίας – *PG* 91, 136). In 810, when Charlemagne's envoys demanded that the *filioque* be inserted in the Creed of Constantinople, Pope Leo III roundly refused to do so, although asserting that he was profoundly convinced of the orthodoxy of the Latin tradition (*PL* 102, 971–976). These two convergent examples have lost nothing of their freshness and immediacy, pointing as they do to what is perhaps the only way to an honourable agreement. The Roman Catholic Church will be able to restore the Creed and acknowledge the radical truth to monopatrism once the Orthodox Church likewise recognizes the authenticity of the *filioque* understood in the sense of the traditional δἰ Υἱοῦ.

THE FILIOQUE CLAUSE:
AN ANGLICAN APPROACH

DONALD M. ALLCHIN

I. The Moscow Statement of 1976

The history of Anglican-Orthodox relationships is a long and slowly moving one. Contacts were made in the seventeenth and eighteenth centuries, and became more frequent in the nineteenth century. In the last fifty years official exchanges have been constant. The appointment of an international Joint Doctrinal Commission in 1931 marked a new stage on the way. Although the meeting of 1931 was not followed up, the idea of such a Commission was not forgotten. In the 1960's a new and more representative Commission was set up, and held its first full meeting in Oxford in 1973. After two years of further intensive work the full Commission met again in Moscow in 1976 and issued an agreed statement which covered the subjects of "The Knowledge of God", "The Inspiration and Authority of Holy Scripture", "Scripture and Tradition", "The Authority of the Councils," "The Church as the Eucharistic Community" and "The Invocation of the Holy Spirit in the Eucharist". Not the least important section of the agreed statement is that which deals with the *filioque* clause, which follows directly on the treatment of "The Authority of the Councils". It reads as follows:

"19. The question of the *filioque* is in the first instance a question of the content of the Creed, i.e. the summary of the articles of faith which are to be confessed by all. In the Niceno-Constantinopolitan Creed (commonly called the Nicene Creed) of 381, the words 'proceeding from the Father' are an assertion of the divine origin and nature of the Holy Spirit, parallel to the assertion of the divine origin and nature of the Son contained in the words 'begotten not made, consubstantial with the Father'. The word ἐκ-

● Donald M. ALLCHIN (Anglican) is Residentiary Canon of Canterbury Cathedral, a member of the International Anglican/Orthodox Doctrinal Commission, and Chairman of the Council of the Fellowship of St Alban and St Sergius.

πορευόμενον (proceeding), as used in the Creed, denotes the incomprehensible mode of the Spirit's origin from the Father, employing the language of Scripture (John 15:26). It asserts that the Spirit comes from the Father in a manner which is not that of generation.

"20. The question of the origin of the Holy Spirit is to be distinguished from that of his mission to the world. It is with reference to the mission of the Spirit that we are to understand the biblical texts which speak both of the Father (John 14:26) and of the Son (John 15:26) as sending (pempein) the Holy Spirit.

"21. The Anglican members therefore agree that: (*a*) because the original form of the Creed referred to the origin of the Holy Spirit from the Father; (*b*) because the *filioque* clause was introduced into this Creed without the authority of an ecumenical council and without due regard for Catholic assent; and (*c*) because this Creed constitutes the public confession of faith by the people of God in the eucharist, the *filioque* clause should not be included in the Creed." [1]

Two years later in the Lambeth Conference of 1978, the bishops of the Anglican Communion agreed to commend the work of the International Commission, to receive the Report of Moscow 1976, and to recommend "that all member churches of the Anglican Communion should consider omitting the *filioque* from the Nicene Creed, and that the Anglican-Orthodox Joint Doctrinal Commission through the Anglican Consultative Council should assist them in presenting the theological issues to their appropriate synodical bodies and should be responsible for any necessary consultation with other churches of the western tradition". [2]

What was the context of this agreement? Something of the nature of the discussion at the Moscow meeting can be seen in the account written by the Orthodox theological secretary, Father Kallistos Ware, which makes considerable use of quotations from the minutes. On the one side it becomes clear that the Anglicans did not see this proposal as a mere gesture of ecumenical good-will. Anglicans have long recognized that in this matter their position is anomalous, at least as regards the position of the clause in the Creed. The view commonly held is that the *filioque* clause owes its

---

[1] *Anglican-Orthodox Dialogue: the Moscow Statement Agreed by the Anglican-Orthodox Joint Doctrinal Commission 1976*, ed. K. Ware and C. Davey, pp. 87–88. This book contains a useful history of the dialogue written by C. Davey, London, SPCK, 1977, pp. 4–37.
[2] *The Report of the Lambeth Conference, 1978*, London, CIO Publishing, 1978, pp. 51–2. This recommendation was endorsed and reaffirmed at the meeting of the Anglican Consultative Council in London, Ontario, May 1979.

position in the Creed to a decision of the papacy, over-riding an earlier conciliar decision. But Anglicans in general do not recognize such an authority in the papacy. The members of the Commission, however, wanted to go further than this. It was not only a question of the form of the Creed of 381, it was also a question of the intention of those who framed it. Hence the carefully phrased formulation of paragraph 19, about the parallel between the begetting of the Son and the proceeding of the Spirit; hence the first of the reasons given for the recommendation made to their churches by the Anglican members of the Commission that the *filioque* clause should no longer be included in the Creed. Here is a question of faith which lies behind the subsequent development of divergent theologies.

But as the minutes of the meeting also make abundantly evident, there was no intention on the part of the Anglican members of the Commission to make any condemnation of the *filioque* doctrine as such, still less of the whole Latin tradition of trinitarian teaching of which it is a part. Indeed one member of the Commission proposed that an addition to the statement should be made in terms such as these. "We make this proposal without prejudice to the teaching of Augustine on the double procession of the Holy Spirit, which is found in other Anglican formularies, and without implying any condemnation of the Roman Catholic, Lutheran and other churches which use the *filioque*." [3] This proposal was not taken up, but I think it is clear that even those Anglican theologians who feel seriously dissatisfied with the *filioque* tradition of trinitarian theology would not wish either to condemn or outlaw it. Both traditions of trinitarian theology contain elements of value. They bring out complementary aspects of the truth. Before so great a mystery a sane theological pluralism is not undesirable.

It is in this light that the remarks in paragraph 20 are to be understood. The distinction made may be elementary, but it is certainly vital, and relates directly to the preceding paragraph's account of the intention of the Creed of 381. It also marks a place where there is not disagreement between East and West; the Spirit is sent by the Son. But the reference to the Johannine texts was certainly not meant, at least by the Anglicans present, to foreclose the large questions of New Testament exegesis which lie behind the elaboration and development of differing formulations of trinitarian doctrine. All these questions were left open, and the hope was expressed that they might be further explored in future discussion. As one of the senior Ortho-

---

[3] *Op. cit.*, p. 63.

dox members of the Commission (Archbishop Basil Krivocheine) remarked, the document "did not condemn the *filioque* doctrine".[4]

II. The seventeenth century discussion

Concern about the doctrine of the *filioque* is not something new in post-Reformation Anglicanism. At the time of the Reformation there was anxiety as to whether it could be proved with sufficient clarity from the scriptures, since the most obvious proof text, John 15:26, seemed to work against this. Thus for instance, we find the reformer, Roger Hutchinson arguing "that he proceedeth also of Christ, these St Paul's words be a sufficient record. 'If any man have not the Spirit of Christ he is none of his.' For he cannot be Christ's Spirit, not proceeding of him . . . Further our Saviour Christ, to teach that the Holy Spirit proceedeth from him equally as he doth from the Father, breathed on his disciples and said, 'Receive the Holy Ghost,' and 'Lo, I send the promise of my Father upon you.' " [5] Here as we see there is no distinction being made between a temporal mission and an eternal procession of the Spirit, a failure to distinguish which seems common at this period.

In the seventeenth century, however, other difficulties about the *filioque* come to the fore. In the gradual articulation of an Anglican theological position over against Rome on one side and Geneva on the other, appeal to the authority of the Fathers played an increasing role; and in controversy with Rome appeal was also made to the existence and testimony of the contemporary eastern churches. It was clear that the question of the *filioque* could not be evaded. If we were to appeal to the witness of the East, it must be proved that the East was not in error on a fundamental point of faith. Where was the right in this question, in terms of history and of theology?

It must be said straight away that the great majority of Anglican theologians in this classical period of Anglican theology followed in the western tradition of trinitarian theology. As typical we may cite a work written towards the end of the century, and primarily concerned to defend the doctrine of the Trinity against Socinian attacks. In his *Vindication of the Doctrine of the Trinity*, William Sherlock writes on this subject in relation to the text of the Athanasian Creed: "But the difficulty of this is with reference to the dispute between the Greek and Latin Church about the *filioque*, or the Spirit's proceeding from the Father and from the Son. The reason why the Latin Church insists on this is to preserve the unity and

---

[4] *Ibid.*, p. 67.

[5] *The Works of Roger Hutchinson*, Parker Society Edition, Oxford, 1842, pp. 126–7.

subordination of the Divine Persons to each other. The Son is united and subordinate to the Father, as begotten by him; the Holy Ghost is united and subordinate to the Father and Son, as proceeding both from the Father and from the Son. But if the Holy Spirit proceedeth only from the Father, not from the Son, there would be no union and subordination between the Son and the Spirit, and yet the Spirit is the Spirit of the Son as well as of the Father, and that these Three Persons be one God, it is necessary that there should be an union of Persons as well as one Nature. But then the Greek Church confessed that the Spirit proceedeth from the Father by the Son, though not *from* the Son; and *by* and *from* are such niceties that we confess we understand not the manner of this Procession of the Holy Spirit to be such as ought to have made a dispute, much less a schism, between the two churches. The Greek Church acknowledges the distinction of Persons, and their unity and subordination; that there is one Father, not three Fathers, one Son, not three Sons, one Holy Ghost, not three Holy Ghosts; that the Unity in Trinity and Trinity in Unity is to be worshipped; which is all this Creed [sc. the Athanasian] requires as necessary to salvation." [6] Even allowing for the controversial context in which this book was written, we see here a clear reiteration of the western tradition, and a desire, which is characteristic of a large part of Anglican writing since the sixteenth century, not to multiply those articles of faith which are considered necessary to salvation.

But, of course, we can find more detailed and penetrating discussions than that of William Sherlock. Pre-eminent among them is the treatment of the subject by John Pearson (Bishop of Chester, 1673–86) in his *Commentary on the Creed*, for more than two centuries a standard work used in the training of the clergy. In the course of his exposition of this article, Pearson declares: "Our sixth and last assertion (sufficient to manifest the nature of the Holy Ghost, as he is the Spirit of God) teacheth the Spirit to be a Person proceeding from the Father and the Son . . . Now this procession of the Spirit, in reference to the Father is delivered expressly, in relation to the Son is contained virtually, in the scriptures." And there follows a lengthy discussion of the New Testament texts to support this assertion. "From whence it came to pass in the primitive times, that the Latin Fathers taught expressly the procession of the Spirit from the Father and the Son, because by good consequences they did collect so much from those passages of the scriptures which we have used to prove that truth. And the Greek Fathers,

---

[6] W. Sherlock, *A Vindication of the Doctrine of the Trinity*, 1690, pp. 16f., quoted in *Anglicanism*, ed. P. E. More and F. L. Cross, pp. 277–8.

though they stuck more closely to the phrase and language of the scripture, saying: that the Spirit proceedeth from the Father, and not saying, that he proceedeth from the Son; yet they acknowledge under another Scripture expression the same thing which the Latins understand by procession, viz. that the Spirit is of or from the Son, as he is of or from the Father; and therefore usually when they said, *he proceedeth from the Father*, they also added, *he received of the Son*."

Pearson continues with a brief account of the development of the dispute between Greeks and Latins, supported by extremely ample footnotes, and concludes as follows: "Now although the addition of the words to the formal Creed without the consent and against the protestation of the Oriental Church, be not justifiable; yet that which was added is nevertheless a certain truth, and may be so used in that Creed by them who believe the same to be a truth; so long as they pretend it not to be a definition of that Council, but an addition or explication inserted, and condemn not those who, out of a greater respect to such synodical determinations, will admit of no such insertion, nor speak any other language than the scriptures and their Fathers spake." Thus in the body of his text Pearson, who is clearly convinced of the truth of the doctrine, maintains, though with qualifications, the rightness of maintaining its expression in the Creed. When we turn to the last of his footnotes on this passage we find a slightly different shade of meaning. In the preface to the reader, Pearson explains that he has purposely kept all material demanding a knowledge of Latin, Greek and Hebrew out of the body of the text, so as to make his work accessible to the less learned. Writing, as he was, during the period of the Commonwealth when the use of the *Book of Common Prayer*, and hence the liturgical recitation of the Creed, was forbidden, he was particularly anxious not to raise doubts about the authority of its text as known and received. In his notes, however, he does not hesitate to take a more critical view. Here he concludes: "Thus did the Oriental Church accuse the Occidental for adding *filioque* to the Creed, contrary to a General Council, which had prohibited all additions, and that without the least pretence of the authority of another council; and so the schism between the Latin and Greek Church began and was continued, never to be ended until those words ἐκ τοῦ Υἱοῦ, or *filioque*, are taken out of the Creed. The one relying upon the truth of the doctrine contained in those words, and the authority of the Pope to alter anything; the other denying or suspecting the truth of the doctrine, and being very zealous for the authority of the ancient councils. This therefore is much to be lamented, that the Greeks should not acknowledge the truth which was acknowledged by their ancestors, in the substance of it; and that the Latins should force the Greeks to make an addition to the Creed, without as great an authority as hath prohibited it, and to use that language in the expression of this doctrine which never was used by any of the Greek Fathers." [7] Here there is surely implied a suggestion that the Latin Church should be prepared to remove the clause from the Creed, for the sake of a unity which otherwise cannot be restored, particularly if the Greeks are willing to acknowledge "the substance" of the truth which it seeks to express. And if this is the case for the Latin Church, how much more for the English Church which does not recognize the authority of the Pope to order such matters independently of a council?

Pearson was not the only Anglican writer of this time to see that there were two sides of the question. In a book written in 1664, *A Rational Account of the Grounds of the Protestant Religion*, Edward Stillingfleet, later Bishop of Worcester, begins with a chapter entitled "The Defence of the Greek Church", in which he argues that whatever defects and errors it may contain, the Greek Church remains a true church, which is not guilty of heresy on any fundamental article of faith. On the question of the *filioque* he states a case against the West, adding: "For you may see the Greeks want not great plausibleness of reason on their side, as well as the authority of Scripture and Council, plain for them, but not so against them." [8] Twenty-five years later in the upheaval caused by the dethronement of James II and the introduction of William III, these theological discussions suddenly touched on practical politics, and Stillingfleet was intimately involved in a proposal to remove the *filioque* clause from the Nicene Creed, and to make a declaration about the Athanasian Creed making it clear that the condemnatory clauses relate "only to those who obstinately deny the Christian faith".

This proposal formed part of a much more general proposition for a revision of the *Book of Common Prayer*, intended to make possible the inclusion of the main bodies of Protestant dissenters within the Church of England. It is striking that in a move designed primarily to meet the problems of Independents and Presbyterians, the Eastern Orthodox should also have been considered. Timothy Fawcett, in a recent study of the scheme of *The Liturgy of Comprehension, 1689*, shows that it was Stillingfleet and Gilbert Burnet (Bishop of Salisbury) who were particularly concerned about the text of the Creed. He illuminates the background to the hand-written note

---

[7] J. Pearson, *An Exposition of the Creed*, ed. E. Burton, London, Bell, 1857, pp. 492–6.
[8] E. Stillingfleet, *Complete Works*, Oxford, 1844, p. 53.

in the copy of the prayer book used by the Commission which adds after the relevant words in the Creed: "It is humbly submitted to Convocation whether a note ought here to be added with relation to the Greek Church, in order to our maintaining Catholic Communion." [9] For reasons of a political nature, all these plans came to nothing at that time, and no revision of the liturgical texts took place. Nonetheless it had been seriously envisaged.

III. Developments in the nineteenth century

The renewed interest in patristic theology and the increased concern for the eastern churches which followed on the Oxford movement of 1833, might have been expected to bring new attention to the *filioque* question in nineteenth century Anglican theology. But in fact it seems that it was only amongst those who had a quite special interest in Eastern Orthodoxy, notably William Palmer of Magdalen College, and J. M. Neale, that this was the case. In his published works on the history of the eastern Church, Neale merely repeats the judgment of John Pearson on the question of the *filioque*. In his private correspondence of the same time, he notes: "I wished to seem to pronounce no judgment, but to leave the reader to form his own . . . I am convinced with Palmer that the Latin doctrine, if consistently carried out, would become heresy, and that the Holy Ghost does not proceed from the Son at all, except by way of Temporal Mission, and then not according to his Divinity, but only according to his operations. However, of course, I don't say all this in the book." [10] In an unsigned article in *The Christian Remembrancer* for October 1864, almost certainly written by Neale, while it is argued that for pastoral reasons it would not be possible to remove the *filioque* from the Creed, a proposal is put forward that the Church of England might perhaps make a declaration that in retaining the clause in the Creed, "we by no means assert that the Eternal Procession of the Holy Ghost from the Father and the Son is an article of faith; and nothing of necessity is to be held as implied in the additional clause except the temporal mission of the same Holy Ghost from the said Son".

J. M. Neale died in 1866. It is interesting to speculate what part he might have played in the discussions on the future of Anglican-Orthodox relations, which took place in England in 1870, during the visit of Archbishop Alexander Lycargus of Syros and Tinos, and on the more substantial controversy which followed the Bonn Conferences of 1874 and 1875. As it was, the

---

[9] *The Liturgy of Comprehension 1689*, London, Alcain Club Series, 1973, p. 104.
[10] *Letters of J. M. Neale*, ed. by his daughter, M. S. Lawson, London, Longmans, Green & Co., 1910, p. 131.

proposals made at Bonn in 1875 were strongly contested by E. B. Pusey, who was adamant in his defence of the Latin tradition. In one of his last writings published in 1876 he criticized the Bonn proposals as making improper concession to the Greek point of view.[11] Pusey's personal authority in the Church of England at this time carried very great weight. Nevertheless in 1888, at the Lambeth Conference of that year which first adopted the Lambeth Quadrilateral as the Anglican basis for negotiations towards unity and in which, of course, the Nicene Creed is specifically mentioned, the question of the revision of the English text of the Creed was proposed by the Committee on Authoritative Standards of Doctrine and Worship. This Committee concluded: "In relation to the doctrine of the Holy Spirit, while we believe that there is no fundamental diversity of faith between the churches of the East and the West [here there is a reference in a footnote to the proposals of the Bonn Conference in 1875] we recognize the historical fact that the clause *filioque* makes no part of the Nicene Symbol as set forth by the authority of the undivided Church. We are of the opinion that, as opportunity arises, it would be well to revise the English version of the Nicene Creed and of the Quicunque Vult." [12] This proposal was not, however, followed up.

In our own century, the question has naturally continued to feature in all official Anglican-Orthodox dialogue, and particularly in the meeting of the Joint Doctrinal Commission of 1931. Here reference was made back to the terms of the Bonn Agreement of 1875, and the Anglican delegates made appeal to the theology of St John of Damascus, and seem to have hoped that the formula "through the Son" would form an acceptable point of meeting between the two sides. Comparing the discussion of 1931 with that of 1976, it appears that in the more recent case a clearer distinction was made between the level of faith as expressed in the text of the Creed, and the level of theological explication as expressed in the two contrasting, but possibly complementary traditions of trinitarian teaching.

IV. Contemporary considerations

If we come to ask what is the state of Anglican theological opinion on the subject at the present time, we should have first to recognize that immensely varied positions are taken. In a period when theologians question the foundations of traditional Christology and trinitarian theology, it is clear that this

[11] See E. B. Pusey, *On the Clause "And the Son" in regard to the Eastern Church and the Bonn Conference: a Letter to the Rev. H. P. Liddon, D.D.*, Oxford, 1876.
[12] *The Five Lambeth Conferences*, London, SPCK, 1920, p. 172.

particular issue will appear to many as somewhat trivial. To others, and they perhaps a majority, the variations of teaching as between Latin and Greek traditions will seem wholly acceptable divergences within a general unity of faith. Here we are faced with great mysteries. Let us be tentative and humble in our approach to them; let us hear what is to be said on both sides.

At the other extreme there are those, few in number but not without weight, who have found themselves in agreement with those Orthodox theologians who have seen in the teaching of the *filioque* one of the primary sources not only of the schism between East and West, but also of the ills of western Christendom. Notable among them was the late Dr D. J. Chitty, who maintained this position with historical learning and acute theological intuition. A more widely held position, and one which was represented amongst the Anglican members of the Commission, would see the question of the *filioque* as a symptom rather than a cause of an underlying difference between East and West about the doctrine of the Holy Spirit. While unconvinced by the logical neatness of the former position which seems to involve the over-simplifying of large and highly complex theological and historical issues, those who hold this view would point to the widely expressed conviction in the West at the present time that something has gone seriously wrong with our theology of the Holy Spirit. They would also point to the fact that many of the controversies of the sixteenth and seventeenth centuries about the doctrine of redemption, or the doctrine of the Church and the sacraments, seem to have been carried on with curiously little reference to the doctrine of the Holy Spirit. It is a striking fact that at the present time, if we take the instance of the eucharist, western revisions of the eucharistic rite have almost always tended to make the action of the Holy Spirit in the sacrament more clearly evident. In some Reformation texts it was scarcely mentioned. What is to be seen in the revisions of the texts is also to be seen in the consensus statements on eucharistic doctrine, where it has often been a new awareness of the role of the Spirit in the eucharistic action which has helped towards the resolution of old problems about the nature of the presence or the nature of the sacrifice. What is true of the eucharist would, I believe, also be true of the doctrine of the Church as a whole, since the Church needs to be seen as the communion of the Holy Spirit no less than the Body of Christ. Here are areas where we have much to learn from the Orthodox tradition, and could recognize much truth in Vladimir Lossky's insistence on the reciprocity of the action of Christ and the Spirit in the Church.

But the question of the relationship of the second to third person of the Trinity has wider implications. Has not the technical language of "subordination" led to unfortunate and unintended consequences? One of the most acute theological minds in the eighteenth century Methodist revival, Ann Griffiths, confessed that while she had thought of the Father and the Son as co-equal, she had thought of the Holy Spirit "as a functionary subordinate to them".[13] She saw this as an error striking at the very root of Christian life.

But this error has surely been widespread and has had a variety of consequences. In the life of the Church, where the person and work of the Holy Spirit are little regarded or understood, it seems as though the inner and the outer, the subjective and the objective, the personal and the corporate, the spiritual and the material, too easily fall apart and come into conflict with one another. The life of the Church will be read in terms of a constant struggle between the group and the individual. In the worship of the Church, no less than in its faith, either the objective, given structures will be emphasized at the expense of what is inner and personal, or the subjective elements will be stressed to the detriment of what is common and received. It becomes increasingly difficult to see how thinking and feeling, how lucidity and enthusiasm are to be held together and coordinated.

For it seems as if this point of doctrine touches our understanding of the nature of man and his relationship to God. The vision of an inherent inter-relationship between man and God, expressed in the eastern tradition by terms such as "Godmanhood" or "theocentric humanism", tends to be lost. God is more and more banished into a transcendent realm, or is understood simply as the ground of man's being, his deepest subjectivity. Man is more and more understood not in relationship with God, but in isolation from him or in opposition to him. The thought and experience of man as constantly transcending himself into God, finding himself by losing himself in encounter with God and with his neighbour, becomes obscured. A more balanced doctrine of God which expressed anew both the distinction between the persons and their inherent inter-relationship would do much to restore a more balanced, richer understanding of man, in whom Word and Spirit work together in mutual harmony and support. It would help us to see more of what is meant by man's creation in God's image and likeness.

These are some of the issues which an exploration of this subject raises, and which are of urgent significance for the present development of the whole Christian tradition. The study of this question can be the occasion for a creative reappropriation of the content of our faith in God as Father, Son and Holy Spirit. This possibility is coming to be more widely seen. It is

---

[13] A. M. Allchin, *Ann Griffiths*, Cardiff, Writers of Wales Series, 1976, p. 49.

noteworthy that in May 1979 the Anglican Consultative Council linked its recommendation about the *filioque* clause with a plea for a reconsideration of the centrality of the Church's faith in God as Trinity. Here are questions where Christian East and West have much to gain from one another, not least in learning to find a new language to speak of the divine mystery, a language at once humble and yet decisive, clear and yet imaginative. And here our very handling of this ancient controversy can be of help to us, as we learn to enter into different points of view and trace the development of differing traditions of teaching and reflection. To adapt the words of Bishop Stillingfleet in 1664, "there being confessed to be depths on both sides, it might teach us a little more modesty in handling these matters and much more charity to those who differ about them". Only in a deepening sense of amazement and wonder before the generosity of the divine being shall we together be able to receive the gift to acknowledge the glory of the eternal Trinity, the majesty of the divine unity.

● I am deeply indebted to my friend Canon Edward Every for his kindness in allowing me to see the text of his detailed study of this subject now in preparation.

THE FILIOQUE IN THE OLD CATHOLIC CHURCHES: THE CHIEF PHASES OF THEOLOGICAL REFLECTION AND CHURCH PRONOUNCEMENTS

KURT STALDER

I. The Bonn Reunion Conferences of 1874–75

When the Catholics excommunicated by the Bishop of Rome for rejecting the 1870 papal dogmas found themselves obliged to organize independently in order to perpetuate the true Catholic Church of the early centuries, they also committed themselves to work to recover the visible unity of the Church. This goal had been a serious concern of some of their leaders even before 1870. The establishment of the Old Catholic Church with this commitment provided them with the ecclesiastical basis and opportunity for taking the initiative towards achieving it. In the so-called "Bonn Reunion Conferences" of 1874–75, their initiative accomplished the first step. In addition to Old Catholic theologians, various members of Evangelical, Anglican and some other churches took part, and so did some members of Orthodox churches. This was why the Old Catholic theologians had to concern themselves with the *filioque* question, not merely as a matter of historical research as hitherto, but in personal encounter, and this at a time when most Old Catholic churches were still only in process of constituting themselves.

From the start the authoritative Old Catholic theologians were agreed that the *filioque* had been inserted in the ecumenical Creed in the West, in a canonically illegitimate way. Only gradually, however, at once in some places, much later elsewhere, did the Old Catholic churches draw official consequences from that agreement, by dropping the *filioque* from the Credo in the mass.

Insight into the course of events which had led to the insertion of the *filioque* into the Creed did not bring merely polemic impulses but promoted an intensification of ecclesiological reflection, above all on the need for

---

● Kurt STALDER, Old Catholic, is professor of New Testament at the Theological Faculty of Bern, Switzerland.

certain questions to be made the subject of ecumenical conciliar discussion and decision by the whole Church, and also on the relation between the responsibility of the local church and of the Church as a whole. This in turn contributed to the formation of the ecclesial conception of a local church with an episcopal and synodal constitution.

As regards the actual dogmatic question of the *filioque*, the discussions of the 1875 Reunion Conferences at Bonn produced agreement on two sets of theses, termed "articles" or "paragraphs". First the following four articles were adopted:

"1. We agree in accepting the ecumenical creeds and the dogmatic decisions of the ancient undivided Church.

2. We agree in recognizing that the addition of the *filioque* to the Creed was not made in an ecclesiastically legitimate way.

3. We all profess the presentation of the doctrine of the Holy Spirit as given by the Fathers of the undivided Church.

4. We reject any conception and any mode of expression which involves the assumption of two principles or ἀρχαὶ or αἰτίαι in the Trinity."

At a later session the following six "paragraphs" were adopted on the procession of the Holy Spirit and the inner-trinitarian relations of Father, Son and Spirit. Their mode of expression was based on the writings of St John Damascene[1].

"We accept the teaching of St John of Damascus on the Holy Spirit as expressed in the following paragraphs, in the sense of the teaching of the ancient undivided Church.

"1. The Holy Ghost proceeds from the Father (ἐκ τοῦ Πατρὸς) as the beginning (ἀρχὴ), the cause (αἰτία), the source (πηγὴ) of the Godhead (*De recta sententia* n. 1, *Contra Manich.* n. 4).

2. The Holy Ghost does not proceed from the Son (ἐκ τοῦ Υἱοῦ), because in the Godhead there is but one beginning (ἀρχὴ), one cause (αἰτία) through which all that is in the Godhead is produced (*De fide orthodoxa*, i, 8: ἐκ τοῦ Υἱοῦ δὲ τὸ Πνεῦμα οὐ λέγομεν, Πνεῦμα δὲ Υἱοῦ ὀνομάζομεν: "We do not say that the Spirit is out of the Son, but we do designate him the Spirit of the Son").

3. The Holy Ghost proceeds from the Father through the Son (*De fide orthodoxa* i, 12: τὸ δὲ Πνεῦμα τὸ ʺΑγιον ἐκφαντορικὴ τοῦ κρυφίου τῆς

---

[1] *Report of the Reunion Conference at Bonn*, 10–16 August 1875, pp. 103–104, quoted by C. B. Moss, *The Old Catholic Movement, its Origins and History*, London, 1948, p. 269. As, however, the official text does not translate the Greek but paraphrases it, an actual translation has been added, in double quotes in each case.

θεότητος δύναμις τοῦ Πατρὸς, ἐκ Πατρὸς μὲν δι' Υἱοῦ ἐκπορευομένη: "the Holy Spirit, the power of the Father revealing that which is hidden of his Godhead, which proceeds out of the Father through the Son"). *Ibid.*: Υἱοῦ δὲ Πνεῦμα οὐχ' ὡς ἐξ αὐτοῦ ἀλλ' ὡς δι' αὐτοῦ ἐκ τοῦ Πατρὸς ἐκπορευόμενον: "Spirit of the Son, not that he proceeds from him, but because he proceeds through him from the Father". *Contra Manich.* n. 5: διὰ τοῦ λόγου αὐτοῦ ἐξ αὐτοῦ τὸ Πνεῦμα αὐτοῦ ἐκπορευόμενον: "his Spirit, which proceeds out of him through his Logos". *De hymno Trisag.* n. 28: Πνεῦμα τὸ ῞Αγιον ἐκ τοῦ Πατρὸς διὰ τοῦ Υἱοῦ καὶ Λόγου προϊόν: "the Holy Spirit which proceeds from the Father through his Son, the Logos". *Hom in sabb.* s. n. 4: τοῦτο ἡμῖν ἐστὶ τὸ λατρευόμενον . . . Πνεῦμα ἅγιον τοῦ Θεοῦ καὶ Πατρὸς. ὡς ἐξ αὐτοῦ ἐκπορευόμενον, ὅπερ καί τοῦ Υἱοῦ λέγεται, ὡς δἰ αὐτοῦ φανερούμενον καὶ τῇ κτίσει μεταδιδόμενον, ἀλλ οὐκ ἐξ αὐτοῦ ἔχον τὴν ὕπαρξιν: "this is he who is to be worshipped by us . . . the Holy Spirit of God the Father, as he who proceeds from him, who is also named (Spirit) of the Son, as he who is revealed by him and is communicated to the creation, not however as he who has his being out of him".

4. The Holy Ghost is the image of the Son, who is the image of the Father. (*De fide orthodoxa*, i, 13: εἰκὼν τοῦ Πατρὸς, καὶ τοῦ Υἱοῦ τὸ Πνεῦμα: "the Son is the image of the Father, and the Spirit is that of the Son"); proceeding from the Father and resting in the Son as the power radiating from him, (*De fide orthodoxa*, i, 7: τοῦ Πατρὸς προερχόμενον καὶ ἐν τῳ λόγῳ ἀναπαυόμενον καὶ αὐτοῦ οὖσαν ἐκφαντικὴν δύναμιν: "[the Holy Spirit] who is the power of the Father, which proceeds from him and rests in the Logos and is his power of revelation"); *ibid.* i, 12: Πάτερ . . . διὰ λόγου προβολεὺς ἐκφαντορικοῦ πνεύματος: "The Father . . . who through his Logos produces the revealing Spirit".

5. The Holy Spirit is the personal "productio" of the Father, belonging to the Son but not from the Son, because he is the Spirit of the mouth of the Deity, and utters the word. (*De hymno Trisagion*, n. 28: τὸ Πνεῦμα ἐνυπόστατον ἐκπόρευμα καὶ πρόβλημα ἐκ Πατρὸς μὲν, Υἱοῦ δὲ, καὶ μὴ ἐξ Υἱοῦ ὡς Πνεῦμα στόματος θεοῦ, λόγον ἐξαγγελτικόν: "the Spirit, the hypostasis, who proceeds out of the Father and is produced by him, (is) the (Spirit) of the Son, but not *out* of the Son, but as the breath of his mouth which is expressive of the Logos").

6. The Holy Spirit forms the mediation between the Father and the Son and is united to the Father through the Son. (*De fide orthodoxa*, i, 13: μέσον τοῦ ἀγεννήτου καὶ γεννητοῦ καί δἰ Υἱοῦ τῷ Πατρὶ συναπτόμενον: "[the Spirit, who] links the Unbegotten with the Begotten and through the Son is united with the Father")."

These theses, though unofficial in character, assumed for succeeding decades the significance of a mutually recognized foundation which was repeatedly referred to, even though opposition to it was raised by some Orthodox theologians.

II. The period from 1875 to 1942

Even at the first Bonn Conference the proposal was made to set up a commission for further study of dogmatic questions. An Anglican proposal in particular was that it should be examined whether "the Creed could possibly be restored to its primitive form, without sacrifice of any true doctrine which is expressed in the present western form".[2] The suggestion was not, however, carried out. Joseph Langen did, it is true, publish two works that derived from the conference proceedings: *Die trinitarische Lehrdifferenz zwischen der abendländischen und der morgenländischen Kirche*" (The Trinitarian Doctrinal Difference Between the Western and the Eastern Church),[3] in which he mainly tried to give an account of the Patristic material, and *Johannes von Damaskus* (John Damascene).[4] Apart from these, however, he did not express himself any further on the subject. Nor did Döllinger. There was then no discussion for almost two decades. It was clear, however, that if it were to be taken up again it would primarily have to be in conversations between Orthodox and Old Catholics.

These came about, however, only after the International Old Catholic Congress of 1892 in Lucerne, where both Professor Friedrich and Archbishop Gul of Utrecht formally expressed the wish for a new step towards unity between the Orthodox and Old Catholic churches. In that same year, or at latest in the following year, the Holy Synod of the Russian Orthodox Church established a commission, subsequently called the "St Petersburg Commission", to report on the state of these problems. Its first report was also conveyed in 1894 to the International Old Catholic Bishops' Conference, which thereupon at its meeting in Rotterdam nominated a commission of theologians, the so-called "Rotterdam Commission", which was to ensure that the studies necessary to clarify these questions were undertaken and their findings submitted.

Unfortunately these commissions never made any personal contacts, only in writing. At long intervals they exchanged three "Statements of Views", the last in 1913. The Russian Revolution put an end to the work. In these

---

[2] *Report* I, 32; C. B. Moss, *op. cit.*, p. 263.
[3] Bonn, 1876.
[4] Gotha, 1897.

Statements, the *filioque* question occupied a central position. At the same time, which is perhaps characteristic, considerable attention was also devoted to the question of the relation between dogma, theologoumenon and private theological opinion.

The jointly recognized initial basis was, as already noted, the Bonn theses quoted above. Both sides acknowledged, therefore, that the Father is the sole ἀρχή, αἰτία, πηγή (beginning, cause, source) of the Godhead both of the Son and of the Spirit. However, the Rotterdam Commission also held the view that the *filioque*, to the extent that it understands the Son only as a "secondary" or "contributory cause" in the procession of the Spirit, is not essentially different from the διὰ τοῦ Υἱοῦ ("through the Son") which is also acknowledged by the Eastern, and moreover is not a dogma but merely a theological opinion, which anyone may hold. The St Petersburg Commission, on the other hand, regarded these expressions as calling in question the μία αἰτία ("*one* cause"), and therefore called for greater precision. No progress was therefore achieved in clarifying the problem and in advancing the discussion.

In subsequent decades the necessary conditions for resuming the interrupted reflections did, however, exist, thanks to the activity of influential theological teachers who with exceptional intensity kept alive awareness of the fundamental importance of trinitarian questions, thanks also on occasion to the demands of ecumenical meetings. No use was made of them, however.

III. The work of Bishop Urs Küry

A new stage opened with the writings of Bishop Urs Küry. What had been achieved so far was indeed taken up, but also critically examined. Above all, earlier modes of expression were not merely compared or even played off one against another; instead, an advance was made into the heart of the matter itself. We are thinking, for example, of his Berne Inaugural Lecture in 1942 on "The Significance of the *filioque* Controversy for the Concept of God in the Western and Eastern Church," [5] and above all of the final section of his article on the concluding phase of the work of the St Petersburg and Rotterdam Commissions: "Fundamental Theological Considerations on the *Filioque* Question".[6]

---

[5] Printed in *Internationale kirchliche Zeitschrift*, Berne, 33, 1943, pp. 1–19.
[6] *Internationale kirchliche Zeitschrift*, 58, 1968, pp. 81–108.

In this latter article, Urs Küry examines the works of W. Bolotov[7] and reaches the following conclusions:

a) With Bulgakov he considers it as unfortunate that the tradition and terminology of western trinitarian theology moves so much in abstractions and, with Bolotov, he feels it is not conscious enough of the inadequacy of its expressions. The starting point ought rather always to be, rigorously and concretely, God's trihypostatical aseity (102).[8] The two elements in this criticism must be borne in mind together if their relevance is to be clear.

It follows, then, that "The terms αἰτία (cause) for the first hypostasis and αἰτιαταὶ (caused) for the second and third hypostases are, as Bolotov himself noted, unavoidable but inadequate. They are unavoidable because they maintain the idea of the Father's monarchy in the sense just explained, namely that the Trinity, as act of mutual love within the divinity, is the self-revelation of the Father in the Son and in the Holy Spirit. They are inadequate because they mislead us into thinking of the Father as an abstract principle" (102f.). This unfortunate fact is aggravated by unsuitable translations into Latin and German. Moreover if "these terms are questionable even in reference to the Father's *monarchia*, they are most emphatically so if in speaking of the procession of the Holy Spirit, the Father is termed 'first cause' and the Son 'second cause'. The controversy on this point which still preoccupied the Petersburg and Rotterdam Commissions, may be regarded from this point of view as obsolete. There must be no talk in this abstract way at all of 'cause', nor of the Father as *principium non de principio*, nor of the Son as *principium de principio*, nor again of the Holy Spirit proceeding from the Father *principaliter*. This terminology makes it impossible to tackle the problem whether and how the Son 'shares' in the procession of the Holy Spirit from the Father. The formula which the Rotterdam Commission retained, of the Son as 'joint cause' or 'secondary cause' in the procession of the Holy Spirit from the Father, is to be abandoned" (103).

If the generation of the Son and the spiration of the Spirit are subsumed under the general term of procession, and "two processions" are referred to without distinction, the defectiveness of the abstractions is patent: "By this subsumption the concrete distinctiveness of the coming of the Son from the Father or of his having come from the Father, and of the issuing of the

---

[7] "Theses on the *filioque* question", *Revue internationale de théologie*, 1898, pp. 681–712; and S. Bulgakov, "Capita de Trinitate", *Internationale kirchliche Zeitschrift*, 26, 1936, pp. 144–167, pp. 210–230, and 35, 1945, pp. 24–55.
[8] The figures between brackets in this section all refer to *Internationale kirchliche Zeitschrift* 58, 1968.

Holy Spirit out of the Father is blurred. In the New Testament the 'procession' of the Holy Spirit from the Father is expressed by a different word (ἐκπορεύεται, John 15:26) from the 'procession' of the Son from the Father (ἐξελθὸν, John 8:42). In the Vulgate, on the other hand, the word *procedere* is used both times and has passed into Latin theology and come to prevail in it. The resulting want of clarity in terminology is even worse in German (or in English) when the procession of the Holy Spirit is said to be *from* the Father which does not render exactly the term *ek* 'out of' " (103f.).

Döllinger drew attention to these problems of difference in terminology several times at the Second Reunion Conference at Bonn in 1875. According to the Report II, 13.25.38, "the two expressions ἐκπορεύεσθαι and *procedere* are not completely identical; the former says more in one respect and less in another than the latter, and contains something that applies only to the relation of the Holy Spirit to the Father." Furthermore, "we admit that the relation of the Son to the Spirit is not entirely the same as that of the Father to the Spirit, because paternity in the wider sense, or the property of being the source of the divine persons, does not belong to the Son, but only to the Father. To that extent the eastern Church is justified in rejecting the *procedere ab utroque* or *a Patre Filioque*, since that Church attaches to the ἐκπορεύεσθαι a different meaning from that of the *procedere* of the Latins, namely, that of the causality that belongs to the Father alone (μόνος γὰρ αἴ-τιος ὁ πατήρ: the Father alone is he who causes), whereas the Latins left out of account the difference between the action of the Father and that of the Son in relation to the Spirit . . ." We may well consider that Döllinger indicated an important point here but did not succeed in giving full clarification. This will only be possible if it is realized that the two "processions" out of the Father are two fundamentally different acts, each with a special content, and have to be expressed by the concrete terms of generation and spiration. The difference between them must not be blurred. But it is blurred if the two concepts are so linked by subsumption under the term "procession" that there is talk of *one* procession of the Holy Spirit "from" the Father and "from" the Son.

From this point of view it must also be improper to interpret the two abstractly conceived *processiones* as *productiones* in such a way that it is only through them that the Son and the Holy Spirit as αἰτιατοὶ (those caused) in the ontological sense "originate" out of the Father as αἰτία (cause). Consequently the idea that the Holy Spirit is a joint *productio* of the Father and the Son is to be rejected. The relation in which the Holy Spirit stands to the Father is other than that in which he stands to the Son. The former alone is a "relation of origin" and could – in the imprecise and abstract terminology of western theology – be interpreted in the sense of a *productio*. The relation of the Holy Spirit to the Son, on the other hand, is of a quite different kind (104f.). On the basis of the idea that the *processiones* are to be understood as *productiones*, it is therefore one-sided and wrong "to interpret the relations arising through the *processiones exclusively* as relations of origin. The *relationes originis* are indeed in a certain sense the primary, but not the only, relations within the Godhead. Certainly the relations of the Son and the Holy Spirit to the Father are to be called relations of origin – in the light of the idea of the trihypostatical self-revelation of the Father in love – but not the relation in which the Son stands to the Holy Spirit and the Holy Spirit to the Son. With the Fathers of the ancient Church, this relation may be described as one of 'belonging properly to': the Holy Spirit belongs to the Son (ἴδιον)" (105).

b) As fundamental thesis for the understanding of the inner-trinitarian relations, Urs Küry following Bulgakov recognizes that the "duality" of Son and Holy Spirit as compared with the monarchia of the Father, means that "the Son in his relation to the Father is not to be separated from the Holy Spirit nor the Holy Spirit from the Son. *Each* of the hypostases manifesting the Father depends not only from the Father but also from the correlative hypostasis which manifests the Father. The being of the Son depends *a patre spirituque*, the Holy Spirit does not proceed abstractly from the Father alone, but *through* the Son *or Patre filioque*. The 'and' which western theology allows only at one place" (102) applies in all trinitarian relations, provided it is not understood in the sense of a causal *productio* or *relatio originis*. In short, it can be formulated as an "axiom following from God's trihypostatical aseity" that "the relations within the Godhead are to be understood throughout as threefold" (105).[9] From this, Küry concludes that "we must agree with the thesis maintained by both Bolotov and Bulgakov that both the eastern 'from the Father alone' and the western 'filioque' – provided the thesis of the threefold character of the inner-trinitarian relations is maintained – are *admissible* as free theological opinions. Both formulas safeguard a legitimate concern, even if in an inadequate way".

The formula "from the Father alone", provided it is not understood in an exclusive sense, safeguards the idea of the Father's monarchia (though of course the question would have to be put to Bulgakov whether the addition

---

[9] The expression "threefold relations" or "threefold character of the relations", which occurs several times, appears to mean that each relation involves all three hypostases and that such a relation is correctly described only if it is shown that and in what way each of the three hypostases shares in it.

of "alone" can in fact be understood except in an exclusive sense). In order to prevent the formula, which has been adopted in the *Confessio orthodoxa*, being construed in the exclusive sense, Döllinger in 1875 in Bonn rightly declared: "We can accept this statement as valid, because of the addition: so far as the Father is beginning and source of the Godhead." Döllinger also declared: "If the question is framed in this way: Does the Spirit proceed *only* from the Father?, the answer will be affirmative or negative according to the sense attached to the word 'proceed'. It will be affirmative if what is meant is that power or activity which belongs only to the Father by which he is the source of the Godhead and the spiration of the Spirit is wholly his work, both that done by him as person and that effected by the Logos who only possesses through or from the Father the power radiating or breathing forth the Spirit . . . The reply must be negative if the formula means that the Son is excluded from any cooperation in the production of the Spirit." For our part, we consider that Döllinger's formulation that the Son must not be excluded from any collaboration in the "production" of the Spirit is incorrect. The point is not that the Son is involved in the "production" (*productio*) of the Spirit, but that the procession of the Holy Spirit takes place "ὑπάρχοντος τοῦ Υἱοῦ", and that the existence of the Son is the "condition" (Bolotov) or presupposition of the spiration of the Spirit by the Father. This is pertinently and sufficiently expressed by the formula διὰ τοῦ Υἱοῦ (through the Son). This "ecumenical theologoumenon" is to be accepted unreservedly, as was done by the Old Catholics in Bonn in 1875 on the basis of a catena of relevant statements from the writings of John Damascene. On the other hand, the "from the Father alone" is only acceptable with the proviso stated above: so far as the Father is beginning and source of the Godhead.

On the other hand, the western *filioque* is also admissible as a free theological opinion so far as it is a reminder that should not be ignored of the threefold character of the relations within the Godhead (in contrast to the eastern "from the Father alone"). That means, however, that the *filioque* must not be understood in an exclusive sense, either. As Bulgakov argued, beside it the *ex Patre Spirituque* must also have its place, if the relation expressed by the *que* is not thought of as a relation of origin. The Holy Spirit does not proceed from the Son as a second principle of origin (consequently Döllinger's formulation quoted above, that the Son possesses through or from the Father the "radiating or spirating power", is at least imprecise). Nor can it be said that the Holy Spirit proceeds out of the Father and the Son as *unum principium*. This Augustinian φιλοσοφούμενον (Bolotov) must in fact be rejected. But the *filioque* is to be affirmed in that in a different way from the Greek διά, with which it is not identical, in the sense already explained, it presupposes the existence of the Son for the existence of the Spirit, as its "condition", and so maintains the threefold character of the relations within the Godhead (105–107). And the expression found in the proposal quoted above, section (5) ad init., regarding the "doctrine expressed in the present-day western form", which would not have to be sacrificed in any case in restoring the original form of the Creed, can accordingly only mean for us that "the existence of the second hypostasis is the presupposition or 'condition' of the existence of the third: the Holy Spirit proceeds from the Father ὑπάρχοντος τοῦ Υἱοῦ" (107).

c) In conclusion, Urs Küry expresses the view that "the question of the mode of procession of the Holy Spirit out of the Father and of the participation of the Son in that procession, is certainly in need of the universally binding dogmatic formulation which it has not yet received even to this day, but which it could only be given by the decision of a future ecumenical council. What we can already do now, however, until a comprehensive consensus has been established, is to use the terms coined in an unmistakably *schismatic* spirit in the course of the history of dogma, θεοπρεπῶς, that is to say, in a way worthy of God (as the Orthodox theologian Ossinin said at the Second Bonn Reunion Conference). That is only possible, however, if the eastern and western theologians speak together in the spirit of the love of God, which is what is ultimately at stake in the dogma of the Trinity . . ." (107–8).

IV. Church pronouncements on the basis of the theological position reached through the work of Bishop Küry

The theological position attained in the articles of Bishop Urs Küry and which met with general recognition, was given official church expression in two pronouncements of the International Old Catholic Bishops' Conference. First in the "Declaration of the International Old Catholic Bishops' Conference on the *Filioque* question" of 1969–70,[10] and then in the "Doctrinal Letter of the International Old Catholic Bishops' Conference" addressed at the same period (1969–70) to the Ecumenical Patriarch Athenagoras I.[11] The second of these devotes only seven lines to the *filioque* question, but in contrast to the first document they expressly emphasize that "we firmly reject in fact any theological doctrine which makes the Son a joint cause of the Spirit". For the rest, the second document maintains the same line as

---

[10] *Internationale kirchliche Zeitschrift*, 61, 1971, p. 69f.
[11] *Internationale kirchliche Zeitschrift*, 61, 1971, pp. 65–68.

the first; the sentence quoted is obviously merely intended as clarification. We shall consequently deal only with the first, the Declaration. Although this is even shorter, it deals exclusively with the *filioque* question, and constitutes the official elucidation of a question which had previously been left in suspense. It is not, however, a theological statement addressed to all and sundry, but a document addressed to an actual partner in discussion by whom it particularly wishes to be understood because it deals with a question that concerns them both.

The introduction recalls that the addition of the *filioque* to the original text of the Creed was made at a time of estrangement between the eastern and western Church, and has occasioned manifold controversies that are still not wholly resolved. It confirms that the way the *filioque* was inserted in the ecumenical profession of faith is judged by the Old Catholic churches to have been uncanonical, and for that reason the addition in question had been removed from the only Creed they admit.

As regards the dogmatic question of the *filioque*, the following statement is made: "Holy Scripture teaches us on the question of the eternal procession of the Holy Spirit that the Spirit of truth proceeds from the Father (John 15:26). The Council of Constantinople in 381 included this teaching of the word of God into the Creed and stated that the Holy Spirit proceeds from the Father. The Old Catholic Church has always accepted this teaching of the ecumenical council as its own and attributes the highest degree of dogmatic authority to it.

"Furthermore we maintain that in the most Holy Trinity there is only one principle and source, namely the Father. We affirm the formulation of the eastern Church that the Holy Spirit proceeds from the Father alone, if it is added, so far as the Father is the ground and source of the Godhead. Further thought about the relation of the Son as the second person of the Holy Trinity to the eternal procession of the Holy Spirit must remain within the limits set by the trinitarian dogma of the ancient Church."

V. The beginning of the "dialogue of faith" between the Old Catholic Churches and the Orthodox Church

On the basis of these official pronouncements, the "dialogue of faith" was opened between the Orthodox and the Old Catholic churches, to examine whether the presumed agreement in faith could in fact be actually verified. Obviously this examination had to extend also to the problems connected with the *filioque*. The theological position which the Old Catholic delegation had arrived at during the preparatory stage is characterized by the following:

How the procession of the Spirit is distinguished from the generation of the Son is incomprehensible. The fact that there is such a distinction is revealed in the sending of the Spirit by the Son. This temporal mission must be distinguished from the eternal procession. That does not mean, however, that God in his revelation in time is other than the eternally self-subsistent. For even in time the Spirit is not sent by the Son in the same way as by the Father; the Son sends him from the Father (John 15:26) and the Father sends him in the name of the Son (John 14:26). It can indeed be said that the Spirit is sent by the Father and by the Son, but the more precise expression is: by the Father through the Son. And thus even the different manner of the temporal mission reveals the Father as sole beginning (that is, his "monarchia"). The relevant sections from the Letter and the Filioque Declaration of the International Old Catholic Bishops' Conference are also quoted.

The joint texts of the Mixed Orthodox-Old Catholic Dialogue Commission then affirms that according to the testimony of the New Testament and the doctrine of the ancient Church, the Holy Spirit proceeds from the Father, the source and beginning of the Godhead. Then a distinction is drawn between this procession solely from the Father (the words "as far as the Father is ground and source of the Godhead" contained in the Old Catholic Bishops' Conference Filioque Declaration are not appended to this statement, but are presupposed to it in meaning) and the temporal mission of the Spirit by the Son which can also be termed a procession from the Father and from the Son. On the one side, therefore, the eternal relation of the origin is mentioned, on the other the temporal mission. Nothing is said, either positively or negatively, about eternal relations which are not relations of origin. But since the relations in the temporal mission correspond not only to the eternal relations of origin but also to the other eternal relations, the silence of the text about the latter leaves the impression that eternal relations and temporal mission do not stand in any proper connection. That is, of course, unsatisfactory but it is simply the inevitable consequence of the fact noted by Küry that "the question of the mode of procession from the Father and of the participation of the Son in that procession has not yet received any universally binding dogmatic formulation and to that extent must remain open . . .".[12] In a text of this kind, therefore, the "only from the Father" could be stated only in regard to the eternal relation of origin, and the "through the Son" and perhaps also "and from the Son" only in regard to the temporal mission; the important pertinent question of the eternal relations which are not relations of origin had to remain open. To

---

[12] *Internationale kirchliche Zeitschrift*, 58, 1968, p. 107.

avoid misunderstanding it is, however, important to note that it is not so much an open question between Old Catholic and Orthodox theology, as in Orthodox theology itself.

In conclusion we recall Bishop Urs Küry's view that conversations held in a spirit of love between eastern and western theologians with a view to a future ecumenical council should seek to clarify the question of the mode of procession of the Spirit from the Father and that of the participation of the Son in that procession. We should like to take up this suggestion, widen it, and if possible even reinforce it. For some considerable time now it has been remarked, not without reason, that the reality and presence of the Holy Spirit is constantly either not appreciated enough or almost not at all, and that this affects the thought and action of the churches and of individual Christians. On occasion we even come across ways of behaviour and argument which show that people can have at the back of their minds, if only unconsciously, the assumption that the Holy Spirit is in some way less than the Son. The question arises whether it is completely unreasonable to fear that aberrations of that kind may find support in the *filioque* in the Creed, though quite contrary to its intention. But precisely for that reason and because it leaves many questions open, the form of the Creed without the *filioque*, which we regard as the ecumenical one and advocate ourselves, does not seem to us to meet all requirements. An extension of the ecumenical Creed does not indeed seem to us the most urgent of tasks. On the other hand we do think it a fundamental ecumenical task to reach a theological consensus first of all on the controversial question of the procession of the Spirit, but also on the generation of the Son and the inner-trinitarian relations which are not relations of origin. It would also not have to leave out of account, either, the essential connection of all these questions with the Church's self-understanding and practice and the relation between God and world.

THE FILIOQUE IN RECENT REFORMED THEOLOGY

ALASDAIR HERON

This must of necessity be a brief and highly selective paper – much more so than its title might seem to imply. It cannot pretend to offer a comprehensive survey of the handling of the *filioque* question in, let us say, the Reformed theology of the twentieth century, let alone touch on all the various issues which the question has been seen by Reformed theologians to involve. My aim is the much more modest one of sketching in bare outline some of the broad approaches to the matter which can be found in Reformed thinking. I hope this may be of some value in indicating the range of strategies which have been and are currently being employed – strategies which of course have analogies and parallels in other traditions as well.

That there is indeed a good variety of attitudes to the *filioque* within the Reformed churches is only to be expected. Even among the Eastern Orthodox theologians, who are on the whole united in a certain dislike of the *filioque* clause, there are views differing considerably in detail, as Fr Bobrinskoy's paper[1] well shows. The deep antipathy of Vladimir Lossky and his school to the *filioque* (and to the other features of western theology which they associate with it) is not shared to the same degree by all, though it is the outlook which has been most forcibly drawn to the attention of the West in recent decades. In the West in general – and the Reformed family is no exception – the spectrum of opinion is even wider, running as it does all the way from committed subscription alike to the clause and to the theology it expresses, through varying degrees of qualified enthusiasm, to outright rejection of both.

● Alasdair HERON (Reformed) is lecturer in systematic theology at the University of Edinburgh, Scotland.
[1] Cf. page 133 of this volume.

1. Committed subscription

Many Reformed theologians today would, like many of their Protestant, Anglican, or Roman Catholic counterparts, strongly defend the theology of the *filioque*. Some would support it chiefly by appeal to the arguments hammered out in the medieval controversy with the East – especially by Anselm in the *De Processione Spiritus Sancti* and by Aquinas in the *Summa Theologica* I, *qu.* 36, *art.* 2-4 – and underlying the statements of the Councils of Lyons (1274) and Florence (1439). Others, while not necessarily binding themselves so firmly to that particular line of theological development, would look still further back and regard the matter as having been settled by the Council of Toledo in 589, or indeed by Augustine's explanation that the Holy Spirit proceeds from both the Father and the Son, albeit *principaliter* from the Father (*De Trinitate* XV. xvii, 29).[2] Others again, while not feeling it incumbent upon them to explore these venerable records in any detail, would be satisfied by the fact that the Reformers in the sixteenth century do not appear to have had any serious doubts about the *filioque*, and that Reformed orthodoxy subsequently accepted it without demur. So, for example, the *Westminster Confession*, §2 (iii), in what is virtually a paraphrase of the *Quicunque vult*, is content to affirm as a matter of course: "The Father is of none, neither begotten nor proceeding; the Son is eternally begotten of the Father; the Holy Ghost eternally proceeding from the Father and the Son." [3]

The outstanding Reformed advocate of the *filioque* in the last generation was none other than Karl Barth. In his discussion,[4] he gave a powerful restatement of what was essentially the Anselmian position. To it he added his own characteristic emphasis, insisting that the *filioque* is a barrier blocking the road to any kind of access to the Father otherwise than through Jesus Christ, and hinting broadly that what he regarded as the wilder effu-

---

[2] So, for example, Louis Berkhof: "And the long drawn dispute about the question, whether the Holy Spirit proceeds from the Father alone or also from the Son, was *finally settled* by the Synod of Toledo in 589 by adding the word 'filioque' to the Latin version of the Constantinopolitan Creed . . ." *Systematic Theology*, London, Banner of Truth Trust, 1958, p. 96, my italics.

[3] The relevant statement in the *Quicunque vult* (the "Athanasian Creed", so-called) runs: "The Father is from none, not made nor created nor begotten. The Son is from the Father alone, not made nor created but begotten. The Holy Spirit is from the Father and the Son, not made nor created nor begotten but proceeding." J. N. D. Kelly, *The Athanasian Creed*, London, A. & C. Black, 1964, p. 19. On the acceptance of this creed by the Reformers, see Kelly, *op. cit.*, pp. 48–9.

[4] *Church Dogmatics* I/1, §12, 2.3, second English edition, Edinburgh, T. & T. Clark, 1975, pp. 473–87.

sions of some modern Russian theologians might conceivably be connected with their non-subscription to it.[5]

However one may assess Barth's particular arguments, his energetic defence of the *filioque* is a significant element in the present situation in Reformed thinking. It also serves to underline the fact that adherence to the doctrine is by no means always simply the product of mere convention or arbitrary antiquarianism. Whatever may be said for or against the way in which the *filioque* theology was developed and defined, it has bequeathed a complex and cohesive structure of dogmatic argument which has been and can still be marshalled in its support. Indeed, within the theological horizon of an Anselm, an Aquinas, or indeed a Barth, the *filioque* appears not only *defensible* but actually *required* in order fully to articulate the bond between the Son and the Holy Spirit, and through it, the integrity of the Trinity. This strand in Reformed thought can by no means be ignored. If the tradition in which it stands and on which it builds is no longer to be upheld, good reasons for departing from it will need to be found if its adherents are to be persuaded.

2. Criticism and rejection

At the other end of the scale, some Reformed theologians would be willing to abandon the *filioque* altogether, for any of several reasons:

a) First of all it must be said that not a few theologians – and the great majority of members of Reformed churches – would be likely not so much to reject the *filioque* as to be totally uninterested in the whole question. This has nothing to do with the objections of the Eastern Orthodox churches to the doctrine, but simply with the fact that it has no significant place in their own perspective. Those who belong to churches which make little or no use of the Nicene Creed – and its regular or frequent use is exceptional rather than normative in most Reformed churches – are only rarely likely to encounter the topic at all; and, when they do, are commonly inclined to look upon it as an abstruse theological curiosity about which one need not overly trouble oneself. Whatever theological judgments one might feel tempted to make about such a situation, it is a factor which must be reckoned with in any assessment of the contemporary ecumenical developments. A willingness to jettison the *filioque* which rested on nothing more than a sublime indifference to the whole matter would scarcely constitute a genuine step towards rapprochement with the East!

b) A more consciously theological dissatisfaction with the *filioque* is felt

---

[5] *Ibid.*, p. 481.

by some who sense that it sits only uneasily within the framework of trinitarian doctrine, quite apart from the question of the eastern objections to it. A prominent Reformed critic along these lines has been George S. Hendry, whose critical dialogue with Barth's statement of the matter led him to the conclusion that the *filioque* is an inadequate solution to a genuine problem.[6] Hendry's concern was not primarily to reach an accommodation with the East, but rather to analyse and evaluate the internal logic of the western understanding of the Trinity as sketched out by Augustine. Clearly, however, reassessments of this kind *could* also lead towards a reshaping of western thought in a pattern more congenial to the East.

c) Finally, some Reformed theologians have, in common with some representatives of other western traditions, found much food for thought in the sustained critique offered by Lossky and other Orthodox thinkers of a whole range of distortions and imbalances which they claim to detect in western theology and ecclesiology, and which they believe to be connected with the *filioque*. Among the charges itemized against it, we may note especially the following:

In the doctrine of the Trinity, a tendency towards monistic, indeed Sabellian, thinking, in which the distinct hypostases of the Father, Son and Holy Spirit are dissolved into an (effectively undifferentiated) "Godhead", with the consequent displacement of a trinitarian by a unitarian view of God himself – a displacement which can indeed be detected in much western theology and piety right down to the present day.

In relation to christology, a subordination of the Holy Spirit to the person of Jesus Christ which tends towards a "depersonalizing" of the Spirit, a reduction of him to a mere "power" flowing from Christ, and so loses sight of his sovereign freedom and initiative as the Spirit who, like the Word, is one of what Irenaeus called "the two hands of God". No longer does he "blow where he will"; rather, "it goes where it is sent".

In soteriology, a similar downgrading of the Holy Spirit, enfeebling the sense of his creative and restoring energy, his activity in the incarnation, life and resurrection of Jesus, and his work as the divine restorer of the cosmos. Salvation is thus narrowed down to the event of the cross, seen as standing in total isolation, and interpreted simply as a sacrifice, a punishment or an

---

[6] *The Holy Spirit in Christian Theology*, London, SCM Press, 1965, pp. 45–52. For a critique of both Barth and Hendry, see Alasdair Heron, " 'Who Proceedeth from the Father and the Son': the Problem of the *Filioque*", *Scottish Journal of Theology*, Vol. 24, 1971, pp. 149–66.

example, and to the "benefits" flowing from it, and "christomonism" obscures the action of the whole Trinity in the work of redemption.

In ecclesiology, an unbalanced emphasis on the "objective" rather than the "subjective", on the "given" rather than on the "yet to be received", on established and settled authority, whether of Church or of Bible, rather than on creative freedom in the Spirit, on the past rather than the future, and even on rational understanding, focused upon the Word made flesh, rather than upon personal engagement in the living pilgrimage of faith, hope and love in the power of the transforming Spirit. This imbalance, it is further argued, provokes its natural reaction in the opposite direction: hence arises the excessive subjectivism of much western Christianity, especially in Protestantism generally. Thus the *filioque* effectively runs out into an *ecclesiaque* or an *homineque*, each equally, though in different ways, symptomatic of the lack of an adequate pneumatology.[7]

While few if any Reformed theologians have been willing simply to accept this indictment and to plead guilty on all counts, some have felt that there is at least a measure of truth in these charges against the West. This is not necessarily to concede that the *filioque* as such is the root of the problem, much less that the surrender of the *filioque* would resolve all these other matters. It is, however, to admit the possibility that the *filioque* is in some way bound up with wider divergences between East and West; and with that, to concede that the western approach is not the only possible or correct one, and that it may indeed benefit by learning from the eastern. It is difficult to estimate how widespread at present is this attitude in the family of Reformed churches, for by and large the contemporary Reformed outlook is still consciously western and Augustinian, and burdened by a long history of western feelings of superiority to the Greek East. But a more open ecumenical outlook has certainly begun to develop in modern times, encouraged both by increasing contact with Orthodox theologians and churches and by a certain growth of fresh interest in the theology of the Greek Fathers

---

[7] This last point is in fact made by T. F. Torrance in *Theology in Reconstruction*, London, SCM Press, 1965, p. 231. But he is drawing out "with a little exaggeration" (*ibid.*) a line of thought suggested by the eastern criticism of western theology, though he does not make the connexion in exactly the same fashion as I am here suggesting. His thesis is not that the *filioque* leads on to an *ecclesiaque* or an *homineque*, but rather that these run directly counter to its real intention, which has been obscured by the influence of other factors in western thought. This I believe to be true; but the negative outworkings of misapplications of the *filioque* are also part of the total story – as indeed his own argument most effectively demonstrates. So I trust I may be forgiven for giving his expressions a slightly different twist!

– not to mention a new critical awareness of what has been aptly called the "Latin captivity" of western theology.[8]

This new approach is to be found particularly in the work of Thomas F. Torrance.[9] He believes that much of the eastern criticism of western theology is justified and also that the unilateral insertion of the *filioque* in the Creed should be revoked. The positive intention of the *filioque* to assert the indissoluble link between the Son and the Spirit can, he argues, be safeguarded in other ways; indeed, he holds that it is in fact maintained in the classical eastern position, though not expressed in the western fashion. Beyond that, however, he also sees both the classical eastern and western conceptions of the Trinity as one-sided and liable to distortion. Their reconciliation cannot therefore be achieved simply by attempting to combine them in a new formula which will either simply adapt one to fit the other, or juxtapose them in effectively unreconciled tension. The path he advocates is a return behind and beyond the positions sketched out for the West by Augustine and for the East by the Cappadocians to the distinctive Alexandrian line of thought represented by Athanasius, Didymus the Blind, and Cyril. In their presentation of the Holy Spirit as ὁμοούσιον ("of the same substance") *with the Son* as well as with the Father, he detects a dynamic insight into the Trinity which differs equally from the western *filioque* and from the eastern ἐκ μόνου τοῦ Πατρὸς, and which, if fully exploited, could correct both in a fresh, integrated vision of the triunity of God which will not fall neatly into either the Cappadocian or the Augustinian pattern.

Torrance's distinctive proposals deserve this special mention here as they differ somewhat from those presented elsewhere in this collection. They do admittedly make heavy demands on minds trained to run along the well-worn paths of the traditional eastern and western approaches: given their radical nature, it could hardly be otherwise. While it remains to be seen whether it will be possible for his suggested programme to be widely accepted, it does rightly underline the extent to which deep rethinking by East and West is needed if the *filioque* issue is to be resolved in a way that will bring significant theological advance.

---

[8] So e.g. Robin Boyd, *India and the Latin Captivity of the Church*, London, Cambridge University Press, 1974.
[9] See especially chapters 10–14 of *Theology in Reconstruction*, and the more recent papers collected in his *Theology in Reconciliation*, London, Geoffrey Chapman, 1975. The latter do not often address the *filioque* issue directly, but well illustrate his approach to the doctrine of the Trinity through the Alexandrian theologians. They also show how he finds the formula "through the Son" a more adequate expression of the dynamic unity of God and of the centrality of Jesus Christ.

A rather different critical appraisal of the *filioque* from a Reformed stand-point is that offered by Jürgen Moltmann. As his contribution is presented elsewhere in this volume, it is not necessary to summarize it again here.[10] It may be observed, however, that he comes at the matter from the other side, seeking more to balance and knit together the eastern and western concerns by finding room for their favoured formulations, albeit in qualified senses. Clearly, this aspect of the question also requires attention, though it may be that a fully adequate reconciling framework can only be developed with the help of the further explorations suggested by Torrance.

So far I have mentioned only a few individual theologians, who may, however, be taken as representing the range of views in recent Reformed thinking. What then of developments within the Reformed churches and in ecumenical dialogue? The *filioque* has been discussed in conversations be-tween Orthodox and Reformed churches, but no general recommendations for its removal from the Creed have been made as a result: there is no equivalent to the Anglican/Orthodox *Moscow Statement*.[11] It is, however, worth recording that in 1977 the General Assembly of the Church of Scotland instructed its Panel on Doctrine to review the question. The Panel's report to the Assembly of 1979 surveyed the history of the *filioque* and the main theological issues involved in it, and concluded with the following rec-ommendations, which the Assembly accepted:

"In the light of what has been said, the Panel on Doctrine concludes that the *filioque* clause in the Nicene Creed should be regarded as open to revision in the interests of a better understanding between the eastern and western churches. It does not believe that any useful purpose would be served by unilateral action on the part of the Church of Scotland alone, nor that a mere change in the wording of the Creed unaccompanied by wider theological rapprochement would advance the ecumenical movement. It suggests that a policy along the following lines would be appropriate:

"i) The Church of Scotland recognizes the historical and theological ob-jections of the Eastern Orthodox churches to the *filioque* clause. While it has a different understanding from them of the authority of ecumenical councils, it regards it as regrettable that the insertion of the *filioque* should have been brought about in a unilateral and divisive fashion, and hopes that more universal agreement on the terms of the Creed may be reached. It

---

[10] See p. 164 of this volume.
[11] The *filioque* was discussed in the North American Reformed/Orthodox dialogue, but no conclusion was reached upon it. See the report, *The New Man*, ed. J. Mey-endorff and J. C. McLelland, New Brunswick, Standard Press, 1973.

also recognizes that some of the arguments traditionally used in the West to justify the clause are of doubtful validity.

"ii) The General Assembly remits to the Inter-Church Relations Committee to seek dialogue on the question of the *filioque* with other churches in East and West, in the hope that such dialogue may make it possible for the clause to be either (a) universally accepted in an agreed sense, or (b) admitted as a valid optional expression of proper trinitarian doctrine, or (c) modified, removed or replaced by some other more widely acceptable formula.

"iii) For the present the Church will continue to use the western form of the Creed, and to affirm the procession of the Holy Spirit 'from the Father and the Son'. In so doing, however, it recognizes the original formulation still used in the East as equally valid."

These recommendations, especially the second – which is admittedly a somewhat awkward one – were deliberately framed to leave open as many options as possible instead of prematurely foreclosing the choice of ways forward. This accurately reflects the character of the present situation. It is impossible to predict with assurance what direction future dialogue may take, or what solutions may yet be proposed. But in the Reformed tradition, as elsewhere, there is emerging a sense that the dialogue must be entered into, and fresh solutions looked for.

C.
OPENING A NEW DEBATE
ON THE PROCESSION OF THE SPIRIT

THE QUESTION OF THE PROCESSION OF THE HOLY SPIRIT AND ITS CONNECTION WITH THE LIFE OF THE CHURCH

HERWIG ALDENHOVEN

Introduction

That the Holy Spirit is related to the Father and the Son has hardly ever been challenged in Christian theology. But once the question is raised of the nature of this relationship, the answers begin to diverge. It is here that the controversy over the *filioque* is located. Is it appropriate to affirm that the *Holy Spirit proceeds from the Father "and from the Son" (filioque)* or should we say only that he proceeds from the Father? There is a tendency in many quarters to dismiss such discussions as futile speculation. This is understandable when we remember the extent to which, throughout the history of doctrine in the West, the entire doctrine of the Trinity has been isolated from actual experience and never seemed more than abstract speculation. It is not my intention here to deal further with this attitude and the reasons for it. My purpose is simply to show that, correctly understood, the question of the *filioque* is very intimately related to the activity of God in our human life.

The community of human beings which believes in Jesus Christ experiences God as Father, Son and Holy Spirit. Here, access to the Father can never be direct but always only in and through the Son and the Spirit. In what follows *our constant assumption is that Son and Spirit are related to the Father*, even where this is not stated in so many words. But if our experience of God, our encounter with the hidden Father, is direct experience of the Son and the Spirit, the mode of this direct experience is different in each case. For example, in the life of the community God addresses us as Son through the words and lives of óthers, whereas as Spirit he enables us to respond to this address, to this approach, with our own lives as we should,

• Herwig ALDENHOVEN (Old Catholic) is professor of systematic theology at the Theological Faculty of Bern, Switzerland.

and to constitute a community in the one Spirit. It must be pointed out here, once for all, that this differentiation between our experience of the Son and our experience of the Spirit cannot be taken to imply any division between Son and Spirit. When we are addressed by the Son, this is also the work of the Spirit, of course, since it happens in the power of the Spirit, and Christ, too, is the basis of our response in the power of the Spirit. This fully accords with the classical trinitarian doctrine of the περιχώρησις (*circumincessio*, the mutual interpenetration or passing into each other of the persons of the Trinity). But we must be careful *to distinguish between those experiences where the experience is primarily of the Son and those where it is primarily experience of the Spirit*. From the standpoint already mentioned, which is only one of the many possible standpoints, of course, the address or approach to us is primarily God's mode of operation as Son-Logos, and our equipment to respond believingly and to constitute a community is primarily God's mode of operation as Holy Spirit. *To speak of Son and Spirit is meaningful only if this distinction is made*. Moreover, only if this distinction is made can we understand theologically even those personal human encounters in the rich diversity of relationships which are indispensable for community.

The distinction between Son and Spirit, their unity notwithstanding, emerges most clearly in the question of community. But it emerges in other questions, too. For example, we experience God as Son and Spirit in each case differently in knowledge of the truth and in the communication of life. That is to say, however, that the way in which we understand the relation of the Spirit to the Son and the Father cannot be separated from our understanding of community, knowledge and communication of true eternal life. What is at stake here is the unity of belief in God and the reality of life.

I. The question of the filioque

The question of the *filioque* is directly related not to the activity and work of God but to the relation of the Holy Spirit to the Father and the Son within the divine Triunity. But this inner-trinitarian relationship cannot be separated from the activity and work of the persons of the Trinity and therefore from the life of the Church.

In itself the formula "filioque" *is ambiguous*.[1] It cannot, therefore, be

---

[1] Historically speaking, three main uses of the *filioque* formula seem to me distinguishable: (1) the early use of the *filioque*; (2) Augustine's doctrine of the *filioque*; (3) the systematic *filioque* doctrine of medieval scholasticism, particularly in Anselm of Canterbury and Thomas Aquinas. In the first use, the *filioque* refers to the essential unity of Father, Son and Spirit and does not form part of this present discussion. The

accepted or rejected as such; the standpoint from which it is understood must in each case be stated. But on the other hand we cannot ignore the fact that there is not only a *filioque* formula but also a very specific *filioque doctrine* which has become the dominating one in later western theology. This doctrine differs from other possible interpretations mainly in the following points:

a) The procession of the Spirit from the Son as well as from the Father is understood as an eternal original relationship in the strict sense, i.e. *the Spirit has his origin (principium)* and the cause *(causa)* of his being not only in the Father but *also in the Son.*

b) *Father and Son* together, therefore, are *a single principle* in relation to the Spirit, just as the three divine hypostases are together *one* principle in relation to created reality. The statement that the Son is joint or secondary cause in relation to the Spirit also accords in a different way with what was said under (a).

c) The Spirit depends, therefore, in a strictly ontological way on the Son. The relationship is understood as an original relationship. *In relationship to the Spirit, therefore, an absolute, ontological and logical 'priority' is due to the Son,* and, correspondingly, an absolute, ontological and logical "posteriority" is due to the Spirit. In what follows, our quarrel will be with this doctrine and not with the *filioque* formula as such.

A basic axiom for all reflection on the Trinity is that *the Trinity at work in the world is none other than the Trinity as such.* Otherwise the activity of God would not be a revelation of his truth but a delusory mirage or, to put it another way, would not really be God's activity. On the other hand, it must never be forgotten that God's reality transcends all we can know of him. The fact that the reality of God transcends our knowledge of him does

---

Augustinian doctrine concerns us less than the systematic scholastic doctrine.

As far as the ambiguity of the *filioque* formula is concerned, it should be noted that even so doughty an Orthodox opponent of the *filioque* as Vladimir Lossky left room for the possibility of an Orthodox interpretation of the early Spanish *filioque* (*A l'image et à la ressemblance de Dieu*, Paris, 1967, p. 69).

Whether it is possible to use the formula "filioque" in the present situation without automatically promoting or perpetuating misconceptions – if it means anything at all – is quite another matter. With the passage of time the Old Catholic theology has come to see more and more clearly that it is *not* possible and on the whole therefore, it generally avoids even using the formula. Among western Christians, of course, the outright rejection of the formula also leads to misunderstandings and errors. In the present situation of the western churches, criticism of the formula at any rate prompts reflection on the question itself, whereas an uncritical use of the formula refrains from doing so.

not make this knowledge untrue. Yet it is only true if it is constantly aware that it is surpassed by God's reality. *Even in his revelation*, therefore, or rather, *precisely in his revelation, God* shows himself to be a *mystery*. This necessarily has consequences for our understanding of the Trinity. When we speak in what follows about the *apophatic character of the knowledge of God*, it is this ineffable mystery that is meant.

The issue at stake in the question of the *filioque*, therefore, is the eternal inner-trinitarian relationship of the Spirit to the Father and to the Son, which is disclosed to us in the reciprocal relationship of the activity of the three divine hypostases in the world. But if this knowledge is to be true knowledge of the relations within the Godhead, it must remain aware of its apophatic character, i.e. of the mystery of God which transcends all human knowledge.

We cannot talk of the inner-trinitarian relationships, therefore, as if we were describing a metaphysical ontology of God, but only to the degree to which God himself incorporates us into his inner-trinitarian life, as he does in his saving activity, above all by incorporating us into his love, which is the love of the Father, the Son and the Holy Spirit.

II. Three examples taken from aspects of the Christian life and the life of the Church

The activities of Father, Son and Spirit in the world can be considered from many different angles and the mutual relationships of the hypostases are not the same in each case. But since *their relationships in these activities* are in every case rooted in their inner-trinitarian relationships, the latter can only be rightly understood if the former *are never in conflict with the inner-trinitarian relationships in any of these different aspects.*

Since it would be impossible to list all the aspects calling for consideration here, I shall illustrate my meaning by the three examples already mentioned which are also of great material importance. Firstly, I shall speak of the communication of eternal life from the Father through the Son in the Holy Spirit. Secondly, of the activity of the Son (Logos) and Spirit as the presupposition of our knowledge. Thirdly, of the activity of the three hypostases of the Trinity as the basis of human and ecclesial community.

A. THE COMMUNICATION OF THE TRUE DIVINE LIFE

Like the individual Christian, the Church lives by receiving the true life from God. The important thing here, in the communication of eternal life, is that this eternal life should really be given us as communion with God, as a sharing in his life, in his glory. But this communication takes place from the Father through the Son and, in the Holy Spirit, attains its goal in the recipient, so to speak, directly. The divine life can thus be said to reach the Spirit – and therefore us – from the Father through the Son. What can be said about the divine life, can also be said of the divine essence, the *divina substantia* – understood as the basis of the divine life. We can then speak of the divine essence which is from the Father through the Son in the Holy Spirit, or of the Spirit which derives from the Father through the Son – or, less precisely, from the Father and the Son. But the relation between the Son and the Spirit in the communication of the divine life has not yet been fully described in that statement. It has also to be noted that the activity of the Son which makes the communication of the divine life possible, and indeed the being of this Son in his temporal mission as incarnate, always also already presupposes the activity of the Spirit. By the power of the Spirit, the Son becomes man (Luke 1:35); he acts on earth in the power of the Spirit, offers himself as sacrifice in the Spirit (Heb. 9:14), through the power of the Spirit is raised and exalted (cf. Rom. 1:4), and sends the Spirit which he has himself received (Acts 2:33). But it would contradict all that if an absolute ontological "priority" were to be assigned to the Son in the inner-trinitarian relationship. Seen in this light, *the filioque does not preserve the identity of the Trinity per se with the identity of the Trinity of the salvation history*, as is so often asserted in the West, but actually dissolves this identity.

At this point, a brief glance at the argument that a logical priority of the Son over the Holy Spirit is implicit in *the name "Father"*. But *an absolute logical-ontological "priority" of the Son over the Spirit* cannot be deduced from the fact that the name "Father" is derived from the relationship to the Son and that a name like "Breather" or "Producer" of the Spirit is not usual. The Spirit does not confront us directly as a person like the Son but is, so to speak, a hidden hypostasis. Consistently with this, he is often not even mentioned in the New Testament along with the Father and the Son. The hiddenness of the hypostasis of the Spirit is not in itself sufficient to explain why the Father derives his name only from his relation to the Son and not from his relation to the Spirit as well. But the hiddenness of the Spirit is something quite different from an ontological-logical "posteriority", of course. From a purely logical standpoint, the hidden could undoubtedly also come first.

A *more complete definition* of the trinitarian relationships in the communication of the divine life to us would need to read something like this: the divine life – or divine essence – comes *from* the Father *through* the Son, on whom the Spirit who proceeds from the Father already rests from the beginning, *in* the Spirit, who sees that this life or essence achieves its purpose in us. If all we intend to assert in this statement is that the divine life of the Father is really communicated to us through the Son in the Spirit, then of course the relative clause qualifying the Son in this statement (i.e. "on whom the Spirit who proceeds from the Father already rests from the beginning") can be omitted without altering the meaning.

In this view, which was widely held in the early centuries in both West and East and especially in Alexandria, the focus of interest, it should be noted, is not the question of the original ontological relationships of Father, Son and Spirit within the Trinity but rather the real communication of the divine life in the economy of salvation and the divine unity as the one Father communicates his life to us in Son and Spirit. Here the Spirit must stand in third place since it is in him that God touches us directly. But the Spirit operates on the basis of Christ's work, or, in other words, through the Spirit we are touched by Christ who must therefore stand in second place. But everything derives from the Father as origin, so the Father must take the first place. The order (τάξις) of the trinitarian persons is not interchangeable, therefore, not even between Son and Spirit. Even if our primary concern is not with the question of original ontological relationships, it is surely inevitable, in the nature of the case, that we should speak of an original relationship (a relationship of origin) in the case of the relationship to the Father but not in the case of the relationship between Son and Spirit. The early western and Alexandrian statements along these lines are clearly to be distinguished from the later *filioque* doctrine.

It can safely be said that the development of the *filioque* doctrine in the direction indicated above (cf page 123) was due above all to the fact that *definitions originally developed from the standpoint of the communication of the divine essence* and ourselves as the goal of this communication were *subsequently understood as comprehensive affirmations* concerning the original ontological relationships between the divine hypostases.[2] But, as I have already shown, if these statements are understood as comprehensive affirmations, this represents, even from the standpoint of the communication of the divine life, an illegitimate generalization and absolutization of an originally unobjectionable simplification. But just how inappropriate and dan-

---

[2] In his *Théologie trinitaire de Tertullien*, III (Paris, 1966, p. 106f.), Joseph Moingt, SJ, has this to say about Tertullian, who influenced Latin theology so powerfully and is often considered to be the initiator of the development of the *filioque* in the West: "Nowhere does he countenance the view that the Son himself is the principle of divinity on the same ground and at the same time as the Father. The question raised in ch. IV (sc. of *Adversus Praxean*) is 'economic', since it concerns the origin (status) of the power wielded by the Son and the Spirit. The answer is that the latter admin-

gerous this development is will only become crystal clear as we now go on to consider the aspects of knowledge and community. The personal hypostatic character of relationships within the Trinity does not emerge as clearly in considering the aspect of the communication of the divine life as it does when we consider the aspects of knowledge and, above all, of community.

B. KNOWLEDGE

Only as *the truth comes to meet us in Christ*, the Son of God, and as *the Holy Spirit equips us to know this truth*, is there any such thing as Christian knowledge. But only through faith in Christ do we receive the Spirit and only through the Holy Spirit do we come to faith in Christ. For faith is inseparable from knowledge and knowledge is only possible in the Spirit.

From the standpoint of Christian knowledge, therefore, *the operation of the Son and the operation of the Spirit presuppose each other*, though it is impossible to explain this reciprocity rationally by asserting that one side or the other has an ultimate logical "priority". The unity of the Son and Spirit is in the Father who is their common ground, who operates in them, and to the knowledge of whom their operation ultimately leads. The fact that the Spirit is sent by the Son, for example, cannot be used as an argument to assert an ultimate logical or ontological "priority" of the operation of the Son over that of the Holy Spirit in Christian knowledge. For it is also a fact that it was through the Spirit that the Son came into the world and in the power of the Spirit that he accomplished his work. Moreover, what has been said about the reciprocity of the operations of Son and Spirit applies not only to Christian knowledge in the narrower sense but also, *mutatis mutandis*, to all knowledge, inasmuch as the Logos incarnate in Jesus Christ is none other than the creator Logos, and the Spirit sent by Christ is none other than the creator Spirit. This is something we can only hint at here.

If we assign an absolute logical, ontological "priority" to the operation of the Logos over against that of the Spirit in the process of knowing the truth (and this is the inevitable consequence of the systematic *filioque* doctrine), the logical outcome is an *objectivistic* approach to knowledge of the truth. Among the consequences of this is a *yawning gulf* between such knowledge

---

isters a power which he receives ('from the Father through the Son') . . . It does not follow that he attributes an efficient role to the Son in the production of the Spirit." These remarks refer to the only passage where Tertullian, speaking of the Spirit, uses the formula "from the Father through the Son" (*a patre per filium*). He never uses the formula 'filioque' and only once the formula '*a patre et filio*' (Ad. Prax. VIII), but in this context, the meaning is not "from the Father and the Son" but "as (the third is the Spirit) after the Father and the Son".

and *modern science and philosophy*, which regards any such objectivism as untenable. This truth in particular, which certainly is ignored more often than not even in the natural sciences except for theoretical physics, could perhaps provide the most fruitful starting point for a fruitful encounter between science and theology.

At a different level, objectivism of this kind, which affects not just the realm of knowledge in the strict sense but also the whole approach to life, is accompanied first of all by a subordination of the subject to "objective" reality. When this reaches a certain degree, the subject rebels but, for the most part, fails to transcend objectivism and only, so to speak, stands it on its head, by *regarding surrounding reality merely as an object to be used and exploited.*

At the ethical level, an objectivistic approach to knowledge is accompanied by a *heteronomic ethics* defined from outside. In the end the subject rebels against this and substitutes for it an autonomous ethics, on the basis of which faith in God (Christian or otherwise) is usually rejected.

This is not to say that the development of recent western cultural history as briefly indicated here is to be blamed on the *filioque doctrine*. We are simply pointing out the *close correspondence between this doctrine and the assumptions underlying this development.* Yet even more important is that the *filioque* doctrine makes it impossible to resist these trends theologically, on the basis of a trinitarian faith in God. The only theology capable of doing this is one which sees that the operation of the Son (Logos) and that of the Spirit presuppose each other, while neither precedes the other logically or ontologically but both are grounded in and derive from – and therefore have their logical and ontological "prior" in – the not directly knowable Father who operates in them – and from and in him alone.

As I have already said, the inner-trinitarian relationships cannot contradict those existing in the divine operations. Although we cannot draw from this the *positive* conclusion that Son and Spirit also necessarily presuppose each other in the inner-trinitarian relationships, we can draw the *negative* conclusion that neither can precede the other absolutely, logically or ontologically, in the inner-trinitarian relationships and that allowance must be made for the reciprocity of their relationship, which precisely because of this reciprocity cannot be a relation of origin. Only their relationships to the Father are relations of origin.

C. COMMUNITY

The community of Christians has its roots in the sending of the Son by the Father and in the love with which the Father loved the Son before the foundation of the world and which the Son gives to his own (cf. John 15:9; 17:26). But the sending of the Son cannot be rightly understood apart from the sending of the Spirit. So far as the question of community is concerned, that means specifically:

Christian community can only exist when *human beings are addressed through the words and life of other human beings* and indeed, in such a way that they are thereby addressed *by Christ himself*. But Christian community can also only exist when the human beings so addressed respond with their lives to this address, and indeed, in such a way that *this response is sustained by God just as* the address is, namely, by God *the Holy Spirit*, and the response also becomes in turn an address.

What is involved here is not the sum-total of innumerable personal relationships of the "I-Thou" kind but something much more inclusive which is rooted ultimately in the fact that it is Jesus Christ who addresses us as the Word of God through others and through the whole creation, that we have all received the *one* Spirit and therefore constitute not just the sum-total of innumerable "I's" but one "We". The relationship of address (in the broadest sense) and response (which turns again into address) does not itself alone constitute community, therefore, but is nevertheless *a fundamental and indispensable factor in the creation and continuance of community*.

At first glance, this relationship might seem to allow an interpretation favourable to the *filioque* doctrine. The address in which Christ speaks, it may be said, precedes the response sustained by the Holy Spirit. It is certainly very tempting to take this as indicating a logical or ontological "priority" of the Son over the Spirit. An argument along these lines can, of course, be countered by pointing out that the address of Christ is preceded by all that was mentioned earlier as the work of the Spirit in the incarnation of Jesus and in his equipment for his life and work. It would be odd, however, to affirm reciprocity in the operations of the Son and Spirit in countless other aspects, a reciprocity which rules out any one-sided priority or posteriority for either, and then to have to assign a wholly one-sided "priority" to the Son in this relationship of address through Christ and response in the Holy Spirit. It also seems to me not only inappropriate but even a tacit abandonment in face of this problem if we simply exclude it and make do with pointing out – however correctly – that the operation of the Spirit in the whole also precedes the address through Christ.

The "priority" of the Son is not really as one-sided as appears at first sight even in the relationship of address and response. There is only a limited degree of priority. For the address cannot be considered in the abstract with no reference to the presence of a person capable of being addressed. It must

be seen as a concrete approach to such a person. This means, however, that
the address which originates in Christ presupposes the ability of the person
addressed to respond to this address in the power of the Spirit. *Just as the
response presupposes the address, so too the address which constitutes community, concretely understood, also presupposes the capacity to respond.* But
this means that, from this standpoint too, Son and Spirit presuppose each
other. That the mutual relationship of Son and Spirit is not the same in both
directions is certainly clearer here than in the case of knowledge. That the
"priority" of the Son is limited is also clear from the fact that an absolute
"priority" would not accord with the transposition of response into address.

What has been said is especially important also for the relationship between *apostolic ministry and the laity*, inasmuch as, in the structure of the
Church, the address through Christ is primarily represented by the ministry.
The need of the ministry itself to be sustained by the Spirit is to be understood along the lines of what was said earlier (page 121). Only if we recognize
the reciprocal dependence of Son and Spirit, of address and response, and
of capacity to respond and the transposition of response into new address,
can *an authoritarian view of Church and ministry be excluded on the basis of
the doctrine of God itself.* On the other hand, the logical and psychological
consequence of an assumed absolute "priority" of the Son over against the
Spirit or of understanding the mission of the Spirit as the mere prolongation
of the mission of the Son, is an authoritarian view of the church ministry
charged with this mission. This authoritarianism may take the form either
of a *totalitarian clericalism* or of a *sectarian individualism*. In both cases it
is precisely the partnership of Son and Spirit in address and response which
is missing; *and* the capacity to respond to and the will to address others who
are really capable of responding and therefore of themselves assuming in
turn the role of those making the address. Once again the *filioque* should
not be blamed for the emergence of such distortions; on the other hand, the
filioque doctrine certainly excludes the possibility of rejecting these distorted
developments theologically on the basis of the trinitarian faith in God.

It is just here, in my view, that it becomes clear why the *filioque* cannot
play the part sometimes assigned to it, namely, that of *a means of defence
– both theological and psychological – against religious fanaticism*. In fact,
the exponents of sectarian fanaticism are thoroughly persuaded that they are
sent by Christ and regard the mission of the Spirit as a prolongation of the
mission of the Son, a view which is actually reinforced by the *filioque*. Only
when recourse to the institutional Church is made the main defensive
measure against sectarian fanaticism – and here the Bible, too, assumes the
role of an institution – can the *filioque* be used as a theological argument.

On the other hand, if we wish to guard against fanaticism by pleading the necessity of the community dimension of the Church, the *filioque* actually proves to be an obstacle, as was shown above in reference to sectarian individualism of all kinds.

III. Conclusions

Justice can be done to the already mentioned factors only if we affirm of relationships within the Trinity that the ground (αἰτία) and origin (ἀρχή) of the Spirit, as of the Son, are found in the Father alone but also that the Spirit is related to the Son, as the Son is also related to the Spirit though in a different way. *We have to distinguish clearly here between the fundamental original relationship, on the one hand, and other relationships in the inner-trinitarian life, on the other.*

The hypostatic *difference between Son and Spirit* is then due not to the fact that the Son originates in the Father alone, whereas the Spirit originates both in the Father and the Son but to the fact that Son and Spirit are related to each other and, each in a different way, have their origin in the Father. The fact that *the character and mode of this difference cannot be defined in formal logical terms*, as the systematized *filioque* doctrine in western scholasticism demands,[3] far from constituting a weakness of this conception *indicates rather its apophatic character*, pointing to the *mystery of God* which transcends all human knowledge, and is therefore an essential element in appropriate speech about God.

It is certainly *impossible* then *to identify the persons of the Trinity with an inner-trinitarian original relationship (relatio subsistens)*, as the *filioque* doctrine does. But this, too, is wholly in accord with the apophatic character of our knowledge of God. The character of the persons of the Trinity must remain a mystery. To equate the person with the relationships to the other persons of the Trinity would be to infringe this mystery. While it is true that the person is person only in these relationships and is known and described in its distinctiveness only in these relationships, and while we can and must define the person conceptually by these relationships, we are not at liberty to define it substantially by equating these relationships, with original relationships (*relationes subsistentes*). That would signify an inadmissible – and

---

[3] Certainly there are also considerable differences in the view of the Trinity among medieval western theologians. In the opinion of *Duns Scotus*, which contrasted with the dominant view, the Spirit could be different from the Son even if he did not proceed from the Son. In this respect at least, Scotus showed greater respect for the mystery of God.

even logically indefensible – attack by the intellect on the mystery of the trinitarian person. Since the starting point for reflection on the Trinity is not the single divine substance, as in Augustine, but the Father who reveals himself in the Son and in the Spirit, as in the New Testament, and since our concern cannot be to seek a metaphysical ontology of God, it is difficult to understand what possible interest there could be in equating the trinitarian person with the original relationship. Nor was the issue of trinitarian thinking in the one divine substance universally accepted even by the western medieval theologians – not to mention the Greek and pre-Augustinian Latin Fathers – but only the predominant position. Since Karl Rahner's study on "Theos in the New Testament", it is less and less found among Roman Catholic theologians.

Even the insights contributed by personal and relational thinking to our understanding of the human person do not end up in a definition of the person which equates its substance with its relations. On the contrary, in the last analysis even the human person remains a mystery which while revealed in relationships cannot be dissolved by identification with these relationships. If this mystery were untrue of the trinitarian person, how could it possibly be true for the human person? And conversely, if this mystery applies to the human person, how could it not apply to the trinitarian person? What is at stake in this question is the mystery of God and of humanity, the divinity of God and, inseparable from this, the dignity of the human person. Here, too, therefore, the study of the *filioque* question leads us into the heart of the life of the community of the Church and, beyond this, into the life of humankind in general.

THE FILIOQUE YESTERDAY AND TODAY

BORIS BOBRINSKOY

I. Controversial importance and relevance of an historical debate

1. For more than a thousand years the *filioque* has separated the Orthodox Church and the Christian West. At present we are seeing in all the churches a renewal of interest in the mystery of the Holy Spirit. The theme of the Spirit appears more and more as a universal factor for the renewal of theology and indeed for the whole life of the Church. This renewed experience of life in the Holy Spirit certainly contrasts with spiritual crises which the whole of the Christian world is passing through.

It is in the context of an awareness of such a renewal that we see the necessity for a joint reflection on one of the most traditional and insurmountable obstacles to Christian unity, the Roman dogma of the procession of the Holy Spirit from the Father *and the Son (filioque)*, promulgated at the Council of Lyons in 1274. This medieval polemic between Rome and Byzantium may appear derisory and unreal in the face of the apocalyptic threats which weigh on the modern world and in particular on the Christian world. Is it a sterile quarrel over words or abstract intellectual notions, or is it a confrontation between two total and coherent spiritual visions, of the Christian East and the Christian West, whose existential meaning only becomes clear from within a lived and prayed ecclesial theology?

In the course of the centuries, reflection on the Holy Spirit (and on the mystery of his procession) has taken place within very different spiritual and theological contexts. The danger of anachronism is great in reading and interpreting early pneumatological texts in the light of later theological categories.

Let us mention, simply as a reminder:

a) The "economic" or soteriological approach to trinitarian theology be-

---

• Boris BOBRINSKOY (Orthodox) is professor of dogmatics at the Orthodox Institute of St Sergius in Paris and at the Higher Institute for Ecumenical Studies in Paris.

fore Nicea, from the time of the New Testament onwards, and particularly in the Latin and Alexandrian writers. There is not yet a real dissociation between an "immanent" trinitarian theology and a trinitarian "economy" of salvation.

b) The Arian and Eunomian controversies forwarded the elaboration of a real trinitarian "theology", above all in the work of the great Cappadocians and St Augustine. The establishment of the meaning and context of the word ὑπόστασις by the Cappadocians allowed for a deepening of a theology of the inalienable properties of the trinitarian hypostases, and consequently of the isolation of the idea of "procession" (ἐκπόρευσις), a Johannine term which was finally canonized in the pneumatological article of the Creed of the Council of Constantinople (381).

c) The christological controversy between Alexandria and Antioch in the fourth and fifth centuries very soon showed evidence of different approaches, whether complementary or contradictory, to the mystery of the procession of the Holy Spirit, in relation to the controversial dogma of Christ, God and Man.

d) The important trinitarian work of St Augustine at once bears the mark of his genius, but at the same time constitutes the fruit (perhaps one-sided) of an evolution of Latin pneumatology going from Tertullian to St Augustine. In St Augustine the Latin intuition of the *filioque* finds its theological foundation which became the inheritance of the whole of scholastic and Protestant theology, a theology of trinitarian appropriations, psychological analogies, "relational" understanding of the person, etc.

e) Eastern patristic theology, and modern Orthodox "neo-patristic" theology do not examine directly the mystery of the procession of the Holy Spirit, but since St Theodore of Cyprus, Maximus the Confessor and St John Damascene, down to our days, "react" to the western dogmatic formulations. Patriarch Photius (ninth century) was the first to attempt to work out a coherent doctrine of the procession of the Holy Spirit *from the Father alone*, on the basis of the traditional Byzantine theology; in doing so he perhaps hardened the distinction, certainly necessary but made too sharp in his writings, between the eternal relations of the trinitarian hypostases, and the temporal missions into the world. Until today, the *Mystagogia of the Holy Spirit* constitutes the foundation of the dogmatic teaching of the Orthodox schools.

St Gregory of Cyprus and St Gregory Palamas sought to deepen the discussion in a creative way in the light of the Orthodox vision of the uncreated trinitarian energies. Without departing from the position of Patriarch Photius, they sketched out a creative theological synthesis which has been taken up again in our own times by modern Orthodox theology, starting from the work of Vladimir Lossky (†1958).

2. Modern Orthodox theology is divided between three main tendencies: (1) One which maintains the rigid and absolute traditionalism of the schools, the authors of nineteenth and twentieth century manuals of dogmatic theology (Z. Rossis, C. Androutsos,[1] P. Trembellas,[2] Metropolitan Makary). Their work is certainly based on that of Photius, but it suggests scarcely any link between the problem of the procession and a general theological and ecclesiological synthesis. (2) Those who give the *filioque* a limited and relative value. (3) Those who emphasize its full theological value and importance.

a) Among the efforts which have been made to get beyond the polemical impasse about the *filioque*, we must mention first of all the Russian church historian B. Bolotov. In his famous "Thesis on the Filioque"[3] he made a distinction, which subsequently found much favour, between (a) *dogmas* concerning the truth, which require an obligatory adhesion from all believers, (b) θεολογούμενα which concern what is probable, but which nevertheless have a very high degree of authority, and finally (c) *theological opinions* which are the private opinions of theologians; "their principal distinguishing mark is that they do not have authority".[4] Bolotov considered the procession of the Spirit from (*ek*) the Father, to be a dogma (thesis 1), but reduced the addition of Photius (from the Father *alone*), to the rank of a theologoumenon (thesis 7), and that of St Augustine (*filioque*) to the rank of a private theological opinion (thesis 27). However, this latter "cannot be considered as an *impedimentum dirimens* to the re-establishment of communion between the Eastern Orthodox Church and the Old Catholic Church" (thesis 27).[5]

---

[1] Their teaching is summarized in the classic work of Frank Gavin, *Some Aspects of Contemporary Greek Thought*, London, SPCK, 1936.

[2] Published in Athens in 1959–61 and in a French translation in Paris in 1966–8.

[3] Published in German without any indication of authorship in the *Revue Internationale de Theologie* VI, October-December 1898, No. 24, pp. 681–712, and recently reprinted in a French translation in *Istina*, 1972, Nos 3–4, pp. 261–289.

[4] *Istina, op. cit.*, p. 263.

[5] A very faithful restatement of Bolotov's position can be found in Fr J. M. Garrigues, in this same volume. Although he slightly distorts the position of Bolotov by making him grant the *filioque* the position of a theologoumenon, Fr Garrigues shows a remarkable openness to the Palamite positions, recognizing them as on an equality with the *filioque*, and as constituting complementary theologoumena. What will be the response to these views of traditionally minded theologians in the East (who regard the *filioque* as a heresy) and in the West (who regard it as a dogma of faith)?

b) For his part, Fr Sergius Bulgakov[6] asked whether the problem of the procession of the Holy Spirit, which has taken such an importance in pneumatology, has in its present state "any right to existence; is it not simply a false problem which leads inevitably to a sterile war of words?" He was severe about the polemic, in which the victory won by Catholic theology was more at the level of theological method than of the content of the controversy, from the time of Photius onwards. He took up Bolotov's opinion that the formula "through the Son" introduced into the solemn confession of faith of the Fathers of the Ecumenical Council (Nicea 787) "did not have the strength of a dogma, but belonged to the realm of theology of opinion, of θεολογούμενα". He regarded it less as a dogmatic definition than as a "question to future pneumatology" (pp. 93–94). Fr Bulgakov concluded by condemning this ancient controversy as sterile and a matter of indifference and affirmed that "the *filioque* is not an *impedimentum dirimens* to the divided Church once again becoming one" (p. 134). He thought that "the filioquist controversies had been an *obstacle* to a genuine pneumatology, having no spirit in them. They were conducted in the icy void of scholastic abstraction and never took the universal dimensions of a real, substantial pneumatology" (p. 124). "Would it not have been natural to expect that the existence of such a serious heresy, of such a fundamental dogmatic divergence, would penetrate into the whole life and doctrine of the two churches? For many years, as far as I have been able, I have been looking for the traces of this influence, and I have tried to understand the issues at stake, what was the *living* significance of this divergence, *where* and *how* it was revealed *in practice*. I confess that I have not succeeded in finding it; rather I should go further and simply deny its existence. This divergence exists at no point in patristic teaching on the activities of the Holy Spirit in the world, on his 'mission', his gifts, on the mysteries, on grace . . . We end up with a strange dogma, deprived of dogmatic power" (pp. 124–5).

However, Bulgakov diminishes the very sharp character of these last affirmations when he links the Latin doctrine of the *filioque* with the western Christocentrism which culminates in the dogma of the Pope as Vicar of Christ; "so, he says, the *filioque* is above all in fact a dogma about the Pope" (p. 137, referring to Bolotov).

c) Against this, the importance of the doctrines of the procession of the Holy Spirit, and of their influence on the life of the Church (or of their expression of it) has been vigorously underlined by Vladimir Lossky and those who have followed him.

---

[6] *The Paraclete* (in Russian), Paris, 1936; in French, Paris, 1946.

i) Lossky maintains with force and interior evidence that "for the Orthodox Church, the Trinity is the unshakeable foundation of all religious thought, of all piety, of all experience".[7] Trinitarian dogma controls and determines all the anthropological, spiritual and ecclesiological reflection which we find in Lossky. If, in his classical work, *The Mystical Theology of the Eastern Church*, we do not yet find an explicit working out of this question, the theological premises of the Orthodox doctrine of the procession of the Holy Spirit are already set out with great clarity; the doctrine of the monarchy of the Father, the hypostatic relations always in a threefold pattern, which thus transcend the philosophical way of the oppositions of human logic; the specificity of the role of the divine Persons of the Son and the Holy Spirit at work in the world.

It was above all in a lecture given at Oxford in 1947 that Lossky developed the whole scheme of the problematic of the *filioque*.[8] He affirmed first of all that "the question of the procession of the Holy Spirit has been (whether one likes it or not), the one dogmatic reason for the separation between East and West. All the other divergencies, which historically have accompanied or followed the first controversy over the *filioque*, to the extent that they have any doctrinal content, are linked more or less directly to this primordial point". There, and in a series of lectures, as yet unpublished, which he gave between 1953 and 1957 where his thought deepened and expanded, Lossky showed the real non-sense of filioquism on a properly theological plane. This doctrine seemed to him to bring in an "alien light", that of fallen reason and sensibility, into the "holy of holies of the divine existence".[9]

Finally, it was in this same series of lectures that Lossky took up and developed the intuitions of Palamism attempting to integrate what was positive in the *filioque* into a theology of the eternal trinitarian "manifestations", as developed by Gregory of Cyprus and Gregory Palamas.

ii) Alongside Lossky, Father John Meyendorff from 1950 reopened the eastern patristic material on the procession of the Holy Spirit,[10] renewed our

---

[7] *The Mystical Theology of the Eastern Church*, London, 1958, p. 65.
[8] "La Procession du Saint Esprit dans la doctrine trinitaire Orthodoxe", Paris, 1948; published in English in *In the Image and Likeness of God*, London, 1975, pp. 71–96.
[9] Numerous references to these unpublished lectures will be found in Olivier Clément's study, "Vladimir Lossky, un théologien de la personne et du Saint Esprit", in the *Memorial Vladimir Lossky* of the *Messager de L'Exarchat du Patriache Russe en Europe Occidentale*, Nos 30–31, Paris, 1959, pp. 137–206.
[10] "La Procession du Saint Esprit chez les Pères Orientaux", in *Russie et Chrétienneté*, 1950, Nos 3–4, pp. 158–178.

knowledge of the historical origins of the *filioque* in the West[11] and finally made an appeal to the creative openings sketched out by Palamism.[12]

iii) In our time, Paul Evdokimov,[13] Nikos Nissiotis,[14] Father Dumitru Staniloae[15] and Olivier Clément[16] have followed a common search for the integration of the problem of the procession of the Holy Spirit into the Palamite synthesis, always attempting to make a creative transcendence of the age-old oppositions.

Thus we are witnessing in certain Orthodox circles (and more generally in all the Christian churches) a notable renewal of pneumatology and a rediscovery of its vital significance as a dimension in the whole of theology and of the life of the Church. As to the *filioque*, it is considered in Orthodox circles if not as the cause, at least as one of the symptoms of a pneumatological regression which has touched the life of the Church in depth, with its ministerial and sacramental structures, which has diminished the fullness of the experience of salvation, which distorts the exercise of power and freedom, and which calls into question the very meaning of ecclesial and episcopal collegiality.

II. Historical circumstances and the fact of the addition of the filioque

1. One cannot deny that the doctrine of the *filioque* was to some extent rooted in Latin theology before St Augustine (cf. Tertullian, Novatian, St Hilary, St Ambrose). However, these very early filioquist formulas scarcely distinguish between trinitarian theology on the one side and the economy of salvation on the other. Even for the Bishop of Hippo, the *filioque* remains the expression of a personal and hence provisional theological investigation; his psychological analogies have only an illustrative character.

The conciliar proclamations, first in Spain in the sixth century, the adoption of the *filioque* by Charlemagne, then at Rome in the eleventh century,

---

[11] "At the Origins of the Filioque controversy" (in Russian) in "La Pensée Orthodoxe", No. IX, Paris, 1953, pp. 114–37, and *Byzantine Theology*, New York, 1974, pp. 91–4.
[12] *A Study of Gregory Palamas*, London, 1964, pp. 228–32.
[13] See principally *L'Esprit Saint dans la tradition orthodoxe*, Paris, 1969.
[14] "Pneumatologie orthodoxe", in *Le Saint Esprit*, Geneva, Labor & Fides, 1963, pp. 85–106.
[15] See his essay later in this book.
[16] "A propos du Filioque", in *Le Messager Orthodoxe*, nos. 7 and 8, Paris, pp. 9–22 and 22–32, "De la Transfiguration" (end of the preceding article) *ibid*. 1960, no. 10, pp. 26–31. He takes up the whole historical and theological problem of the *filioque* in a contribution made on the 7th centenary of the Council of Lyons (1274) "Byzance et le concile de Lyon" in *Unité Chrétienne*, Lyons, 1975, No. 37.

gave the doctrine an ecclesial resonance and authority. The Council of Lyons (1274) gave it the force of law and dogma for the whole of Latin Christendom and furnished the decree with an anathema ("damnamus et reprobamus"). The Orthodox East never accepted the dogmatic definitions of the "Council of Union". Despite severe pressure from the civil and religious power, a real resistance of the Orthodox people formed against this artificial and ephemeral "union".

I do not propose to develop here the history of the negotiations for union between the Greeks and the Latins after the Council of Lyons. Let us notice however that the popular feeling aroused after the dogmatic agreement of the Council of Florence (1438–9) was no less than after the Council of Lyons, although the later Council seemed to offer a better common basis for agreement in the final formula for the procession of the Holy Spirit from the Father, "through the Son", but in a strictly filioquist interpretation. We must also add that the theological debates were concerned with the legitimacy of the addition of the *filioque* to the Creed, and with defensive anti-Latin argumentation. The Palamite synthesis, already anticipated by Gregory of Cyprus and applied by him to the theology of the processions was not able to be brought into the discussion.

2. I would also like, in relation to this brief historical survey, to underline the consciousness of the Orthodox Church that beyond the strictly dogmatic content of the problem of the *filioque*, to which I shall return later, the "moral" aspect of the *filioque* is in itself significant, if not of primary importance.

It is perhaps the slavophile theologian A. Khomiakov who has most uncompromisingly formulated this consciousness of the Orthodox Church of having been subjected to a real *moral fratricide* through the dogmatic constraint exercised down the centuries. Only the whole and unanimous Church has the right to define new dogmas or to modify the symbol of faith. By arrogating this right to itself, one part of the Church "was destroying the equality of rights between the various communities, and the central importance of unity of spirit and love, on which were based all the concepts of the primitive Christian community". "This pride of the separated Churches, who have had the effrontery to alter the Creed of the whole Church without the consent of their brethren, was not inspired by love: it was a crime before God and before Holy Church. And how can the faith, the truth, survive intact, where love has been impoverished?" [17]

[17] Texts quoted in A. Gratieux, *A. S. Khomiakov et le Mouvement Slavophile*, Vol. II, Paris, Editions du Cerf, 1939, pp. 83 and 86: cf. pp. 119 and 139.

Father S. Bulgakov, for his part, comments that in the filioquist controversy the dogmatic problem had become an instrument of domination and of self-defence, so that the *filioque* became the symbol of papal absolutism or, on the other side, that of its negation; that is why, for the Greeks at Florence, the question of the insertion of the *filioque* in the Creed was more important than its dogmatic content.[18]

3. It seems to me of great importance to give the "moral" aspect of the adjunction of the *filioque* its true weight. It is not a question for me of casting doubt on the good faith of the Latin West. A by no means negligible amount of misunderstanding is still linked to the estrangement of Rome and Byzantium. I entirely accept the opinion of Fr A. de Halleux that the insertion of the *filioque* into the Creed of Constantinople can have signified at the beginning nothing more than a natural adaptation to local tradition, which showed, no doubt, a regrettable ignorance of the conciliar tradition, but certainly not a subjective distrust of the Eastern Orthodox Church (cf. page 83 of this volume).[19]

It nevertheless remains true that the addition of the *filioque* continues to be a stumbling-block and a scandal for Orthodoxy, as much in the actual fact of it as in its theological content. The wound experienced by the very people of the Orthodox Church is expressed with truth in the rather hard words of Khomiakov quoted above. I think it desirable that the Roman Catholic Church's first step be the removal of the *filioque* from the Creed, primarily as a token of fraternal reconciliation, and as a necessary preliminary to the setting up of a bilateral theological dialogue, *without this suppression of the filioque having ipso facto to signify a denial by the Catholics of the content of the filioque which is traditional for them.* This gesture would have enormous ecclesiological significance, as a spontaneous gesture which would not come at the end of a process of ecclesiastical bargaining or theological compromise, but which, by its very gratuity, would lift people's minds to the level of mutual confidence and love, and would then greatly contribute to lightening the whole climate of church relations and the ancient theological debate.

The second stage would allow for the opening up of a genuine theological dialogue (at present premature) between the churches where a loyal confrontation with our divergences would lead us to a genuine common deepening of the theological question.

---

[18] *Op. cit.*, p. 123.
[19] "Pour un accord oecumenique sur la procession de l'Esprit Saint et l'addition du Filioque au symbole", in *Irenikon*, 1978, No. 4, pp. 451–4–69.

This stage could be followed eventually by a reformulation in common of the pneumatological article of the Creed, which would respond to the theological progress being made and would express the dogmatic agreement which had been reached and would itself be a major stage on the way to the restoration of sacramental communion between our churches.

III. The positive theological content of the filioque

It is true that modern Orthodox theology has itself also made an effort at "spiritual discernment" by drawing a distinction between the *filioque* and "filioquism", thus rediscovering the legitimate theological and soteriological context of the Latin (and Alexandrian) tradition before St Augustine, and before the Western Councils of Lyons and Florence.

1. The legitimate christological context of the filioque

A comparative study of the theological traditions of East and West during the first centuries has led me to the conviction that from the beginning of the third century of the "western" theologies (Latin and Alexandrian) a different emphasis from that of the East was put on the very movement of trinitarian revelation, understood as the revelation of the mystery of salvation.

In the West, the emphasis was placed to a preponderent (though not exclusive) degree on a movement of revelation Father-Son-Spirit, in which the Spirit, as the revelation of the mutual love of the Father and the Son, is communicated to men jointly by the Father and the Son. The Fourth Gospel in particular expresses the promise of the Paraclete, sent by the Father and the Son (John 17 and 20). Starting from this christological diagram of Father-Son-Spirit, theological contemplation, or rather speculation, spontaneously went on to consider the eternal basis of these temporal missions, the inner-trinitarian "procession" or "relations". At a time when the distinction between the temporal mission and eternal procession had not been elaborated (let us not be too quick to see in this an incomplete "archaic" theology) the idea of an eternal procession of the Holy Spirit from the Father *and the Son* (at this stage still a very tentative idea) expressed essentially this same dynamic of the Church's experience of the Spirit, in the Church and in human life in general, as the gift of the Father and the Son.

In such a perspective, the Spirit is seen as acting in the Church above all as the power of growth and fruitfulness which enables us to carry on the mission of Jesus in the world, through history, until the end of the age, in a Church which itself is on pilgrimage to the heavenly kingdom.[20]

This missionary and apostolic perspective of salvation thought of in terms of the Church's growth in time and space is certainly profoundly biblical and traditional, but it has dominated the whole understanding of the Church, its ministries, its mission, its theological language, in a one-sided way. But before passing judgment on the omissions of a partial and incomplete vision, let us first of all keep hold of what is positive and necessary in this aspect of the dynamics of salvation, centred on the mission and expansion of the Church in the world, in and through the power of the Spirit: "Go and teach all the nations" (Matt. 28:19). The Church obeys this commission when, at the end of the Liturgy, that eucharistic "Pentecost", she "sends back" (or rather "sends out") the faithful into the world ("Ite missa est", "Let us go forth in peace"), carrying the Good News having through the eucharistic union themselves become the Good News.

2. OTHER POSITIVE ASPECTS OF THE FILIOQUE

As to the positive value of the Latin theology of the Holy Spirit, I would sum it up in three points which have their place in an Orthodox vision of the Trinity.

(a) *The Holy Spirit is the mutual love and the bond of love between the Father and the Son*. This idea, which is perhaps inspired by the psychological analogies of St Augustine, turns up again in the East in St Gregory Palamas in the fourteenth century, but replaced in an Orthodox *Trinitarian context*.[21] I would add that in Orthodox consciousness of the Trinity, it is not only the Holy Spirit who has the "prerogative" to be the link between the divine hypostases. Each hypostasis gathers together and unites the others in himself, the Father as source in the monarchy, the Son as the One in whom the Father and the Spirit find their resting place.

(b) *The Spirit is the common gift of the Father and the Son*. Orthodoxy

---

[20] Prof. John Zizioulas has in recent years sought in a series of studies and articles to renew the problem of pneumatology and its implications in the life and thought of the Church in the East and in the West. He distinguishes, in perhaps a slightly too schematic way, a western type of pneumatology where the Spirit is given and works in the Church as the power of the Father and the Son, a more balanced eastern pneumatology, where the Holy Spirit makes the Risen Christ present, above all in the Eucharistic community, thus revealing the Lord of the Parousia in the today of the Church. Cf. eg. "La portée de l'Eglise des Apôtres pour l'Eglise d'aujourd'hui" in *Istina* (Paris) 1974. No. 1, pp. 65–94. Also in the summary of a lecture on "The Holy Spirit and the Church" in *Episkepsis*, Geneva, No. 169, 1 June 1967.

[21] Cf. John Meyendorff, *Byzantine Theology, op. cit.*, pp. 186–8.

adds, nonetheless, (i) that the Holy Spirit also gives himself, for every divine gift to creation is a common gift of the Holy Trinity; the Spirit is no stranger to his own coming; (ii) that the Spirit in his turn leads us to the Son, and through him, to the Father. It is therefore no less true to say that in giving us himself, the Spirit gives us the Father and the Son.

(c) *The eternal Son is not extraneous to the procession of the Holy Spirit.* But Orthodox theology adds, (i) in an ineffable manner, (ii) without bringing in the idea of causality, (iii) without calling into question the untransmissable character of the Father's hypostatic property of being the one Source and Principle of the Divinity of the Son and of the Spirit.

IV. The omissions of "filioquism"

1. ORTHODOX CHRISTOLOGY AND THE PROCESSION OF THE HOLY SPIRIT

When we turn to eastern theology, we find, it seems to me, a better balance in the dynamics of revelation. Side by side with the classic diagram Father-Son-Spirit of which I have spoken above, another movement of revelation and of communion in the life of the Trinity can be outlined around the diagram Father-Spirit-Son. This movement, perhaps more interior, brings out above all the presence, the coming to rest, of the Spirit on the Christ, who is the Word incarnate and glorified in the flesh. Recent New Testament exegesis is rediscovering the pneumatological dimension of Christology, particularly in the works of St Luke, and through the Syrian theological tradition. This perspective has brought about at the present day a considerable enrichment in christological thought and in the concept of salvation itself, of the sacraments and of the Church; all in all, it is the foundations of Trinitarian theology itself which have been restored.

It is above all in the life of the Saviour that the Trinity is revealed, that we see the Spirit at work, that the infinite love of the Father is made manifest. Before communicating the Spirit to men, Christ is himself the place of rest, the receptacle of the Spirit's plenitude and perfection. All that we can say of the identity, of the messianic, divine and filial consciousness, of the human psychology of Jesus, must be situated within this moving power, this infinite enkindling of the Holy Spirit. The Spirit is in Jesus as Jesus is in the Spirit. We cannot resign ourselves to reducing this reciprocal indwelling to a simple relationship of unilateral causality. We are dealing indeed with an infinite *coincidence* of the Son and the Spirit, a coincidence of fullness and mutual transparency which can only be expressed in human terms in the concept of reciprocal revelation and love. Before being the gift of Christ, the Spirit reveals Christ's identity. He actuates Christ's presence, both in the time of the Incarnation and in the time of the Church.

The Holy Spirit therefore determines the life of the Church, and not only insofar as he comes from Christ, but insofar as he constantly *prepares* the human heart to receive the coming of the Risen Christ. It is from this ecclesial, sacramental, spiritual experience of Christ, who is anointed by the Holy Spirit (Luke 4:4, 14, 18; Acts 2:33), and of his Body, the Church, herself the bearer of the Spirit, that theological vision attains to the intuition of the eternal mystery of the Holy Spirit, no longer as proceeding from the Son, or through the Son, but as resting on the Son from all eternity. The descent of the Spirit on Jesus at the Jordan therefore appears in the Orthodox trinitarian vision as an icon, a manifestation in history of the eternal resting of the Spirit of the Father on the Son. Thus it is that, following St John Damascene, the Orthodox liturgy for Pentecost proclaims, "the Spirit who proceeds from the Father and rests on the Son".

The incarnation of Christ thus finds its extension through the whole of human history, of which it is the heart and focus. Touched by the same energies and strengthened by the power of the Spirit which dwelt in Jesus as in his Temple, man in his turn is renewed by the Spirit who conforms us to Christ, and who shines out from us in ineffable light into the darkness of the world.

All the theology of the Church, of salvation, of the new man, of the sacraments is profoundly marked by this mysterious movement of reciprocity between Christ and the Spirit who are manifest, give themselves, are sent in such a way as constantly to ensure and renew the equilibrium in the life of the Church between obedience and creative liberty, between institution and prophecy.

This movement of reciprocity of Christ and the Spirit must finally be reflected in trinitarian theology itself. Perhaps without always expressing all the ecclesial implications of the theology of the Holy Spirit, it has nonetheless been a very sure spiritual instinct which has made Orthodoxy reject, as much in the past as today, any attempt to compromise this equilibrium of the Son and the Spirit. This explains the tenacity with which Orthodoxy has constantly resisted the western attempts, in the Councils of Lyons and Florence, to introduce the *filioque* into the Creed.

It has not at all been my desire at all costs to make an opposition between the theological and spiritual traditions of East and West, still less to make them exclusive of one another. I have therefore questioned less the positive element in the western theology of the procession of the Holy Spirit than its omissions, what it does not say and what it cannot account for; the experience of the fullness of the Holy Spirit in the life of the Church and in the life of the Christian, each of which become the spiritual body of Christ himself.

2. OMISSIONS AND INADEQUACIES

a) The "revelatory function" of the Holy Spirit allows us to say, as a counterbalance to the western diagram, that, if it is true that the Son is not extraneous to the procession of the Holy Spirit (without bringing in the idea of causality), on the other hand neither is the Holy Spirit extraneous, exterior to the generation of the Son. One cannot separately conceive of or articulate the two eternal movements of the Trinity; one must remember, following the whole of Orthodox tradition both ancient and modern, that their character is concomitant (St Gregory of Nyssa) and simultaneous (St John Damascene). Any introduction, even purely conceptual and speculative, of anteriority in the generation of the Son relative to the procession of the Spirit, contributes to the rationalization and unbalancing of the trinitarian mystery, to the great hurt of the Church, in which the reign of the Trinity is inaugurated.

b) The notion of a procession of the Holy Spirit from the Father and the Son *tamquam ab uno principio* is radically unacceptable to Orthodox theology, whatever may be the explanations or attenuations of the formula. For Orthodox theology, the Father does not transmit his hypostatic properties, even to the Son. What is common to two hypostases (their attributes-energies, their life, the divine nature itself) is common to all three. If the Holy Spirit is given by the Father and the Son in the sanctifying grace of the Church, he is, then, also given by himself. He appears as the hypostatic gift of trinitarian grace, the grace by which we are incorporated in the eternal banquet of the trinitarian kingdom.

c) The theological idea of the procession of the Holy Spirit *through (per)* the Son is to be found in different theological contexts in Byzantium, in the West and in modern theology. This idea is capable of receiving an Orthodox interpretation, as for example, in St John Damascene,[22] or in the synodical letter of Patriarch Tarasius to the Fathers of the Seventh Ecumenical Council

---

[22] "The Spirit is the Spirit of the Father . . . but he is also the Spirit of the Son, not because he proceeds from him, but because he proceeds through him from the Father, for there is only one Cause, the Father". (Exposition of the Orthodox faith, 1,12; P.G.94, 849 B).

of Nicea (787).[23] The eternal Son is understood as the mediator or the gift of the Spirit and the place of his procession.

But it can also conceal a veiled filioquist doctrine, as was the case at the Council of Florence. The age-old conflict over the *filioque* then clearly recalls this. I do not therefore believe that the compromise formula *per Filium* can of itself offer a satisfactory solution to the conflict, on account of the ambiguities it can contain.

V. The transcending or integration of the filioque into an Orthodox trinitarian vision

1. THE ECCLESIAL EXPERIENCE OF THE MYSTERY OF THE TRINITY

We are witnessing in our time a notable deepening of pneumatology and a discovery of its central place in the whole life of the Church, and in theology. Too *direct* and scrutinizing an approach to the mystery of the procession of the Holy Spirit runs the risk of hardening and emptying out what is inexpressible and shutting the dialogue up in sterile polemics. The history of the controversy confirms this eloquently. It is time to re-immerse our reflection, our theological research, our intellect itself, in the heart of the Church's prayer and love, where the divine Spirit breathes and gives life. It is then, and only then, that the existential meaning of the eternal processions, for the Church and for our salvation, will become manifest and will communicate itself to us.

We have to admit that if the patristic and liturgical tradition of Orthodoxy has preserved this knowledge of the divine mysteries in its sacred deposit, and thus speaks of the reciprocal relations of the Son and the Spirit, the Orthodox theology of the schools has only assimilated and worked out this important aspect of revelation in a very limited way.

I am nonetheless convinced that today, as before, it is only the patristic synthesis, renewed in Palamism and realized today in modern Orthodox "neo-patristic" theology which will be capable of reinserting theological speculation in its living and creative context, that of trinitarian experience and vision which are always living in the Church, the Body of Christ, the Temple of the Holy Spirit. There is, it seems to me, an essential convergence between the most creative patristic intuitions of Byzantine theology (St Gregory of Cyprus and St Gregory Palamas) and contemporary theological research which brings out the pneumatological dimension of Christology and its extension in the Church. In both cases, it is the great spiritual tradition

---

[23] Cf. Mansi, *Collection Conciliorum* XII, 1122.

of the Church which is primary and which introduces us into the mystery of the eternal Son, incarnate in Jesus Christ, dwelling place and source of the Spirit who proceeds from the Father.

To rediscover the place of the Spirit in the mystery both of the personal Christ and of the total Christ, which is the Church, has become one of the urgent necessities of our theological task, whatever Christian confession we may belong to; without this, the very meaning of the mystery of salvation will become atrophied and deformed.

To speak of the fullness of the Spirit in Christ, of the moving of the Lord Jesus in the Spirit, of the transmission of the Spirit by Christ in the Church, is to announce to human beings the fullness of salvation and of new life in the divine Trinity; it is to announce that the Church and humanity cannot be defined in terms of themselves, but that in their ultimate roots they are constituted by that indwelling of the Spirit which makes us Christs and sons, inheritors of the Father's kingdom.

Contemplation of the trinitarian mystery and of the eternal processions then becomes co-extensive with the fullness of our salvation. It is therefore necessary that trinitarian theology should itself be adequate for translating trinitarian experience, both of the Church and in the Church, that it should be an icon of the trinitarian life to which we are invited. Then there can be manifested the full concurrence of theology and life (St Irenaeus).

2. PRESUPPOSITIONS AND CONDITIONS OF THE THEOLOGICAL DIALOGUE

The historical circumstances of the dogmatic formulation of the *filioque* (or of any other dogma) are inseparable from its objective doctrinal content, since truth and love form an undivided unity. The restoration of the genuine spiritual climate of dialogue is therefore an absolute and necessary presupposition for such dialogue. In our time it has become necessary with unparalleled urgency.

The lifting of the anathemas between Rome and Constantinople in 1965 must extend to the whole body of the unilateral acts which have contributed to creating a dogmatic gulf between our churches. The promulgation of the *filioque* as a truth of faith at the Council of Lyons in 1274 must first of all be freed from the anathemas which accompany it. If the Latin dogma of the *filioque* loses, in the eyes of the Orthodox, its constraining character, if the Niceno-Constantinopolitan Creed recovers its common primitive form and becomes again a true "Symbol" of unity and love, then the *filioque* will cease to be seen as a sin against unity and love. It will then be possible for the Orthodox to consider it as a particular theological investigation belonging to a certain region, to a certain period of Christianity, seeking to express a particular aspect of the Catholic faith.

If the doctrine of the *filioque* loses its constraining character it seems to me that it would then be possible to seek, in a dialogue of love and of truth, to integrate it into a far wider trinitarian and soteriological vision, that of the Church of all times and of all places.

*   *   *

These reflections on the *filioque* do not simply constitute a unilateral appeal to the theological conscience of our Catholic and Protestant brethren. In order that the Catholic Church should be able to accomplish its progress towards unity of faith with Orthodoxy, in order that the Latin "dogma" of the *filioque* should be resituated in a full theological and spiritual context, the whole Orthodox Church must also become committed to a profound spiritual renewal of its theological activity, so that eucharistic life may be the true place of trinitarian communion in the Church. The renewal of ecclesial life and thought in the Holy Spirit is, for the whole of Christendom of East and West alike, the necessary condition for the gift of the Spirit of unity, of love and of witness in the world.

A ROMAN CATHOLIC VIEW
OF THE POSITION NOW REACHED
IN THE QUESTION OF THE FILIOQUE

JEAN-MIGUEL GARRIGUES

The specifically ecumenical problem posed by the *filioque* can be summed up as follows: in its liturgical use of the Creed the Catholic Church professes the faith that the Holy Spirit *a Patre Filioque procedit*. Pope Paul VI employed this formula again in his profession of faith in 1968. To many Orthodox Christians today the dogmatic character, so to speak, which the Catholic Church assigns to the *filioque* still seems to be the *impedimentum dirimens* to the union of the Church of the East and the Church of the West.

It could very well be, however, that the *filioque* acquires a meaning ecumenically acceptable to the Orthodox precisely by becoming an integral element in the official teaching of the Catholic faith. When in the exercise of their solemn magisterium in the Catholic Church the bishops and the Pope employ a formula such as the *filioque* (and the same applies to transubstantiation, immaculate conception, papal infallibility), this does not mean that they are canonizing the exact meaning this formula was given in the theological trend which invented it and had used it up to that point. On the contrary, it means that, having been recognized as a normative expression of the faith, the ultimate meaning of this formula must be sought in conformity with revelation, which for the Catholic means in Scripture read in the light of the symphony of Tradition (ecumenical councils, Fathers of the Church). If the *filioque* represents an essential dimension of the Church's trinitarian faith it can only yield up its significance if it embodies a truth unanimously recognized by the Fathers (explicitly or implicitly). Once it has become part of the Church's confession of faith, the *filioque* can no more be regarded as the canonization of the trinitarian theology of St Augustine, St

• Jean Miguel GARRIGUES (Roman Catholic) is a monk and priest of the Diocesan Church of Aix-en-Provence in France and teaches Patristic Dogmatics at the Catholic Institute of Toulouse.

Anselm or St Thomas Aquinas than the dogma of the Council of Ephesus was the canonization of the Christology of St Cyril of Alexandria. The faith of Ephesus was ecumenically received when by their union formula St Cyril and John of Antioch abandoned any thought of reducing that faith to their own individual christologies, however excellent these appeared to them, and agreed instead to recognize that formula as embodying the common element of the Church's faith which each of their christologies was trying with greater or less success to express.

It took another three centuries or so (down to the Second Council of Nicea in 787) for the post-Nicene christological faith, formulated for the first time at Ephesus, to disclose its ultimate meaning in the Church, and one still wonders today, in the dialogue with the Nestorian and non-Chalcedonian churches, whether the ecumenical reception of that true meaning was sufficiently complete. And if that is the case with Christology, what are we to say of the Church's pneumatological faith! The first Council of Constantinople at which the Nicene Creed was developed under the influence of the Cappadocian Fathers, was held in the absence of the papal legates (though their presence was canonically required for ecumenicity) and of the western bishops. The latter met at about the same time in Rome in a Council which was dominated by the personality of St Ambrose. St Ambrose, following a traditional trinitarian theology going back to Tertullian, had already in his writings professed faith in the *filioque*. On both sides there was a realization that the pneumatological formulas lacked sufficient ecumenical reception. When East and West met again at Ephesus fifty years later and forbad any addition to the symbol of faith, they opted for the Nicene Creed without the development of the First Council of Constantinople on the Holy Spirit. It was only twenty years later at the Council of Chalcedon that the Niceno-Constantinopolitan Creed was proclaimed and received ecumenically. But by this time St Augustine had developed the *filioque* in his trinitarian theology and Pope St Leo had officially professed it in a letter to the Church in Spain. On the basis of one and the same Creed, which the easterners believed excluded the *filioque* (cf. the reaction of Theodoret of Cyrrhus) and the westerners believed implied it, the pneumatological development would in future follow at first parallel lines and then, after the Photian crisis and the schism of 1054, conflicting lines.

The medieval period was poisoned by the polemic atmosphere prevailing between East and West from which not even very great thinkers and saints were exempt. Trinitarian theology was subtly systematized on both sides to exclude the other's position. For example St Anselm and then St Thomas Aquinas demonstrated that if the divine Persons are subsistent relationships, the Father and the Son in their reciprocal relationship can constitute the unique principle of the procession of the Holy Spirit. The fact that the West, profiting from the difficult political situations in the East, managed for a time to impose this trinitarian theology on the East at the Councils of Lyons and Florence, does not mean that the *filioque* had been really received ecumenically in this form, as was soon demonstrated by the Orthodox Church's rejection of those Councils. On the contrary, Gregory of Cyprus and then Gregory Palamas, on the basis of the apophatic distinction between God's essence and energies, argued that while the energy of the Spirit may proceed eternally from the Father and the Son, it by no means follows from this that the Person of the Spirit proceeds from the Father and the Son. But they were no more successful in persuading the Latins with their doctrine of energies than were the Latins in persuading them with their doctrine of relationships. Each side had the impression that the other was trying to lead it "ad obscurum per obscurius". To pursue this road again would only lead to the same result. Not that the doctrine of trinitarian relations has no patristic basis. (The principles are found more explicitly in the easterners St Gregory Nazianzen and St Maximus the Confessor than in St Augustine.) And the doctrine of the divine energies rests on an insight which was widespread in almost all the eastern patristic writings. Both these theologies are valuable and would benefit by mutual receptivity. But for all the obstinacy displayed on both sides in turning them into dogmatic statements, they are essentially medieval developments and cannot claim to be the norm for the concordant faith of the Fathers of the undivided Church concerning the relationship between the Spirit and the Son in the Trinity.

The dogmatic core of the relationship of the Spirit to the Son in the Trinity depends on the mystery of the Holy Spirit as the divine Third Person (cf. the sequence of the baptismal formula in Matt. 28:19 which controls the Niceno-Constantinopolitan Creed). As Bolotov stated in his famous *Theses on the Filioque*: "The Spirit is the third hypostasis of the Holy Trinity. His very being presupposes the existence of the Father as well as that of the Son, because the Holy Spirit proceeds from the Father and because the Father is Father only of the Son. As soon as God, προβολεὺς τοῦ Πνεύματος, is named *father*, He is thought of as having a Son. Without incurring the danger of too great inexactitude, therefore, it can be said that ὑπάρχοντος (ὄντος, ὑφεστῶτος) τοῦ Υἱοῦ ἐκ τοῦ Πατρὸς ἐκπορεύεται τὸ Πνεῦμα τὸ ῞Αγιον (whereas the Son exists, the Spirit proceeds from the Father)." And further on: "The begetting of the Son-Word is a condition proper to God (θεοπρεπῶς) for the *unconditioned* procession of the Holy Spirit, the motive and the basis (and therefore the logical 'prius') for the procession of the Holy

Spirit from the Father." And in a note: "If the Holy Spirit as well as the Son is of the essence of the Father, why then – as the Arians and the Macedonians asked – is the Holy Spirit not the Son? They were told: Because the Spirit is ἐκπορευτὸν from the Father and not γεννητὸν (by generation). Why then is the Spirit not γεννητὸν (begotten)? Because only the Only-begotten, i.e. the Son, is γεννητὸς. Therefore the Son by his being as Begotten, also determines the τρόπος τῆς ὑπάρξεως, the *modus existendi*, of the Holy Spirit, his being non-begotten."

On the basis of the scriptures and the symphony of the Fathers of the Church, the only strictly dogmatic content of the *filioque* which can claim any rightful place in the Church's confession of faith, is that the Holy Spirit goes forth (ἐκπορευόμενον) from the Father *as Father, i.e. as begetter of the unique Son*. Understood in this way, the *filioque* simply spells out the dogma of the Third Person, whom the Niceno-Constantinopolitan Creed presents to us as proceeding from the Father who begets the unique Son. If the Roman Catholic Church wishes to demonstrate that when it confesses the *filioque* it does no more than affirm the fact, universally recognized by the Fathers, that the procession of the Spirit depends on the generation of the Word in the bosom of the Father, without any desire to turn into a dogma one of the theological explanations of *how* this dependence works, then it would be desirable for the Pope and the Catholic bishops to point out, as did Pope Leo III, that the dogmatic version of the Niceno-Constantinopolitan Creed is the original Greek text confessed by the Councils and this version already contains the full catholic faith in the Holy Spirit; the *filioque* being no more than a Latin explanation which does not claim to add anything to the conciliar dogma. But the Roman Catholic Church will be able to do this only if the Orthodox churches for their part, taking note of this solemn declaration, abandon the view that there is more in the *filioque* than the Catholic Church sees in it and accepts the liturgical development of the Latin Church without branding it as heretical. One would hope that on this plane the Orthodox will show just as much broadmindedness to a traditional expression in the Latin Church as they do today to the christological expressions of the non-Chalcedonian churches.

Although in the light of the concordance of the Fathers of the undivided Church the *filioque* cannot be interpreted as a unilateral addition to the Niceno-Constantinopolitan dogma, the Creed of which was received by the whole Church at the Council of Chalcedon, it remains true that, as an explanation of the dogma, it is still (as Bolotov has shown) a theologoumenon whose precise status in relation to the dogma needs to be clarified at the ecumenical level. Specifically a distinction must be made between the universal and strictly ecumenical range of the theologoumenon on the one hand, and its particular interpretation of Latin trinitarian theology on the other.

The validity of the *filioque* as a theologoumenon in relation to the dogma has its limit in the fact often insisted on in the East, that it cannot cancel the "monarchy" of the Father, i.e. the truth that the Father is the source of the divinity and the principle of its unity. Photius described this limit in the formula which the Orthodox hold dear: "The Holy Spirit proceeds from the Father alone." In his seventh thesis, however, Bolotov points out that this formula itself is a theologoumenon; it makes clear the truth of the monarchy of the Father which is implicit in the dogma but leaves in obscurity the truth that the procession of the Spirit depends on the generation of the Word in the bosom of the Father. For although the Spirit does originate in the Father alone as the source of the divinity, He does not originate in the Father in isolation but in the one only Father as the unique Father of the only-begotten Son. The unique monarchy of the Father is manifested first of all in his unique generation of the only-begotten Son and, paradoxically, it is this latter generation which by its uniqueness guarantees that he is the unique principle of the Spirit in a radically different mode in the ἐκπόρευσις. If the dogma had to be stated in terms of the two theologoumena which develop it, we should have to say: "I believe in the Holy Spirit who goes forth from the one only Father insofar as He begets the only Son (ἐκ μόνου τοῦ Πατρὸς, ὡς τὸν Μονογενῆ γεννῶντος, ἐκπορευόμενον). These two θεολογούμενα are so deeply rooted in the mystery of the procession of the consubstantial Third Person that a genuine conciliar reception would probably have professed them together dogmatically and we may hope that this will one day be done when the loving reunion between East and West takes place. Unfortunately it was impossible for this "ecumenical theologoumenon" (as Bolotov calls it in his second thesis) with its two facets to be expressed in its radiant simplicity and in its dogmatic unity, because since the patristic period each facet has been framed in the narrower setting of *one* particular theology.

The mystery of the divine monarchy, understood as the incommunicable hypostatic distinctive property of the Father in the trinitarian theology of the Cappadocians and of Theodoret of Cyrrhus and St John Damascene, led a dominant trend in the eastern tradition to regard the mediation of the Son merely as a passive and quite non-causal condition of the procession of the Spirit from the Father alone. For these Fathers the Spirit derives his hypostatic existence from the Father alone but as the Third Person in the trinitarian order he exists in the mode of existence peculiar to him in the light of the fact that the Son was begotten as the Second Person in this order. In the formulation: "The Spirit goes forth from the Father *through the Son*" (ἐκ τοῦ Πατρὸς δι' Υἱοῦ ἐκπορευόμενον), this theological version of the theologoumenon of the mediation of the Son was officially professed at the Seventh Ecumenical Council by the Patriarch St Tarasius and approved by Pope Hadrian. From the characteristic apophatic perspective of Cappadocian trinitarian theology, the Son's mediation in the procession of the Holy Spirit is seen as fulfilling the role of *negative condition*, not so much in the procession of the Spirit who derives his whole existence from the Father, as in his eternal manifestation which makes him known as the Third Person. The subordination of the level of the eternal relationships in which the Son and the Spirit are manifested to the level of their origin in the Father by generation and ἐκπόρευσις respectively, already foreshadows the medieval Byzantine solution based on the apophatic differentiation between the unknowable essence of divinity in God and the manifestation of the Persons of the Trinity in their eternal relationships in the form of energies.

The understanding of the mystery of the monarchy in the trinitarian theology of the Alexandrians and the Latins, on the contrary, namely as consubstantial communion proceeding from the paternal source in the Son and then, in him and from him, in the Spirit, led to the view that the mediation of the Son is the relational presence of the paternal source enabling the Son to share with the Father in communicating the divinity to the Spirit. From this characteristic kataphatic perspective of western theology, the role of the Son in the procession of the Spirit is that of a *positive condition*. Moreover this procession is seen not as the original relationship of ἐκπόρευσις from the Father in distinction from the genesis of the Son but as the final moment in the communication of the consubstantial divinity which "proceeds" (πρόεισι) in the sequence of the divine Persons (the procession of the Son and then of the Spirit is spoken of generically).

This theological view of the theologoumenon of the Son's mediation in the procession of the Spirit found expression in Augustine's formula: "The Spirit proceeds from the Father as principle (*principaliter*) and, through the non-temporal gift of the Father to the Son, from the Father and the Son in communion (*communiter*)." The same theological view was expressed at the Council of Ephesus in the ninth anathema of St Cyril of Alexandria: "The Holy Spirit is not known as something alien to the essence of the unique Son but he proceeds (πρόεισι) naturally from that essence, in no sense existing as any different from him in respect of identity of nature, even if the Spirit is correctly known as having his own proper character" (PG 74, 444B).

The two theological statements of the mediation of the Son in the procession of the Spirit (ἐκ τοῦ Πατρὸς διὰ τοῦ Υἱοῦ ἐκπορευόμενον; ἐκ τοῦ Πατρὸς καὶ τοῦ Υἱοῦ προϊὸν = *qui ex Patre Filioque procedit*) are simply two variations of one and the same theologoumenon, attempting to explain the *how*, either as a negative condition or as a positive condition. But when the Church confesses the one or the other (ninth anathema of Ephesus, profession of St Tarasius at Nicea II), it is not claiming to make a theological approach to the *how* into a dogma but simply wishing to recognize in its faith the dogmatic *fact* which remains a mystery: the Spirit proceeds from the Father only inasmuch as the latter begets the only Son. "In necessariis unitas, in dubiis libertas."

The Council of Florence, of course, proclaimed the substantial identity of the διὰ τοῦ Υἱοῦ and the *filioque*. It may be objected that this Council was not accepted in the East. But on this precise point it was supported by an incontestable fact, one which Bolotov points out in his theses 19 to 27: the Fathers lived in the communion of the undivided Church even though they had different theological explanations of the nature of the mediation of the Son in the procession of the Holy Spirit from the Father, though not on the fact of this mediation.

One of the Fathers of the Church, St Maximus the Confessor in the seventh century, was able to produce a synthesis of patristic thought as a whole. His life itself was a bridge between the East and the West. He combined the two insights in a single extremely concentrated formula: "Just as the Holy Spirit exists by nature according to the essence of the Father, so too He is by nature according to the essence of the Son, inasmuch as He goes forth essentially from the Father through/by reason of the begotten Son" (PG 90, 672 CD).

But it is not just this attempted ecumenical synthesis which should warn us against any unilateral dogmatizing of either of these trinitarian theologies, but even more the uncertainties of their exponents.

On the Latin side we have the hesitation of St Hilary, with his acute mind and familiarity with the eastern *altera pars*, in face of the seemingly obvious *utroquist* position: " 'Everything the Father has is mine; that is why I said: All the Spirit tells you will be taken from what is mine' (John 16:15). He receives from the Son, therefore, he who is sent by him and proceeds from the Father. *I ask whether to receive from the Son and to proceed from the Father are not the same thing.* If we believe that there is a difference between receiving from the Son and proceeding from the Father, it is nevertheless certain that to receive from the Son and to receive from the Father are one and the same thing" (PL 10, 215A).

On the eastern side it is the subtle St Gregory of Nyssa who refuses to exclude completely the possibility of a causal role of the mediation of the Son in the procession of the Spirit, sensing as he does the difficulty of defining the eternal relationships which differentiate the divine Persons of the Son and the Spirit in the order of the Trinity otherwise than by the principle of the trinitarian causality of origin between them: "Just as the Son is united to the Father and receives his being from him, without being posterior to him in his existence, *so the Holy Spirit in turn receives himself from the Son who is contemplated prior to the hypostasis of the Spirit solely from the standpoint of causality*, although there is no room for temporal intervals in this eternal divine life. Consequently, apart from the argument of causality, the Holy Trinity contains within itself no distinction" (PG 45, 464).

As we listen to two such eminent representatives of the two trinitarian theologies playing "devil's advocate", we realize the impotence of human thought and language to convey the *how* of so great a mystery. Unity can only come about, therefore, as we recentre the theologoumenon (with the two divergent interpretations of the *how*) on the dogmatic *fact* to which it bears witness: the Holy Spirit proceeds from the one only Father only inasmuch as the latter is Father of the unique Son. As St John Damascene says – and he is one Father of the Church unlikely to be suspected of filioquism: "I say that God is always Father, having always his Word originating from himself and, through his Word, having his Spirit going forth from himself" (PG 94, 1512 B).

When the ecumenical unity of East and West is rediscovered at the level of trinitarian faith it will be possible to initiate a peaceful dialogue between the two theologies of the *how*: the theology of relationships of origin which the West canonized and sought to impose on the East at the Councils of Lyons and Florence, and the theology of the eternal manifestation of the Persons in their uncreated energies, to which the East gave dogmatic status at the Palamite Councils of Constantinople. Any attempt to make unity of faith in the Holy Spirit possible by the confrontation of these two systems would inevitably lead the contemporary ecumenical dialogue into the same cul-de-sac as those to which the former controversy led, even though each side can boast of having converted a John Beccos or a Maximus the Greek to its own view. The unity of faith is much too serious to be dealt with at the level of theological confrontations, however interesting and valuable these may be. Those who engage in such confrontations must know when to bow out with a nod in the direction of the fact of faith which takes precedence over their debates, provides their basis but also radically transcends them. The decisive word rests with the People of God assisted by the Holy Spirit through its ministries and gifts.

What follows is a summary of my position which I believe not to be in contradiction to the official teaching of the Roman Catholic Church.

I differentiate between three levels in the question of the *filioque*:

1. The dogmatic core, implicit in the consubstantiality of the Spirit as the Third Person of the Trinity as confessed in the Niceno-Constantinopolitan Creed. This dogmatic core, acknowledged by the concordant voices of the Fathers of East and West, may be formulated as follows: the Spirit goes forth from the Father inasmuch as only Father, therefore inasmuch as He is He who begets the only Son. This dogmatic core expresses two trinitarian truths unanimously affirmed by the Fathers of both East and West: on the one hand the monarchy of the Father, and on the other hand the respective order of the Persons of the Son and the Spirit as originating in him. At this level nothing is said concerning the "how" of this order. In the ecumenical consensus of the undivided Church this "how" was not considered a *necessitas* requiring *unitas*.

2. The two theologoumena, Cappadocian-Byzantine and Latin-Alexandrian. In these an attempt is made to state the "how" of the trinitarian order between the Second and Third Persons:

– either by regarding the generation of the Son as negative condition of the fact that the ἐκπόρευσις of the Spirit, of which the Father is the unique cause, is not a second generation; the Cappadocian-Byzantine theologoumenon is stated as follows: the Spirit goes forth from the Father alone through the Son; in Greek: ἐκ μόνου τοῦ Πατρὸς διὰ τοῦ Υἱοῦ ἐκπορευόμενον;

– or by regarding the generation of the Son as positive condition (cause, but not as primary principle) of the consubstantial procession of the Spirit in the communion of Father and Son; this Latin-Alexandrian theologoumenon is stated as follows: the Spirit proceeds from the Father and the Son; in Greek: ἐκ τοῦ Πατρὸς καὶ τοῦ Υἱοῦ προϊόν; in Latin: *qui ex Patre Filioque procedit*.

Ecumenical agreement can be established between East and West only if each of the churches acknowledges that the trinitarian formula to which it clings is only a theologoumenon. In other words, that (a) it is only one expression of the dogmatic core (cf. previous section) implicit in the Niceno-Constantinopolitan Creed to which it adds nothing normative for faith (even in such a liturgical usage as that of the Creed in the Roman Mass); (b) the theologoumenon of the other church, attested by a venerable patristic tradition which could not be discredited by its own theologoumenon, is neither heretical nor less orthodox; (c) the two theologoumena, professed by Fathers who lived in communion in the undivided Church, are intended to express the same divine reality, even if it is in a way which is beyond our understanding, which is so limited in face of the ineffable mystery of the Trinity.

We must not forget that both traditions wished to safeguard the same mystery of the trinitarian monarchy, each by means of its own theologoumenon. As long ago as 1904 it was said by Mgr Sergius, later Patriarch of Moscow, with reference to the dialogue between the Orthodox and the Old Catholics: "For the Old Catholics, to say that the Son and the Spirit in their eternal procession are utterly independent of one another, that they are not in contact with one another, would mean violating the very monarchy which is so vigorously defended in the East."

In fact, as we have seen, these two theologoumena are merely two particular theological formulations of the same ecumenical theologoumenon. They were worked out by the Fathers from two key words whose semantic connotations were not at all the same in Greek and in Latin but which an imperfect ecumenical meeting between East and West caused to be taken as equivalent, thus making it impossible for there to be any complementarity between the two approaches to the trinitarian mystery. The two words are the Greek ἐκπορεύεσθαι and the Latin *procedere*. We are accustomed in French (and in English) to translate both by the verb "to proceed", itself derived from the Latin. But the apparently obvious identity proves on closer examination to be fallacious.

In Greek ἐκπορεύομαι is the middle voice of ἐκπορεύω which in turn derives from the verb πορεύω meaning "to make to go", "to convey". It is connected with the noun πόρος "passage" (cf. Bosphoros: "straits") and by the verb πείρω "to go quite through", with the root περ or παρ which has given the preposition *per* in Latin and *par* in French. In the middle voice πορεύομαι, implying the subject in its action, consequently signifies "to pass", "to go across", intransitive, or, in a verb etymologically closer to the Greek word: "se porter" in the sense of "se transporter", "to betake oneself". For in fact the Latin verb *portare* has the same meaning and etymological root as the Greek verb πορεύω. The Greek form of the Nicene Creed, ἐκ τοῦ Πατρὸς ἐκπορευόμενον, should not therefore have been translated by *qui ex Patre procedit* but, more exactly, by *qui ex Patre se exportat*, which might be rendered in French by "qui se porte hors du Père", "qui sort du Père", in English perhaps "who goes forth out of the Father", "who issues from the Father". Might we suggest to our Orthodox brethren in the West, who in their liturgy use languages derived from Latin, to try to translate with this kind of rigorous striving for precision the Greek formula of the Creed, and not to borrow, however convenient this may be, the derivatives of the Latin term *procedere*, which in the triadology of the Fathers has become a technical term and bears a meaning which can imply a *filioque* which the very meaning of the Greek formula inherently excludes?

If the Greek term ἐκπορεύεσθαι as such denotes a passage out of that from which one issues in distinction from it, the Latin term *procedere* has the inverse connotation. *Cedere* means "to go from by giving place to", "to retire", hence in French "céder", "to yield", "give way" and, as in English, "to cede". With the prefix *pro* which means "forward", the form *procedere* means to go forward giving place to that from which one moves away and to which by that very fact one remains connected. The head of a procession, for instance, as it advances, gives way to the cortège which keeps it connected with its starting point. St Thomas Aquinas pointed out that the Latin term *processio* is the most general there is to designate any relation of origin: as a line proceeds from a point, a ray from the sun, the stream from the spring (1a, q.36, art. 2). In the examples he gives, what is expressed is not, as in the Greek ἐκπόρευσις, a passage out of the origin which distinguishes what comes out from it, but the progression starting from the origin of what moves forward while maintaining with it a homogeneous link of communion: it is the same stroke which proceeds from the point into the line, the same light which proceeds from the sun in the ray, the same water which proceeds from the spring into the stream. The origin is not apprehended first of all as the principle from which a distinction issues but as the starting-point of a continuous process.

The same meaning as the Latin *procedere* is found in the Greek verb προχωρεῖν which comes from χωρεῖν; like the Latin *cedere*, this means "to go from by giving place to" and is connected, it would appear, with the same etymological root (χωρεῖν, χῆρος, χάζειν; *cedere, cadere*) meaning "leaving a space between". The formula of the Latin Fathers *qui a Patre Filioque procedit* would therefore have to be rendered in Greek by ἀπὸ τοῦ Πατρὸς καὶ τοῦ Υἱοῦ προχωρῶν. It is a striking fact that the Greek trinitarian term περιχώρησις was translated into Latin in the Middle Ages by *circumincessio*, but that they did not as a consequence think of rendering the cognate term *processio* by the Greek περιχώρησις, which is its exact equivalent. We speak of trinitarian "circumincession" because the divine Persons are not separated from one another because the same consubstantial being proceeds in each from the or those Person(s) to which that Person remains linked in the trinitarian order. We speak therefore of the "procession" of the Spirit because in him the divine nature advances from the Father and the Son, in relation to whom it maintains him in consubstantial communion according to the order of the trinitarian perichoresis in which the divine nature is manifested. As V. Lossky would put it: "In the order of the divine manifestation, the hypostases are not respective images of the personal diversities, but of the common nature: the Father reveals his nature by the Son and the divinity of the Son is manifested by the Holy Spirit." Manifestation does not mean here temporal economy but procession within the eternal immanent movement of trinitarian communion in which the divine nature advances from the Father into the Son and from the Father and the Son into the Holy Spirit.

The "ecumenical theologoumenon" was formulated in fact in the seventh century by St Maximus the Confessor: "Just as the Holy Spirit exists by nature according to the essence of the Father, so too he is by nature according to the essence of the Son, inasmuch as he goes forth essentially from the Father through/by reason of the begotten Son" (PG 90, 672 CD). It might be formulated as an explication of the normative formula of the Niceno-Constantinopolitan Creed, in the complementarity of Greek and Latin trinitarian language. This would give something like: The Holy Spirit, by going forth out of the one only Father who begets the unique Son, proceeds in origin from both; in Greek: ἐκ μόνου τοῦ Πατρὸς τὸν Μονογενῆ γεννῶντος ἐκπορευόμενον καὶ ἀμφοῖν προχωρῶν; in Latin: *Ex unico Patre unicum Filium generante se exportans, ab utroque procedit*. It will be noticed that I interpret part of each of the two theologoumena in such a way as to make it compatible with the other, but I believe there is a good basis in each of their two traditions for doing so. I translate the ἐκ μόνου τοῦ Πατρὸς by "from the one only Father" rather than by "from the Father alone". In support of this I refer to Bolotov's seventh thesis: "The Fathers of the Church say that the Son is the 'Unique born of the Unique', but avoid this expression when speaking of the Spirit, as if to prevent the thesis that 'the Holy Spirit proceeds from the Father *alone*' from being set in antithesis to the theological idea 'and shines through the Son'." By preferring the translation "from the one only Father who begets the unique Son", we consider we restore to the theologoumenon the dogmatic transparency which its polemical connotation may have obscured. In the same way, I express the Latin *filioque* not by *qui ex Patre Filioque procedit*, but by *ab utroque procedit*, which I render in French by "qui procède *a partir* des deux" – "in origin from both". Even though the actual phrase *qui ex Patre Filioque procedit* is found in St Augustine, the latter always recognized that the character of principle expressed in the Latin *ex* referred only to the Father. Moreover, providence decreed that the formula which passed into Roman liturgical practice was not *qui ex Patre filioque procedit* but *qui a Patre filioque procedit*, in which the Latin *ab* locates the *filioque* on the level of a condition and not of cause as primary principle, and so does not set it in contradiction to the *ex Unico Patre*. Relieved in this way of their polemical narrowness, the two theologoumena convey their profounder meaning as mutually necessary expressions of one and the same ecumenical truth of faith.

3. The third level is that of the two medieval systems, the scholastic and the Palamite, each claiming to explain the "how" of the trinitarian order between the Second and the Third Persons:

- either by radicalizing the apophatic character of the eastern theologoumenon and explaining that the Son is the condition of the Spirit only with reference to his eternal manifestation as energy negatively distinct from his origin as Person in the Father alone;
- or by rationalizing the kataphatic character of the western theologoumenon and explaining that the Son is the cause of the procession of the Spirit because, together with the Father in their reciprocal relationship, he constitutes the unique principle of the relation of origin of the Person of the Spirit.

Whatever the value of these two theologies and the patristic basis which underlies them both, they were systematized in a setting of estrangement and controversy between East and West which made them increasingly resistant to each other throughout the unhappy history of the quarrel between them. On this point the churches must not let themselves be imprisoned by theological developments, however venerable. Communion must be restored by focusing on ecumenical confession of the dogmatic core, in recognition that it is to this alone that their respective theologoumena bear witness. Once unity in the confession of the trinitarian faith has thus been recovered, a new climate of love will make it possible for the mind of the Church to express in authentic ecumenical consensus the explicit dogmatic truth which the western Councils of Lyons and Florence and the Palamite Councils of Constantinople attempted to formulate unilaterally.

It is already possible to glimpse the common truth contained in the medieval theologies of subsisting relations and manifestation as energies, if one returns to their common source – St Gregory of Nazianzen. St Gregory the Theologian was in fact the first Father of the Church to express the trinitarian mystery in terms of relations and manifestation. But far from opposing these two terms as the medieval theologies sought to do by speaking of *subsisting* relations and of *energetic* manifestation, St Gregory considers them as strictly equivalent. "What then is lacking to the Spirit to be the Son? For if nothing is lacking, he would be the Son. We say that he lacks nothing, for nothing is lacking to God; but *it is the difference of the manifestation*, so to speak, *or of the relation between them which creates the difference of their name.* Nothing is lacking to the Son, either, to be the Father – for filiation is not a lack – but for all that he is not the Father" (Fifth Theological Oration, 9,1-7). Even if, for St Gregory, there flows from the trinitarian relations the order in which the trinitarian Persons commune with one another in the same consubstantial divinity, these relations do not for all that signify degrees in the divinity but simply posit the difference of the names of the Father, the Son and the Spirit in their personal "proprieties" – distinctive characteristics.[1] "*The Son is not the Father*, since there is one only Father, *but he is what the Father is; the Spirit is not the Son* by the fact that he is from God (the Father), since there is but one Only-begotten, *but he is what the Son is.* The Three are One from the point of view of the divinity and the One is Three from the point of view of the 'proprieties' " (*ibid.* 9, 15-19).

If, however, for St Gregory the Theologian the distinctive characteristics which differentiate relationally the trinitarian Persons are not names of the one and indivisible divine substance, they are not for all that names of "energy". "Father is neither a name of substance nor a name of energy; it is a name of relation, of the how the Father is in respect to the Son and the Son in respect to the Father" (Third Theological Oration, 16, 12-14). Even if the trinitarian relationships do not appear *ad extra* except in the energies by which the Living God naturally expresses the hypostatic character of his liberty which is love, they are already, within the bosom of the consubstantial perichoresis, the eternal manifestation of the difference of the divine Persons in respect to one another. The Father is manifested as Father by begetting the Son and by that fact the Son is manifested as the Son of the Father who is all that the Father is; the Father is manifested as one only Father of the unique Son by causing the Spirit to go forth through the Son and by that fact the Spirit is manifested as being the Spirit of the Son who is all the Son is. (We translate the διὰ τοῦ Υἱοῦ by "de par", "through"; in the New Testament, at Rom 12:1; 15:30; I Cor 7:2; II Cor 10:1 and frequently, διὰ with the genitive means "through", "by reason of", both "by" and "for" in the sense of "for the love of God".)

The Holy Spirit who comes forth in his personal originality as Spirit from

---

[1] The only truly catholic and orthodox sense that the expression "subsisting relation" can bear is that already expressed by St John Damascene: "Each of the trinitarian Persons contains the divine unity by his relation to the others no less than by his relation to himself" (PG 94, 828 C).

the one only Father of the Only-begotten through and by reason of this unique Begotten, proceeds in origin from the two in the consubstantial perichoresis of the Trinity, while being, by his relation to the Son, what the Son is, just as the Son, by his relation to the Father, is what the Father is, that is to say, God.

THEOLOGICAL PROPOSALS TOWARDS THE RESOLUTION OF THE FILIOQUE CONTROVERSY

JÜRGEN MOLTMANN

The original text

A resolution of the external, magisterial, canonical and liturgical problem of the *filioque* can be found if the western churches recognize, where they have not already done so, that the *filioque* clause is a later interpolation into the credal statement of an ecumenical council. The intention of the *filioque* in the West – an intention which originally involved no polemic against the East – was merely to make more precise the trinitarian affirmations of the Creed. Similarly in the East, the Creed's statements were made more precise with the help of the interpretative gloss, ἐκ μόνου τοῦ Πατρὸς – though admittedly this clarification worked in the opposite direction from the western. If, then, so far as the substance of the issue is concerned – and regardless of the particular ecclesiastical and political motives involved at that time – we are concerned here with *interpretative* formulae, but not with attempts at unilateral correction of the common Creed, then the interpolation can also be withdrawn and treated as an interpretation of the original text in a particular situation of theological controversy. This does not prejudice the theological discussion of "filioquist" and "monopatrist" understandings of the Trinity. With the withdrawal of the *filioque* an ecclesiastical controversy can be ended; but at the same time a theological enquiry into the doctrine of the Trinity must be opened up. The one makes no sense without the other.

What the original text leaves open

The Creed avoids any comment upon the participation of the Son in the procession of the Spirit from the Father. It also says nothing about the relations between the Son and the Spirit. This reserve may be comprehensible in the context of the contemporary struggle against the pneumatomachi,

• Jürgen MOLTMANN (Reformed) is professor of systematic theology, University of Tübingen, Federal Republic of Germany.

who understood the Spirit as a creature, subordinate to the Son. At any rate, it cannot be interpreted as a dogmatic decision of the conciliar Fathers against any participation of the Son in the going-forth of the Spirit from the Father. Their concern was to emphasize the complete divinity of the Holy Spirit, and that was why they spoke only of his procession from the Father. Earlier formulations of the Cappadocian theologians most certainly speak of a relation of the Son to the Holy Spirit in order to understand how the Holy Spirit is both "Spirit of the Son" and "Spirit of Christ". From a dogmatic standpoint, however, it can only be seen as a weakness that neither in the Creed of 381 nor later was a binding formula found to settle the question of the part played by the Son in the procession of the Holy Spirit from the Father, or alternatively in the shaping of the personal identity of the Spirit. Many eastern and western theologians have accordingly characterized the affirmations of the Creed concerning the Holy Spirit as incomplete, and recommended the attempt to find a new, common formula.

It is in the question thus left open in 381 that the theological differences between the triadology of the eastern Church and the trinitarian doctrine of the western have their substantial root. For this reason, the separation between the churches cannot be overcome simply by returning to the original text of the Niceno-Constantinopolitan Creed, but only through a common answer to the question of the relation of the Son to the Holy Spirit, and of the Holy Spirit to the Son.

God remains true to himself

Before we can look for the common answer to this question, one premise must be clarified. It has to do with the relation of the divine Trinity to the economy of salvation. This problem is often posed in terms of the relation between the "economic" and the "immanent" Trinity. Yet this terminology is imprecise, for it appears to speak of two different trinities. The truth of the matter is that we can speak only of the *one* Trinity and of its economy of salvation.

From this it follows that the divine Trinity cannot appear in the economy of salvation as something other than it is in itself. Therefore one cannot posit temporal trinitarian relations within the economy of salvation which are not grounded in the primal trinitarian relations. This means that the relation between the Son and the Holy Spirit cannot be restricted to the temporal sending of the Holy Spirit through Christ. Rather there must be an inner-trinitarian basis for the temporal sending of the Spirit through Christ, the Son of God. Otherwise we should have to suppose some kind of contradiction in God himself. Even with all the necessary apophatic pres-

ervation of the mystery and the unsearchable freedom of God, we must for
God's sake hold fast to this, that God cannot contradict himself: "God
remains faithful – for he cannot deny himself" (II Tim. 2:13). If God cannot
contradict himself, then he remains true to himself precisely and especially
in his economy of salvation, for it is that which reveals him himself, and
offers access to him. One cannot say, therefore, that something holds true
in God's revelation, but not in God's being. His truth is his self-consistency,
and it is this that makes him the Faithful and Trustworthy, in whom human
beings can believe with their whole heart.

The procession of the Spirit from the Father

The Holy Spirit "proceeds from the Father" (John 15:26). The Father
"breathes forth" the Holy Spirit in eternity. The Holy Spirit does not
proceed from the Son. So the interpretation is correct which states that the
Holy Spirit proceeds from the Father "alone". This "alone" is meant to
designate the uniqueness of the procession of the Spirit from the Father,
and to guard against any blurring or confusing of the relations within the
Trinity. The singularity of the procession of the Spirit from the Father, and
with it the uniqueness of the Father as the prime source of the Spirit, has
also never been contested by the theologians of the western Church. Although their *filioque* has been the occasion of this misunderstanding, they
have never in any way seen the Son as "competing" with the Father in the
matter of the procession of the Holy Spirit. The *filioque* was never directed
against the "monarchy" of the Father, albeit at the same time this formula
was intended to counter tendencies to subordinationism in the doctrine of
the Trinity, and to a subordinationist dissolution of the Trinity in its own
economy of salvation. It is not disputed in the West that the Son (John
16:27) and the Holy Spirit (John 15:26) both come forth in their different
respective ways from the Father, that the Father is therefore the primary
source of both – in their distinct fashions – and that both the Son and the
Spirit glorify the Father in eternity. The unoriginated Father was always
recognized as the "first person" in the Trinity. And where the Father was
called αὐτόθεος the West too found it impossible to apply this term to the
Son and the Holy Spirit. For this reason, the formula which speaks of the
procession of the Spirit from the Father, without the addition of the *filioque*,
should be accepted.[1]

---

[1] See also G. S. Hendry, *The Holy Spirit in Christian Theology*, London, Westminster,
1965, pp. 30ff, with his critique of Barth's retention and reformulation of the *filioque*.
Similarly, A. I. C. Heron, " 'Who proceedeth from the Father and the Son': the
Problem of the *Filioque*", *Scottish Journal of Theology*, 1972, pp. 149–166.

On the other hand, the exclusive gloss "from the Father *alone*" should be understood to refer only to the procession of the Spirit, i.e. to his divine existence (*hypostasis*), but not to his inner-trinitarian personal form (*Gestalt*) in his relations to the Father and to the Son. This is demonstrated by the argument of the eastern Church for the interpretative addition of the "alone" itself: that God the Father is the one cause, ground and source of deity. This argument shows only that the Holy Spirit receives his divine *existence* and his divine *being* "solely" from the "source of divinity", which is the Father. Nothing is so far said here about the *relation* of the Father as Father or as "breather-forth" to that which he "breathes" or brings forth, namely the Spirit. Nor is anything said concerning the *personal form (Gestalt)* which the Holy Spirit receives in his relation to the Father and to the Son. It is not because of the Fatherhood of the Father, but for the sake of the monarchy of the first person of the Trinity, that the *filioque* was and is contested – and indeed with justice, so long as the *filioque* is set in this context.

The procession of the Spirit from the Father of the Son

The Holy Spirit "proceeds from the Father", affirms the Creed. The first person of the Trinity is however *the Father* only in respect of the Son, that is, in the eternal begetting of the Son. God the Father is always *the Father of the Son*. He is never simply "universal Father", like Zeus, Jupiter, Vishnu or Wotan. He is not called "Father" merely because he is the unique cause on whom all things depend. Nor is it for the sake of the authority and power which all authorities and powers in heaven and on earth, in religion, state and family, hold from him. It is solely and exclusively in the eternal begetting of the eternal Son that God shows himself as "the Father". He is uniquely "the Father of Jesus Christ", and only through Christ, the only-begotten Son, and in the fellowship of this "firstborn" among many brothers and sisters, is he also "our Father". In order to maintain this crucial distinction, we propose to speak, thoughtfully and emphatically, of "the Father of the Son".

The Father is in eternity solely the Father of the Son. He is not the Father of the Spirit. The procession of the Spirit from the Father therefore presupposes the eternal begetting of the Son by the Father, for it is only in it that the Father is and is shown to be the Father. Just as "Son" is a theological and not a cosmological category, as became clear in the Arian controversy, so too is "Father" a theological one, not cosmological or even political/religious. The doctrine of the Trinity makes this unmistakeably clear.

"The Spirit is the third ὑπόστασις of the Holy Trinity. His being presupposes the existence of the Father and also of the Son, since the Holy Spirit proceeds from the Father, and since the Father is Father only of the Son. Accordingly, as soon as God the προβολεὺς τοῦ Πνεύματος is named *Father*, he is thought of as having a Son." [2]

If then God as Father breathes forth the Holy Spirit, the Spirit proceeds *from the Father of the Son*. His procession therefore presupposes (1) the generation of the Son, (2) the existence of the Son, and (3) the mutual relation of the Father and the Son. The Son is the logical presupposition and the material precondition for the procession of the Spirit from the Father, but he is not an additional accompanying source for him. The procession of the Spirit from the Father must be substantially distinguished from the generation of the Son by the Father, and yet related to it.

If, furthermore, the Holy Spirit does not only proceed from the Father because the Father is the "source of divinity", but because he is the Father of the only-begotten Son, then he derives also from the Fatherhood of God, that is, from the relation of the Father to the Son. While it is quite wrong to draw from this the further conclusion that the Spirit proceeds "from the Father and the Son", one must hold equally firmly to the fact that the Spirit proceeds from the Father in the eternal presence of the Son, and that therefore the Son is not without a part in the matter. "The eternal Son is not a stranger to the procession of the Holy Spirit" (P. Boris Bobrinskoy). The Son is eternally with the Father, and in him. The Father is never and acts nowhere without the Son.

"Since the Holy Spirit proceeds from the Father during the existence of the Son, ὑπάρχοντος τοῦ Υἱοῦ, and since the Father and Son are to be thought of as immediately accompanying and in contact with each other, the moment of the ever-present procession of the Holy Spirit is so understood that the Holy Spirit proceeding from the Father is already recognized by the Son as a complete hypostasis." [3]

"The Holy Spirit proceeding from the Father as a complete hypostasis comes through the Son, is manifested through the Son, and reveals through him his own being which he has from the Father. He shines out through the Son." [4]

Both Orthodox and western theologians should be able to agree with these expositions of B. Bolotov's, for they protect the procession of the Spirit "from the Father alone", and yet bring the Son so closely together

---

[2] B. Bolotov, "Thesen über das *Filioque*". Von einem russischen Theologen, *Revue Internationale de Theologie*, 24, 1898, p. 692.
[3] *Ibid.*, pp. 694f.
[4] *Ibid.*, p. 695.

with the Father that the relation of the Son to the Spirit is made directly apparent. This leads to the proposal that in the interpretation of the text of the Creed we should speak of

"*the Holy Spirit, who proceeds from the Father of the Son*".

What the Holy Spirit receives from the Son

According to the line of thought so far developed, a participation of the Son in the procession of the Spirit from the Father can be spoken of only indirectly, that is, as mediated through the Fatherhood of the Father. A direct relation of the Son to the Spirit cannot yet be articulated. Statements that the Son is not "strange to" or not "without part in" the procession of the Spirit use double negatives to circumscribe what either cannot be positively expressed, or ought to be left unspoken. Yet this remains unsatisfactory.

In order to advance from indirect circumscription to direct affirmation, let us start from the well-known sentence of *Epiphanius*, according to which the Holy Spirit "proceeds" from the Father and "receives" from the Son. We understand this in an inner-trinitarian fashion, and not as if the Spirit "proceeded" from the Father in eternity, and thereby derived his origination, but "received" from the Son purely within time.

If we take the sentence as describing the original relations within the Trinity, we must ask further: As what does the Holy Spirit proceed from the Father, and what is it that he receives from the Son? Our proposal is this: the Holy Spirit receives from the Father his own perfect divine *existence* (ὑπόστασις, ὕπαρξις), and obtains from the Son his relational *form (Gestalt)* (εἶδος, πρόσωπον). Just as the procession of the divine existence of the Spirit is to be ascribed *to the Father*, so too must we recognize that his form, his "face", is stamped *by the Father and by the Son*. That is why he is also called "the Spirit of the Son". The hypostatic procession of the Spirit from the Father is not to be separated from his relational form by which he is linked to the Father and the Son, though the two must be clearly distinguished. When the theology of the eastern Church declares that the Holy Spirit proceeds from the Father "alone" because the Father is "the source of divinity", it only expresses the divinity of the ὑπόστασις of the Holy Spirit over against ever kind of divine creation, but not his inner-trinitarian and interpersonal form.

The distinction here introduced between ὑπόστασις and πρόσωπον, or in Latin between *persona* and *facies*, may at first sight seem surprising. But it does make it possible to differentiate between the relation of the Holy Spirit to his divine source and his relations to the Father and to the Son. If ὑπόστασις is translated as *persona*, the translation imports over and above the literal meaning of the Greek (which can be rendered as *modus subsistentiae*) an additional relational character. This relational form of the person must probably be rendered in Greek by πρόσωπον. Thus the western concept of *persona* includes both the aspects which are indicated by ὑπόστασις as τρόπος ὑπάρξεως and by ὑπόστασις as πρόσωπον. The first brings to expression the relation of the ὑπόστασις to the divinity of God, the second the relation of one ὑπόστασις to the other ὑποστάσεις. To put it in western terms, the divine persons *subsist* in respect of the divinity of God; they *exist* in respect of each other. The western tradition has developed this differentiation in the doctrine of the *trinitarian relations*, according to which *relations* and *persons* are to be understood as complementary: the relations in the persons, and the persons in the relations. The eastern tradition has approached the substance of the matter which concerns us here both in its teaching concerning the *inner-trinitarian manifestation* of the triune God and in that of the *inner-trinitarian energies*. These post-Nicene trinitarian doctrines certainly do not all lie on the same level, but the insights they offer may be drawn upon to clarify our problem.

In this connection, we understand ὑπόστασις and ὕπαρξις in such a way that they express the *being* of the Holy Spirit in respect of his divine origin; while the concepts of πρόσωπον and εἶδος refer to his *form* in his trinitarian relations. If ὑπόστασις is an ontological concept, *form* is an esthetic one. They do not compete with or replace each other, but are mutually complementary.

Pure *form* is the highest beauty, for beauty lies in the perfect form, so far as this form is expression of inner substance and evocative of love. Form comes to be seen when it is illuminated and reflects the light. Then form is transfigured. For Paul, the object of such transfiguration is commonly the "face" (πρόσωπον). The glory of God shines in "the face of Christ" (II Cor. 4:6). The glory of the Lord shines upon us all "with unveiled face" (II Cor. 3:17). At last we shall see God "face to face" (I Cor. 13:13). If we speak of the "form" of the Holy Spirit, we mean by this his "face", as it is manifested in his looking towards the Father and the Son and in their looking towards him. This is the Holy Spirit in his inner-trinitarian manifestation, as the icon of Rublev so marvellously portrays it.

The *procession of the existence* of the Spirit has a substantial, but of course not a temporal, priority over his *reception of his form* in the relations we have described; for the existence of the recipient logically precedes his receiving. Therefore procession and receiving are not the same. If procession refers to the unique relation of the Holy Spirit to the Father as "source of divinity", receiving describes the form of the Spirit as from the Father and the Son. In the description of the relational form of the Holy Spirit, the *filioque* has its proper place. It must however be kept quite distinct from the procession of the Spirit. The Syrian Orthodox Church of South India expresses this with particular clarity in its prayer for the feast of Pentecost:

"When we say 'Father', the Son and the Holy Spirit come from him. When we say 'Son', the Father and the Holy Spirit are recognized through him. When we say *Ruho* (Spirit), the Father and the Son are perfect in him. The Father is the Creator, unbegotten; the Son is begotten and does not beget; the Holy Spirit (Ruho) proceeds from the Father and receives from the Son the person and the being of the Father." [5]

So we recommend for the interpretation of the text of the Creed:

"The Holy Spirit, who proceeds from the Father of the Son, and receives his form from the Father and from the Son."

The problem of generalizations in the doctrine of the Trinity

The "begetting" of the Son by the Father and the "procession" of the Spirit from the Father are different. If both of these are subsumed under the general category of *processio*, and "two processions" are spoken of, the danger of such abstraction becomes immediately apparent. The concrete particularity of the Son in relation to the Father and of the Spirit in his relation to the Father is overlooked. It is then only too easy to form a conception of the Spirit as a second Son, or of the Son as another Spirit. For this reason we ought not at this point to construct any general category to cover both the begetting of the Son and the procession of the Spirit. We must remain concrete, and tell first of the one, then of the other. We are not dealing with two different "comings forth", or with two different "events".

The "procession" of the Spirit from the Father and the "receiving" of his inner-trinitarian form from the Father and the Son are also distinct. The western *filioque* blurs this difference. This can only too easily give the impression that the Holy Spirit has two sources of his existence, in the Father and in the Son. For this reason we ought not to "sum up" the matter as is done with the formula "and from the Son", which leaves unexplained what in the Holy Spirit comes from the Father and what from the Son.

---

[5] Quoted from N. J. Thomas, *Die syrisch-orthodoxe Kirche der südindischen Thomas-Christen, Geschichte – Kirchenverfassung – Lehre*, Würzburg, 1967, p. 67. In Syriac the Greek word *ousia* is used for "substance" and the Syriac *q'nomo* for "person".

Again, we must remain concrete, and can only tell successively of the relation of the Father to the Holy Spirit and of the Son to the Holy Spirit.

The justified rejection of the undifferentiated *filioque* formula was defended by Orthodox theologians by appeal to the *monarchy of the Father*; but this too is in its own way undifferentiated. Certainly the uniqueness of the Father over against the Son and the Holy Spirit can be underlined through the Cappadocians' introduction into the doctrine of the Trinity of the Aristotelian concept of "cause" (αἰτία, ἀρχή) – though even in the early Church this was not undisputed. If, however, the Father is simply described as the "cause" of the divinity of the Son and of the Holy Spirit, the concrete difference between the generation of the one and the procession of the other is again blurred. It is as *Father of the Son*, not as *monarch of the godhead*, that the Father in eternity "breathes forth" the Holy Spirit. The admission of the category of "cause" is of course understandable in the context of the warding-off of the undifferentiating doctrine of the *filioque*; but it conceals similar dangers in itself. It carries over the universal relation of God to the created world, his universal monarchy, into the inner-trinitarian life of God. But we cannot use "monopatrism" to drive out dangerous "filioquism" from the doctrine of the Trinity without running into fresh difficulties. The concept of the sole causality of the Father also threatens to blur the concrete inner-trinitarian relations. The category of "cause" can therefore only be used here in a qualified sense: it is not a suitable general concept to cover inner-trinitarian generation and spiration, begetting and procession.

Basically, in the Cappadocian doctrine of the Trinity both deity and personal relations coincide in the first person. The first person is the "source of deity" as well as the Father of the Son and the Breather-forth of the Spirit. Thus the first person must guarantee *both* the unity of the godhead *and* the threefoldness of the persons. If these different senses are not strictly distinguished from each other, the result is either the disintegration of the Trinity into tritheism, or the subordinationist reduction of the Trinity to monotheism. It would be helpful for this reason to remove the concept of the "first cause" from the doctrine of the Trinity altogether, and to concentrate upon the presentation of the inter-personal relations; for in them, the logical priority of the Father is self-evident.

Dangers also lie in the doctrine of the *three* ὑποστάσεις or *persons* in the Trinity, for it applies one and the same concept to the Father, the Son and the Holy Spirit, and so awakens the impression that they are homogeneous equivalents, namely as ὑποστάσεις, persons or modes of being. These general concepts obscure the concrete differences between the Father, the Son and the Holy Spirit. They differ not only in their mutual relations, but also in respect of their personhood, even if the person is to be grasped in its relations and not apart from them. If one wishes to remain concrete, one must apply a different concept of "person" respectively to the Father, the Son and the Spirit. Their designation as "divine persons" already contains within itself a tendency to modalism. The general categories of ὑπόστασις or person bring to the fore the common and similar in them, not the particular and distinct.

Finally, it is well known how strongly the doctrine of the *divine being*, shared by all three ὑποστάσεις or persons, threatens to dissolve the trinitarian differences away in a Sabellian, modalistic, and ultimately unitarian fashion. The logical and epistemological priority given to the doctrine of the being of God in the West from Thomas Aquinas onwards had the effect of putting the doctrine of the Trinity itself out of action, and rendering it insignificant. The initial and prior thought of the simplicity of the divine being relegated that of the threefoldness to a secondary place. That is why the teaching on the Trinity in the western Church right down to Karl Barth and Karl Rahner has a tendency to modalism. This can only be changed if the indispensable thought of the unity of God is expressed in trinitarian terms, and no longer dominated by the divine being or the divine lordship. The *unity* of God rests *in* the tri*unity* of the Father and the Son and the Holy Spirit. It neither precedes nor follows the triunity.

From this brief survey of the dangers brought by the introduction of general concepts to the doctrine of the Trinity, one must conclude that no such subsuming general categories ought to be applied to it. In the life of the immanent Trinity everything is *singular*. Only because everything in God is *singular* can it be recognized in the ways and works of God as *originating* for anything else. In the doctrine of the immanent Trinity, one ought in principle only to *relate*, but not *subsume*. One must remain concrete, for abstractions bristle with heresies, as history has shown. By contrast, the foundation of orthodoxy lies in relating differentiation. At the centre of Christian theology stands the eternal history, which the triune God is in himself. All recounting requires *time*. For the relating of the triune God, man needs his own time. That corresponds better to the eternal presence of God than the abstraction in concepts which dissolve time away, but only insinuate a timeless eternity.

THE PROCESSION OF THE HOLY SPIRIT FROM THE FATHER AND HIS RELATION TO THE SON, AS THE BASIS OF OUR DEIFICATION AND ADOPTION

DUMITRU STANILOAE

The point of view this paper sets out stems from the positions taken by Fr Garrigues on the Catholic side, and Prof. Moltmann on the Protestant side (cf. the present volume). In my opinion, their expositions indicate the beginning of a movement in the question of the procession of the Holy Spirit, a question that for centuries has remained fixed in the rigid affirmation of the difference between the eastern and the western formulas. Their viewpoints seem to me to be a positive step towards the eastern doctrine even if, in some ways, an insufficient one. I shall therefore try to set out the eastern point of view in a positive way in order to bring a new contribution to the union of eastern and western Christianity on this subject.

Father Garrigues' view: a step in the direction of reconciliation

The step forward which I believe can be seen in Fr Garrigues' exposition is to be found in the fact that he considers Bolotov's formula, "The Holy Spirit proceeds from the only Father as He begets the only Son",[1] to be acceptable for the Catholic Church. Like Bolotov, Fr Garrigues believes that this proposition reconciles, in a formula which could be accepted as a point of faith by both parties, the affirmation that the Holy Spirit proceeds from the Father alone, which he considers to be an eastern theologoumenon seeking to explain the common faith which is expressed in the Niceno-Constantinopolitan Creed by the words, "The Holy Spirit proceeds from the Father", with the *filioque*, which he considers a western theologoumenon, seeking from the western side to explain the same words in the Creed, which are taken to imply, in a non-explicit way, a relation of the Spirit to the Son.

• Dumitru STANILOAE (Orthodox) is honorary professor of dogmatic theology at the Theological Faculty in Bucharest, Romania.
[1] "Thesen über das Filioque", *Internationale Kirchliche Zeitschrift* (1898).

In receiving the proposed formula as acceptable to the Orthodox Church, i.e. the formula which Bolotov and Garrigues regard as effecting a synthesis, we would nonetheless point out that the word *alone* (from the Father *alone*) is not a mere theologoumenon, but a point of faith, since it does nothing more than express, in another form, the monarchy of the Father which is based on the scriptures and affirmed by all the Fathers of the first Christian centuries. Furthermore, the easterners were forced to make use of the word *alone* in order to reaffirm the monarchy of the Father, as a consequence of the fact that the westerners had begun to use the *filioque* which contradicted this monarchy as it was expressed in the Creed itself.

St Gregory Palamas says: "When you hear in the Creed that the Holy Spirit proceeds from the Father, understand at once that we necessarily understand the word 'alone' as well, and so do not think of that word as an addition of ours, but rather think that we have added it in the discussion with you for the sake of the truth which you have destroyed." [2]

On the other hand, since the *filioque* destroys both the doctrine of the Fathers concerning the monarchy of the Father, and the expression of our common faith in the Creed, we consider it to be placed beyond the border of theologoumena and in the realm of error, for it must be accepted that theologoumena are explanations of what is understood implicitly in a formula of faith and not contradictions of it. Otherwise it would be impossible to tell the difference between a theologoumenon and an error. St Gregory Palamas says: "Since He who begets is overflowing divinity and source of divinity . . . and since only the Father is overflowing divinity and source of divinity, as Dionysius the Areopagite and the great Athanasius say, the Son as a consequence is of the Father alone according to nature . . . while he who is according to grace is not of the Father alone but of the Father by the Son. And the Spirit who comes forth from God by nature, proceeds naturally from God, and he who proceeds, overflows from God, overflows from the overflowing divinity who is the Father alone." [3] "Do you see then, that this little word 'alone' which we have added is simply an illustration of the truth? For whether we use it or not, the meaning is the same. But your word (*filioque*) is not only an addition in the proper sense of the word, but indeed a contradiction and destruction of the meaning of the true faith." [4] If the expression that the Spirit proceeds from the Father *alone* was only a theo-

---

[2] P. Christou (ed.), *The Works of Gregory Palamas* (in Greek), Vol I. Thessaloniki, 1962, p. 31.
[3] *Ibid.*, pp. 37–8.
[4] *Ibid.*, pp. 38–9.

logoumenon and not a correct explicitation of a point of faith, then one could consider the expression, "the Son is begotten of the Father alone" as also only a theologoumenon. But when one says that Christ is the Son of the Father, "does one not think and does one not understand by that also the word 'alone', that the Son is begotten of the Father alone, even if the word 'alone' is not added?" [5]

But all the same, we consider the Bolotov-Garrigues formula as acceptable to the Orthodox Church, even though we do not consider it as uniting in itself the words "of the Father alone" and the *filioque*. For this formula has also been used in Orthodoxy in the past. St Gregory Palamas says: "The Spirit has his existence from the Father of the Son, because he who causes the Spirit to proceed is also Father." [6] "Recognize that it is not from anywhere else (that the Spirit has his existence) but only from him who also begets the Son (ἐκ μόνου καὶ τὸν Υἱὸν γεννῶντος)".[7]

But although we would consider the formula, "the Spirit proceeds from the Father, who begets the Son" as acceptable to Orthodoxy, we do not think that the *filioque* is contained in this formula (the quotation from Palamas given above would also exclude this), for in this case one would also grant the Son a role in the Spirit's coming into existence, and this would contradict the first part of the proposition. This formula which Father Garrigues considers to be a formula of concord simply underlines the fact that the Father causes the Spirit to proceed from himself in order to communicate him to his Son, in order to be more united with the Son by the Spirit. This formula emphasizes at the same time that the Son remains Son in relations to the Father, in his quality as the Father who is the overflowing source of the Spirit. For only so can the Spirit be for the Son, the Spirit of the Son of the Father; and for the Father, the Spirit of the Father of the Son.

Otherwise the Spirit whom we receive from the Son would no more give us the quality of sons of the Father according to grace, but would rather make us fathers; and the Son himself, if the Spirit also proceeded from him, would also become the Father of the Spirit. In this sense, the Patriarch Gregory of Cyprus says, with St John Damascene: "We call him the Spirit of the Son, but we do not say that he comes from the Son, for these two affirmations are in contradiction." [8] That is to say that if the Spirit also

[5] *Op. cit.*, p. 38.
[6] *Op. cit.*, p. 46.
[7] *Ibid.*
[8] PG 142, col. 240.

comes from the Son, he would no more be the Spirit of the Son, but would be exclusively the Spirit of the Father. Consequently the *filioque* is opposed to our adoption as sons by the Spirit of the Son.

Even Fr Garrigues, feeling that the *filioque* as it is understood in the West cannot have a place in the formula "the Spirit proceeds from the Father who begets the Son", in the course of his presentation makes a modification to the *filioque*. He presents this modified form as a personal proposition believing that it is not opposed to the first part of the formula which he considers in agreement with Bolotov and acceptable to the whole of Christendom.

He modifies the expression: "The Spirit who proceeds from the Father and the Son (*qui ex Patre, filioque procedit*)" into the expression: "The Spirit who proceeds out of the Father and from the Son (*qui ex Patre et a Filio procedit*)." We remark that this modified expression no longer coincides properly speaking with the *filioque*, for it affirms a distinction between the Father and the Son in what they give to the Holy Spirit, while the *filioque* confounds the Father and the Son in the common impersonal substance, following the interpretation of Anselm of Canterbury and Thomas Aquinas, that the Spirit proceeds from the Father and the Son as from a single principle (*tanquam ab uno principio*), an interpretation which Fr Garrigues admits has never acquired an ecumenical character.

We notice again that in his explanation of the formula he proposes, Fr Garrigues uses the word *originates* for the relation between the Father and the Son, and the word *proceeds* for the relation between the Son and the Spirit. For him the difference between these two words corresponds to the difference between ἐκπορεύεται and πρόεισι, as used by the Fathers. He says: "In taking his origin from the one Father who begets the one Son, the Spirit proceeds out of the Father as origin, by his Son." In Greek: ἐκ μόνου τοῦ Πατρὸς τὸν μονογενῆ γεννῶντος ἐκπορευόμενον, ἐξ αὐτοῦ καὶ ἀπὸ τοῦ Ὑίοῦ πρόεισι. In Latin: *Ex unico Patre generante Unicum Filium ortus, ex Patre et a Filio procedit*.

This formula renders the real positive step towards the eastern doctrine, taken by Fr Garrigues, more explicit. But we judge it preferable not to use the word "proceed" for the relation of the Spirit to the Son, since it can give the impression of a confusion of this relation with the procession of the Spirit from the Father. It would be preferable to use the word "procession" for the relation of the Spirit to the Father, and for his relation to the Son, the term "goes out from" doubled with other terms like "shines out from" or "is manifested by", terms which have been used by the eastern Fathers. The use of these latter terms for what the Spirit receives from the Son as distinct from what he receives from the Father can, without doubt, form the basis of unity for the whole of Christianity in the doctrine of the Holy Spirit.[9]

But with a view to this there is a further question to be elucidated. Fr Garrigues believes that the expression "goes out (in his usage: *procedit*) from the Son (*a filio*)", refers only to the eternal relation between the Spirit and the Son. (Perhaps this is why he prefers to say *procedit* and not "goes out".) He does not consider the use of this expression for the sending of the Spirit by the Son to creation. This latter usage he sees as linked to the doctrine of the uncreated energies in the East, which in his view, should be considered as less than a theologoumenon, and also to the western theory which sees the relations between the divine Persons always and exclusively in terms of the relations of origin of one from the others.

We would consider that this lack of interest in the sending of the Spirit into the world, as uncreated energy, comes from the loss in the West of the doctrine of man's deification and adoption by God. In the West the relations between the divine Persons are seen almost exclusively as an inner-trinitarian question, and thus as a question of speculative theology without consequences in practical life, or in the salvation of man understood as his transformation.

In the East the trinitarian relations are seen as the basis for the relation of the Trinity to creation and for the salvation of creation.

Thus, in the East, it is not denied that at the origin of the sending of the Spirit by the Son there is a special eternal relationship between the Son and the Spirit, just as there is such an eternal relationship between the Father and the Son at the origin of the sending of the Son into the world. In the West, on the other hand, one avoids drawing from the eternal relation of the Spirit to the Son, the conclusion that the Spirit is sent to men for a work which consists essentially in the deification and adoption of man.

The trinitarian relations and the Orthodox doctrine of the uncreated energies brought into the world by the Holy Spirit

This fact is closely linked with the misunderstanding of the uncreated energies by which the Holy Spirit works in the world. This fact keeps God shut in on himself, as an object of pure speculation at a distance. The Spirit who, according to Catholic theology, produces a created grace in mankind, himself remains on a transcendent level. He does not, by his energies which

---

[9] It is true that, according to St Gregory Palamas, St Basil uses the word προεισι for the procession of the Holy Spirit from the Father, and he uses the same word for the begetting of the Son. *Op. cit.*, p. 46.

become the energies of man, make himself the subject of these energies in man, united with the human subject, himself as Person come down into the level of human existence, raising man to the divine level, making him Spirit-bearing and deifying him. In this perspective, the sending of the Spirit by the Son to men rather signifies that the Spirit rests in those who are united with the Son, since he rests in the Son. The Spirit does not go beyond the Son, even when we say improperly that he is sent to men. The Son is the only and ultimate resting place of the Spirit. The Spirit dwells in us insofar as we are raised up in the Son. This safeguards us from a theological rationalism on the one side and a purely sentimental enthusiasm on the other.

It must be noticed that the doctrine of the real sending of the Spirit into the world by the Son as the subject of the uncreated energies which he brings is not a doctrine invented by St Gregory Palamas; it has been the conviction and experience of Christians since the time of the apostles. The apostles were clothed with power from on high when the Holy Spirit came upon them on the day of Pentecost (Acts 1:5; Luke 24:29), and with this power they worked miraculous healings. (Acts 3:7; 5:15; 9:34,40). The same Spirit passed from them to those who heard their preaching with faith. The Spirit has purified the saints through the whole course of Christian history.

The Incarnate Word himself promised the real sending of the Holy Spirit by himself, the Spirit whom he receives from the Father, in his character as the Son united with the Father. He says: "When the Spirit comes whom I shall send from the Father, the Spirit of truth who proceeds from the Father, he will bear witness to me" (John 15:26). We shall see, a little further on, that according to St Gregory Palamas, the sending of the Spirit by the Son who receives him from the Father, does not mean that the Son receives the Spirit from the Father only when he sends him out, but that he always has the Spirit within him, given by the Father. He has the Spirit as a "Treasurer" (ταμίας). "For, according to St Gregory Nazianzen, Christ as God and the Son of God is the Treasurer of the Spirit. But the Treasurer (Distributor) does not offer what he gives on his own behalf, although being God of God by nature, he has the Holy Spirit within him, who goes forth (προϊὸν) naturally from him".[10] This means that the Spirit who proceeds from the Father is "placed" or resides in the Son. We must notice that the relation between the Son as Treasurer and Distributor of the Spirit (thus also as a personified Treasury) and the Spirit as content or personified Treasure of the Treasurer, is not only a relation of consubstantiality (for in this case

---

[10] *Op. cit.*, p. 57.

there would no longer be a distinction between them) but a relation between Person and Person, certainly based on the fact that they are of the same essence. Only this interpersonal relationship between the Son and the Spirit makes of the first the Treasurer of the Spirit, and his Distributor. Otherwise, why should the Father not be the Treasurer and Distributor of the Spirit? But we receive the Spirit only through the Son, in order that we may become sons of God by grace. This is why he who gives us the Spirit must be on the one side God, and on the other the Son of God. St Gregory Palamas says just this in these words: "Christ is, and is called, the Treasurer of the Spirit, as he who is the true Son of God." [11] It is, then, his quality as Son, not simply as God consubstantial with another divine Person, which makes the hypostatic Word the Divine Treasurer, the place of the Spirit's repose.

The Fathers of the Church used the words "going forth" or "manifestation" of the Spirit from the Son, rather in this sense of a real sending to creation. St Cyril of Alexandria, for instance, says: "The three hypostases whom we worship are known and confessed as Father without origin, only Son, and the Holy Spirit who proceeds from the Father, not by birth as the Son, but by procession, as it is said, from the Father alone as from a mouth, but who is shown by the Son and who has spoken by the Son in all the holy prophets and apostles." [12] And St John Damascene says: "We say of the Holy Spirit that he is the Spirit of the Son, but we do not say of him that he is from the Son, but that he is revealed by the Son and has been communicated to us by him." [13]

The active repose of the Holy Spirit in the Son

But St Athanasius speaks both of a sending and of a shining forth of the Spirit from the Son, the sending being temporal, the manifestation being considered as eternal. He says: "Since the Son is one, the living and one Spirit must also be the full and perfect life and being his energy (ἐνέργεια) and gift, who is said to proceed from the Father, but who shines out and is sent and given by the Word who is known by the Father." [14] Thus we can say that St Athanasius considers the sending of the Spirit by the Son to creation to be based on his eternal shining forth from the Son.

In a still more explicit way, St John Damascene speaks of a special eternal relation between the Spirit and the Son as the foundation of the sending of

---

[11] *Op. cit.*, p. 56.
[12] Gregory Palamas, *op. cit.*, p. 47.
[13] PG 94, co. 832–833A.
[14] Ad Serap. I. p. 26, 565–568.

the Spirit into the world by the Son when he says: "We have learned that the Spirit is he who accompanies (συμπαρομαρτοῦν) the Word and who reveals his operation (energy)." [15]

But it is the Byzantine theologians of the thirteenth and fourteenth centuries who have made the eternal relation between the Spirit and the Son still more explicit, seeing it as the basis of the sending of the Spirit by the Son. Thus St Gregory Palamas, quoting the former proposition of St John Damascene, adds: "To accompany (συμπαρομαρτεῖν) means to be together (συνακολουθεῖν), as he himself says. Thus the Spirit is not of the Son, but he is of the Father with the Son, insofar as the procession accompanies (συνακολουθούσης) the begetting, without temporal separation or distance." [16]

Basing himself on St John Damascene, St Gregory Palamas, as we have already mentioned, sees not only an inseparable link between the procession of the Spirit from the Father and the begetting of the Son by the Father, but also the "repose" of the Spirit in the Son as in a Treasurer (that is as a personified Treasury). He says: "We must hear the divine Damascene who writes in the Eighth Chapter of his Dogmatic, 'We believe also in the Holy Spirit who proceeds from the Father and reposes in the Son'." [17] For this reason, Christ is called the Treasurer of the Spirit. [18]

The "repose" of the Spirit as Treasure, in the Son as Treasurer, shows the special relation between the Spirit and the Son more than the inseparability between the procession of the Spirit from the Father and the begetting of the Son from the same Father. The Son is the living, personal, spiritual "place" of the "repose" of the Spirit. He is the place where the Spirit dwells as if at home. He proceeds from the Father with a view to his "repose" in the Son. The one cannot be thought of without the other. The procession from the Father and the repose in the Son, as in his own dwelling place, belong together. The procession of the Spirit from the Father finds its final fulfilment in his repose in the Son, as in a personal dwelling place, beloved of the Spirit. But the Son is begotten as a personal dwelling place, happy to have the Treasure of the Spirit in himself, the Spirit who rests in the Son because he has all his joy in him, the fullness of joy. We shall see further

---

[15] PG 94, col. 805 A,B. The expression is almost literally borrowed by St John Damascene from St Gregory of Nyssa, PG 45.17. The word συμπαρομαρτεῖν is also used by St Gregory Nazianzen.

[16] Gregory Palamas, *op. cit.*, p. 53.

[17] PG 94, col. 821 B.

[18] Gregory Palamas, *op. cit.*, p. 56.

on how towards the end of his life, St Gregory Palamas developed the idea of the Spirit as the one in whom the Father rejoices with the Son.

But we also are raised up in the Son, who is the eternal, filial dwelling place of the Spirit and with the Son we too become eternal, filial habitations for the Spirit. This is why the eternal relation of the Son to the Spirit is the basis of the sending of the Spirit to us by the Son.

Aspects of the special relation between the Holy Spirit and the Son as defined in Byzantine theology

Going further, St Gregory Palamas gives a quotation of Dionysius the Areopagite who says the same thing in a still bolder way, stressing more strongly the unity of Father, Son and Holy Spirit. "Considering this, let us worship the Source of life (the Father, source of the Holy Spirit), who pours himself out in himself (in the Son), seeing him resting in himself." [19] The Father, pouring out his life, for he is not a God without life, nor a God shut upon monopersonal egotism, can only fully pour it out in himself (for no other can fully contain him), but in himself as in "another himself" (ἄλλος ἑαυτὸς), as St Gregory of Nyssa somewhere names the Son. The infinite source of life must have a goal for his generosity to which he can give his life, a goal which on the one side must be distinct from himself – to satisfy his generosity – but on the other side must not be outside himself. This unity without confusion – the greatest paradox of love – can only exist between Persons of the same essence.

But already before St Gregory Palamas, the special eternal relation between the Spirit and the Son as the basis of the sending of the Spirit into the world by the Son had received more articulate precision in the thought of Patriarch Gregory of Cyprus (1283–89). He calls this eternal special relation between the Spirit and the Son the "manifestation" or "shining forth" of the Spirit through the Son, thus giving a dynamic meaning to the word "repose".

The Treasure shines out, revealing itself, from the Treasury; it is not hidden within. This "manifestation" or "shining forth" is not, according to Gregory of Cyprus, temporally separated from the procession of the Spirit from the Father, but accompanies it. If St Gregory Palamas, following St John Damascene, speaks of an inseparable accompaniment of the begetting of the Son by the Father by the procession of the Spirit from the same Father, Gregory of Cyprus speaks of an accompaniment of the begetting of

---

[19] Dionysius the Areopagite, PG 3, col. 1104 B, C.

the Son by the manifestation of the Spirit by the Son.[20] The accompaniment of the begetting of the Son by the procession of the Spirit is a manifested accompaniment. For, without doubt, it is only if the begetting of the Son by the Father is accompanied by the procession of the Spirit from the Father, that the begetting of the Son can also be accompanied by the manifestation or shining forth of the Spirit. But if the accompaniment of the begetting of the Son by the procession of the Holy Spirit from the same Father is on the one hand the more profound fact, on the other it leaves it possible for us to think in terms of a certain parallelism between the two cases. But the accompaniment of the begetting and in general of the Person of the Son by the manifest shining out of the Spirit demonstrates that there is an inner dynamic presence of the Spirit in the Son. That is why it employs the expressions "through" or "from" the Son, words which cannot be used of the procession itself. At the same time the shining out of the Spirit through or from the Son constitutes the basis for the shining out of the Spirit through or from the Son to the created world.

But Gregory of Cyprus does not neglect to explain that the shining out of the Spirit through the Son is the consequence of the procession of the Spirit from the Father, and thus one could say the consequence of the link between the procession of the Spirit from the Father and the begetting of the Son by the Father. For this reason Gregory of Cyprus does not avoid the use of some common terms to express the procession of the Spirit from the Father and his shining out from the Son. Thus he says that the Father is the originator (προβολεὺς) of the Spirit in the double sense that he is the cause of the procession of the Spirit from himself, and the cause of his shining out from the Son. By sending him (προβολὴ), Gregory understands the double but inseparable activity of the procession of the Spirit from the Father and his shining out from the Son, on account of the procession from the Father.[21]

In this we see a perfect union between the Persons of the Holy Trinity brought about by the Father. The Father does not beget the Son, and does not cause the Spirit to proceed as two separate actions, as two Persons who remain separated; but the begetting and the procession, although distinct, are united. Consequently the Person of the Son and the Person of the Spirit also remain united, or interior, to one another. But Gregory of Cyprus constantly insists that the Spirit, although he shines out from the Son, on

---

[20] PG 142, col. 250 C. Τὴν διὰ τοῦ Υἱοῦ ἀΐδιον ἔκφανσιν συντρέχουσαν καὶ συνε-πανοουμένην τῇ ἐκ τοῦ Πατρὸς αὐτοῦ εἰς τὸ εἶναι προόδῳ.

[21] *Op. cit.* col. 242 B. Οὐδὲ πάλιν ὅτι προβολεὺς δί αὐτοῦ ἐστιν ὁ Πατήρ. ἤδη καὶ δί αὐτοῦ αἴτιος ἐστὶ τοῦ Πνεύματος.

account of the fact that he proceeds from the Father who also simultaneously and inseparably begets the Son, has his existence from the Father alone. For though the Spirit's manifestation is by the Son, his coming into existence is not by the Son, even if he is united to the begetting of the Son.

The fact that the procession of the Spirit is from the Father alone, but that the shining forth is from the Son, is a consequence of the procession from the Father alone, but united to the begetting of the Son, and this fact is expressed by Gregory of Cyprus by affirming that the shining out from the Son marks a progress in the existence which the Spirit receives from the Father,[22] one might say a fulfilment, the achievement of the end for which he came into existence.

This last affirmation is very bold. At first sight it could give the impression that the Spirit receives his full existence insofar as he shines out from the Son. But if we remember that for Gregory of Cyprus only the Father is the cause of the Spirit's existence, and that for him the shining out of the Spirit from the Son is, in the last analysis, due to the Father, being a sort of crowning of the procession of the Spirit from the Father, then we see that the conception of Gregory of Cyprus opens to us a door of understanding. Without relinquishing the patristic teaching about the monarchy of the Father, this conception puts strong emphasis on the relation of the Spirit to the Son.

Moltmann's theory and the possibility of completing it by the relationship of a person with his "other"

We cannot think of the Spirit without the Son. In a report presented to the 1978 meeting at Klingenthal and then in a lecture given at the Theological Institute in Bucharest, Prof. Moltmann put forward the idea that the Spirit receives his existence from the Father, but that he receives his image (εἶδος) or the character of a Person, from the Son. Formulated in this way the idea is difficult to understand. The personal character of anyone cannot be separated from his/her existence. But in Prof. Moltmann's idea a truth which is worth taking into consideration can be perceived. It represents a new step towards the doctrine of the Fathers, by making a clearer distinction between the Father and the Son in their relations with the Spirit, than the *filioque* formula is able to do.

What is this truth which, in our view, is contained in the idea of Prof. Moltmann and which we think we have been able to make clear from the conception of Gregory of Cyprus?

---

[22] *Ibid.* Τὴν γὰρ εἰς ἔκφανσιν ἐνταῦθα καὶ ἔλλαμψιν τὴν εἰς τὸ εἶναι πρόοδον . . . παρίστησιν.

The truth is this. The Holy Spirit is a distinct Person within the Holy Trinity not only insofar as he takes his place in the communion between the Father and the Son, but by the fact that he is linked by a special, intimate relationship not only to the Father, but also to the Son. Furthermore, each Person of the Holy Trinity is a Person not only insofar as he has a relation with the other, but insofar as he has a different relation with each of the other two. The Holy Spirit does not receive his personal character of his "relational εἶδος" only from the Son. He receives it from the fact of his procession from the Father, which accompanies the begetting of the Son by the Father, thus being placed in relation with the other two divine Persons, that is to say, within the trinitarian communion.

Let us take the analogy of human relations. I cannot live in the fullness of the life of another – and therefore also in my own – except by also living my relation with his other other, thus making it my own relation; that is to say, in living the much richer complexity which is given him in his relationship with his other other. I can say that I know my other in the light of his other other, with whom he is linked. As for me, I must see them both differently, not just one of them. In the same way, I cannot see the other with whom I am in contact at this moment unless I am penetrated by the experience of another other with whom I am linked. This other other gives me the capacity to see and understand better the other with whom I am in relation at this moment. Thus, no one can exist except in relation with two other persons, and not only in a perpetually closed relationship with one other person. The third person (third in a not rigidly fixed order) opens the horizon which can embrace all and frees the relationship between the two from narrowness and from a certain monotony. The personal pronouns which reflect this reality, necessary for every person, are not only "I and thou", but "I, thou and he." In order to say "I" it is not enough to say simply "thou", one must also say "he". This means that for me to express myself as "me", I must express myself not only in a relation to a "thou", but also to a "he", who is linked both to the "thou" and to myself.

The Son sees the Father not only as he by whom he is begotten, but also as him from whom the other proceeds, i.e. the Spirit. But in his link with his other other, or in the procession of this one from himself, the Father does not forget the Son as Son, but insofar as the Third Person also proceeds from him, all the complex richness of his relationship with the Son can be seen. By the Spirit, the Father lives in all the richness, or in all the perfection, of his living relationship with the Son.

In his turn the Son knows in the light of this other, by whom the Father lives in all the richness of his love for the Son – the Son knows his Father and his love towards him more fully. Not only does the Father by his link with the Spirit live his love towards the Son in its fullness, that is to say not only does the Son shine out brightly towards the Father in the light of the Spirit cast by the Father on the Son, but also the Spirit is fully realized from the Father by the Son. Only in this pure love, this complete love among the three, is to be found a love which embraces all, which hides no egotism, no unjust preference such as would follow from a love between the two.

The relationship between all three divine Persons is expressed by St Gregory Palamas in this way: "No one can conceive the Word without the Spirit, if he has understanding (thus it is not only Spirit without Word which is inconceivable). For this reason the Word of God, born of God, has the Holy Spirit coming forth from the Father . . . And this Spirit of the supreme Word is like an inseparable love on the part of the One who begets the Son, who is born in an unspeakable way. In him the beloved Son and Word of the Father rejoices (χρῆται) looking towards him who engenders, and having him as if coming forth from the Father with him and resting in him by the unity of the nature. The Son receives him from the Father as the Spirit of Truth, of Wisdom and of the Word . . . And by him the Son rejoices together with the Father who rejoices in the Son (ὃς τῷ Πατρὶ ἐπ' αὐτῷ χαίροντι συγχαίρει). For this joy of the Father and the Son since all eternity is the Holy Spirit who is common to them in what touches profit (κατα-χρῆσιν) (the reason why he has been sent by both to those who are worthy), but in what touches existence he is from the Father alone, for he proceeds from him alone as far as his existence is concerned." [23]

There is a reciprocity of infinite richness in its complexity between the Three Persons of the Holy Trinity, and it is this which gives them their fully personal character. But there is a special reciprocity between the Son and the Spirit which is reflected in their contact with the world. The Son by himself transmits the Spirit to those who believe in him. But only through the Spirit is the Son known by those who believe. The Spirit shines out from the Son above all after the Resurrection and since the day of Pentecost. But it is exactly on account of this that the face of the Son gains its radiance, and its divine reality (visible or invisible) is intensely felt through the Spirit, or in the measure that the Spirit is communicated by the Son. Thus one can say that the Son makes the Spirit accessible to us, but that the Spirit in his turn makes the Son accessible in his divine interiority, where by the Spirit, we know the Son and rise to the Father in a pure life and in prayer.

---

[23] *Capita theologica*, Philocalia graeca, 2nd ed. Athens, 1893, p. 315.